DIVERSITY
OR
DISUNITY?

DIVERSITY
OR
DISUNITY?

REFLECTIONS ON LAMBETH 1998

JAMES E. SOLHEIM

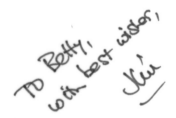

 CHURCH

Church Publishing Incorporated, New York

Library of Congress Cataloging-in-Publication Data

Solheim, James E., 1939–

Diversity or disunity? : reflections on Lambeth 1998 / James E. Solheim.
        p.   cm.

    ISBN 0-89869-310-1 (pbk.)

    1.   Lambeth Conference (1998 : Canterbury, England)
2. Anglican Communion—Congresses—History—20th century.
3. Anglican Communion—Doctrines—Congresses—History—
20th century.   I. Title.
    BX5021.S65   1999
    262′.53—dc21   99-26097
                                        CIP

Church Publishing Incorporated
445 Fifth Avenue
New York NY 10016

5 4 3 2 1

CONTENTS

ACKNOWLEDGMENTS

This book is dedicated to the Lambeth news teams, whose work is really the basis of what is reported here. A meeting like the Lambeth Conference is immensely complex, taking place on many levels and usually behind closed doors. It takes a tenacious press crew to get very far below the surface and, daunting as the task was, the news teams at Lambeth did a remarkably good job.

Headed by Jim Thrall, former deputy director of the Episcopal News Service and now a doctoral student at Duke, the team included others whose skills were honed in covering the Episcopal Church's General Convention: David Skidmore, communications officer and editor from the Diocese of Chicago; Katie Sherrod from Ft. Worth; Nan Cobbey from *Episcopal Life* staff; Ted Malone, the diocesan communications officer from North Carolina; Allan Reeder from Australia; and Jan Nunley, communications officer from Rhode Island who, in addition to some writing assignments, also coordinated press contacts for the eleven women bishops. And to my colleague David Harris, editor of the *Anglican Journal* for the Anglican Church in Canada, whose daily conversations helped me see better what was happening at the conference.

The *Lambeth Daily* staff, under the editorship of Bob Williams from Los Angeles, managed to put out a four-color edition every morning, by the grace of God, with the help of its own news team, including Brian Thomas of New Zealand, Carol Barnwell of Texas and Jane Gitau of Kenya.

Another team followed developments in the four sections as their work unfolded: Nicola Currie from the Anglican Communion Office, Randall Lee from the Evangelical Lutheran

Church in America office in Chicago, Sarah Moore of Sewanee, and Doug Tindal of the Anglican Church of Canada. Without the coverage of the Spouses Conference by Roland Ashby, I wouldn't have been able to add those interesting chapters to the book.

Jim Rosenthal, our missionary to the Anglican Communion Office from Chicago, had the impossible task of coordinating the news office. He was assisted by our own Barbara Braver. Archbishop Robin Eames of Ireland served as episcopal chair of the communications effort, calling both on his experience at three Lambeth Conferences and on his considerable diplomatic skills. These three took more flak than I thought possible for trying to accommodate an occasionally surly press.

Thanks also to Louie Crew who gathered and posted on the Internet many of the reactions to Lambeth, both official and personal. They were invaluable in putting together that section of the book.

Special thanks to Jeff Penn, former deputy director of the Office of News and Information, for his invaluable advice on the structure and content of the book. As a partner during so much of what happened during the turbulent years we spent covering events in the Episcopal Church, his insight and editorial skills were extremely helpful.

Finally, thanks to Frank Tedeschi of Church Publishing, a former colleague at the Church Center, who enticed me into doing the book; and to Donn Mitchell, who faced the difficult task of editing with amazing grace.

INTRODUCTION

THE ANGLICAN COMMUNION WILL NEVER BE THE SAME

Historians should have a fine time sorting out the meaning and import of the 1998 Lambeth Conference. Yet there are several things that are quite apparent: With almost 750 bishops from thirty-seven provinces of the Anglican Communion, it was the largest, most complex meeting in Anglican history. And because the Archbishop of Canterbury invited all bishops, not only diocesan bishops as in the past, the logistics were frightening.

As one watched the bishops process slowly into Canterbury Cathedral, the mother church of Anglicanism, for the opening Eucharist on July 19, it was also apparent that the diversity of the Communion had deepened, that bishops from the developing world were now in the majority. In the three weeks that followed, that dynamic would be crucial as the bishops struggled together with some huge issues, often finding themselves speaking a different language, reading Scripture from their own cultural contexts.

Many observers before and after the conference characterized it in varying terms. Some were convinced that the meeting represented a cultural clash reflecting different missionary strategies of the past. While sexuality was the cloud that loomed over the proceedings, the underlying issue was how Anglicans in different parts of the world lived out Scripture in their daily lives.

In the end the bishops made some major decisions. They overwhelmingly affirmed the belief that the traditional understanding of biblical sexual morality sees monogamous, heterosexual marriage as the only form of sexual expression that honors God. They took a strong stand on international debt and economic justice. They wrestled with the issue of unity and the instruments the Anglican Communion has for expressing that unity—including an expanded role for the Archbishop of Canterbury. They said that no bishop should be forced to ordain or license a woman. They warned that diocesan boundaries should be respected, and they expressed solidarity with Christians who are suffering persecution.

As they packed their bags and headed home it was clear, as one bishop muttered, "The Anglican Communion will never be the same again." The traditional "bonds of affection" that supposedly held Anglicans together had been severely tested, in a few cases even fraying. And the question that lingered in the air was whether this newly reshaped Anglican Communion had a sufficient base of unity that would carry it into the new millennium or whether they had identified limits to diversity that a reshaped leadership would be forced to consider.

At the closing press conference, Archbishop of Canterbury George Carey said, "I believe that our Communion is significantly stronger than when we began, because bishops have met each other face to face, shared their stories of pain, of joy, of hope." He was clearly relieved that no one had walked out of the conference and that the center seemed to have held. It will be up to Carey, in his remaining years as leader, to help Anglicans sort out how they can stay together in the face of some serious disagreements—to determine whether diversity would sow the seeds of disunity.

Perhaps the future of the Anglican Communion lies in what sense the bishops make of the stories they heard in their daily small group Bible studies, how it might be possible to form new bonds of affection based on that deep level of sharing and negotiate new bonds of unity that make sense in the face of continuing disagreements. It was clear to everyone that the ground had shifted, that western churches would no longer dominate and control the agenda or shape the debate.

Carey said early in the conference that, if it were identified only with the sexuality issue, it would be a failure. Yet forces at play for several years before the conference almost guaranteed that beliefs about sexuality would pose the most serious threat to unity.

CHAPTER ONE

NO STRANGER TO
CONTROVERSY

That a Lambeth Conference should be steeped in controversy is not in and of itself noteworthy. The very first worldwide gathering of Anglican bishops at Lambeth Palace in 1867 was convened specifically because of a controversy involving some of the same matters that troubled the 1998 gathering: attitudes toward the culturally and racially different; the authority and interpretation of Scripture; and the apparent inability and possible unwillingness of the Anglican system to define and enforce uniformity.

The issues then focused on the controversial writings of John William Colenso, a missionary bishop in southern Africa who was perceived as a radical, perhaps even a heretic.

"He did not believe that Zulus who failed to become Christians were subject to eternal damnation, nor that the Bible was the Word of God," wrote Clifford Longley in a pre-Lambeth '98 column in the *Daily Telegraph*. Another missionary bishop, Robert Gray, had led an effort to depose Colenso. In 1865, the case went to the

Judicial Committee of the Privy Council in London, which refused to consider it.

"By then the issue had become a crisis of authority for the whole Anglican family," Clifford Longley wrote. At the request of the Canadian bishops, the then-Archbishop of Canterbury, Charles Thomas Longley, invited diocesan bishops from around the world to his official residence in London to discuss the Colenso affair. Longley, the commentator, reported that Archbishop Longley's initiative received lukewarm support from his fellow bishops in the mother country, "and nothing was settled."

Despite its inconclusiveness, bishops from the growing international body known as the Anglican Communion returned to Lambeth Palace roughly every ten years thereafter, sometimes issuing statements that became the heart and soul of positions later taken in the various national churches. Yet a century after Archbishop Longley's first invitation, the conference was again mired in controversy.

The 1968 gathering, the last to actually meet at Lambeth Palace, became something of a scandal. Bishops stayed in hotels, guesthouses, bed-and-breakfasts, or in private homes and ate at some rather fancy restaurants, driving up the costs. The British press exposed the high-living bishops, prompting organizers to change the format and location.

The conference moved in 1978 to the city of Canterbury whose cathedral was the birthplace of English Christianity in 597. St. Augustine, a Benedictine prior who became the first Archbishop of Canterbury, was sent with some forty monks to spread Christianity. The Anglo-Saxon ruler, King Ethelbert, who agreed to be baptized, welcomed them.

Over the centuries the cathedral has been a site of pilgrimage, immortalized in Chaucer's *Canterbury Tales*, the fourteenth-century classic, and T. S. Eliot's *Murder in the Cathedral*, a modern play about the martyrdom of Archbishop Thomas Becket in 1170.

CONCERNS ABOUT UNITY

In 1994 when the present Archbishop of Canterbury, George Carey, issued his invitation to the 1998 gathering, he reminded the bishops that in today's world "the church of Jesus Christ is facing untold odds." He said that "in many parts of the world our brothers and sisters suffer the effects of famine, war and natural disasters."

Carey said the purpose of the conference since its inception has been "to explore issues confronting the church and for bishops to help each other in exercising their ministry of unity."

Meetings in June of 1994 and March of 1995 established three objectives for the 1998 gathering: (1) to maintain and strengthen the theological, spiritual, and personal bonds of our Communion; (2) to stimulate, encourage, and renew the bishops in their episcopal ministry of guarding and interpreting the faith and leading the mission of the church; and (3) to clarify the mind of the bishops on certain designated issues which will be significant for the church's fulfillment of its mission as we prepare to enter the twenty-first century.

While Anglicans should "take great pride in our heritage and rejoice in the foundations laid by our forebears," Carey said in an open letter to the Communion, "the future challenges us. We are at an important point in our development as a Communion. The interdependence of our provinces has much to offer worldwide Christianity."

The Archbishop expressed his hope that the 1998 Lambeth Conference would "lead us in an openly constructive way to look to the future with confidence as we proclaim the good news of Jesus Christ. The story we have to tell is life-changing and we should not falter in the call to make Christ known to all people," he said. "I believe Lambeth '98 will help to focus the minds and hearts of all bishops as the Anglican Communion prepares for the challenges and opportunities of the new century."

A banner leads the bishops of the Episcopal Church U.S.A. into Canterbury
Cathedral for the opening Eucharist of the 1998 Lambeth Conference.
(Photo: Episcopal News Service)

Concerns about unity, of course, did not emerge out of the blue. Faced with the imminent possibility that the Americans were likely to elect a woman to the episcopate, the 1988 conference sought to ward off threats to unity when it passed a resolution urging respect for one another's decisions on the issue. The vote was 423 to 28, with 19 bishops abstaining. It asked the Archbishop of Canterbury to appoint a commission to monitor the process.

The resolution had been shaped by a small group that included Edmond Browning, then Presiding Bishop of the Episcopal Church U.S.A., and Graham Leonard, Bishop of London. Browning was a strong proponent of the ordination of women to all orders, and Leonard was an outspoken opponent who later joined the Roman Catholic Church after the Church of England decided to ordain women. The resolution said the church needed "to exercise sensitivity, patience and pastoral care towards all concerned."

Archbishop of Canterbury Robert Runcie acknowledged that polarization among the bishops on women's ordination posed a threat to unity. In his opening address at the 1988 Lambeth, his topic was "The Nature of the Unity We Seek."

Runcie spoke of Anglicans as "traditionally suspicious of the Lambeth Conference becoming anything other than a conference" because the tradition is "opposed to centralism and encourages the thriving of variety." Yet he said Anglicans "may indeed wish to discuss the development of more solid structures of unity and coherence. But I for one would want their provisional character made absolutely clear; like tents in the desert they should be capable of being easily dismantled when it is time for the Pilgrim People to move on. We have no intention of developing an alternative papacy."

He noted "real and serious threats to our unity and communion and I do not underestimate them." He expressed a hope that the issue of women in the episcopate "won't dominate this conference but we need to recognize that our unity is threat-

ened over the ordination of women to the priesthood and episcopate in whatever we ultimately decide to do. There are dangers to our Communion in this Lambeth Conference endorsing
or failing to endorse such developments. And there are equal
dangers to communion by trying to avoid the issue altogether."

Runcie said that "conflict is particularly painful, because
the glue which binds us together is not so much juridical, but
personal, informal and expressed in worship....So we tend to
shy away from conflict which has destructive potential. This
is, of course, a serious mistake." He added, "Conflict can be
destructive. It can also be creative. We are here not to avoid
conflict but to redeem it. At the heart of faith is a cross and
not, as in some religions, an eternal calm."

While it might be easier to work for local expressions of
Anglicanism, Runcie said that "it is only by being in communion together that diversity and difference have value. Without relationship, difference divides."

The Anglican Communion has reached a stage in its
development "when we must begin to make radical choices or
growth will imperceptibly turn to decay," Runcie added. The
choice is between "unity or gradual fragmentation." The decisive choice is whether or not "we want the Anglican Communion. And if we do, what are we going to do about it?"

In its lead editorial on August 8, 1988, "Avoiding Fragmentation," the London *Times* said: "At this year's Lambeth
Conference, the unity of Anglicanism has been exposed as the
fragile vessel it is. If that enables Anglicanism to gain a better, and long overdue, sense of internal responsibility, that
may be a benefit." Despite three weeks of debate, "the participants were still facing broadly the same direction as they
reached port. They emerged as friends, still unable to agree
about several key issues, but still recognizably members of
the same episcopal college."

In a sermon at the closing Eucharist at Lambeth 1988,
Edmond Browning said, "We have heard much these past

weeks about unity, about communion, about authority. Often these words are heard only as cries of survival, often they are perceived as romantic and sentimental preservation of the structures of the past. The Anglican Communion must empty itself, abandoning not our diversities but our separateness. To have true unity, to have authority, the Anglican Communion must not be a museum of the past but the household of faith for the future."

ROAD TO LAMBETH '98

With these concerns in mind, the design team for the 1998 Lambeth Conference identified four themes for the meeting: (1) "Called to Full Humanity," (2) "Called to Live and Proclaim the Good News," (3) "Called to be Faithful in a Plural World," and (4) "Called to be One."

The first group would be chaired by Archbishop Njongonkulu Ndungane of Southern Africa with Bishop Kenneth Fernando of Sri Lanka as vice-chair. It was assigned questions such as: "What does it mean to be truly human, as individuals and in community? What are the forces which enhance, and which threaten, our humanity?"

Bishop Rowan Williams of Wales would chair the second group, with Bishop Yong Ping Chung of Malaysia as vice-chair. Questions for this group would be: "How is the church to ensure that the faith is faithfully handed on from generation to generation and that it is effectively interpreted in word and deed to the world?"

The third group would be headed by Bishop Fred Borsch of Los Angeles, with Bishop Simon Chiwanga of Tanzania as vice-chair. Acknowledging that Anglicans are used to living with a plurality of views but modern cultures are often more radically pluralistic, it would ask: "What are the implications of pluralism within your own region for the life of the church? How in that context can the church be a sign of God's rule?"

Bishop Jabez Bryce of Polynesia would chair the last group, with Bishop Stephen Sykes of England as vice-chair. Questions put to this group would include: "What is the meaning of the unity for which Jesus prays? How do the Christian churches achieve Christ's bond to each other in a world where economic and commercial forces bind people together and where political and cultural tensions tear them apart?"

At a lecture at Yale Divinity School in October 1997, Bishop Mark Dyer of Virginia Theological Seminary, a member of the design team, said that "the central concern that faces the Communion with every contentious issue that comes before us is: How do we stay in communion with one another? How do we love one another as Christ loves us, in the midst of disagreement and conflict?...How do we remain as one in God and as members of the one Body of Christ, at a time when independence is more valued than interdependence, when the independent decisions of individual dioceses threaten the unity for which Jesus Christ prayed the night before he died?"

For Dyer "the issue is as old as the church herself." He asserted that "the identity of the church as one and catholic, holy and apostolic, is preserved only when the communion of the churches with one another is maintained and the vital character of their interdependence is lived out." The primary challenge is "unity and communion in the midst of diversity."

While it is clear that Anglicans in differing contexts produce "differing attitudes to the faith and cause different elements to be emphasized within our common tradition," Dyer said that "these experiences must be submitted to the discipline and practice of personal prayer and the nurture of biblical teaching and meditation."

The Lambeth Conference provides "a forum for consultation, dialogue and mutual support" and has "avoided becoming an ecclesiastical curia. Nevertheless, the importance of the moral and spiritual guidance should not be underestimated," Dyer said. He pointed to the resolution of the 1988 Lambeth Conference on the ordination and consecration of women to the episcopate as an example of how "the ministry of unity and communion was enabled in the Communion over this most difficult issue."

While the design team worked out the official agenda, other gatherings also identified concerns that would dominate the conference.

Just prior to Lambeth, sixty-eight bishops from around the world who share African ancestry met in the English university town of Cambridge to identify common issues. These "Afro-Anglican" bishops from the United States, England, the West Indies, and the African continent settled on eight key issues—debt cancellation, neo-colonialism, the arms trade, Muslim-Christian relations, refugees of war, the AIDS crisis, inter-Anglican relationships, and church growth.

"The Afro-Anglican conference informed us and prepared us for making positive contributions in the various sections," said Bishop Josiah Idowu-Fearon of Nigeria. Citing a presentation on the issue of international debt, he added, "Had it not been for the Cambridge meeting, we would have been in the dark."

The bishops issued a ten-point statement, "The Cambridge Challenge," that called for a Decade of Reconciliation to "break down the walls which continue to separate us." According to Bishop Orris Walker, Jr., of Long Island, New York, who organized the meeting, the statement "expresses a feeling among bishops of color in the Anglican Communion that there is still too much business as usual and the focus was on the concerns of bishops of the First World." He said "there is a need for a lot of reconciliation. A lot of things passed off as reconciliation are really sort of Anglican courtesy. People have been taught to be courteous and really have not addressed the issues." He suggested a closer examination of the process of reconciliation in South Africa after the apartheid system was dismantled as an example of "where people have confessed their involvement in a bad system and seek one another's forgiveness."

The statement acknowledged the "great diversity and vastly differing contexts" so apparent in the Communion and said such diversity meant "inherent difficulties for the development of a common mind." The statement said that the Cambridge meeting "has provided us with a fruitful reminder of this reality," but said that, despite some differences, "we are in solidarity against the forces and sources of evil and dehumanization."

Idowu-Fearon said that Christians in Africa are "ashamed seeing Christians killing each other in Rwanda," adding that "we feel ashamed when tribal loyalties take precedence over loyalty to Jesus Christ." The bishop's statement referred to a recent genocide in Rwanda in which Anglican clergy were accused of complicity and outright participation in the killing.

THE KUALA LUMPUR STATEMENT

Yet while these official and unofficial efforts to identify common ground proceeded, other developments would accentuate the differences. In February of 1997, about eighty church leaders—many of them bishops and archbishops from Anglican churches in the global South—met in the Malaysian capital of Kuala Lumpur to "reflect on the place of Scripture in the life and mission of the church in the twenty-first century."

"We recognized the importance of our chosen theme for the church at a time of difficulty and confusion in some provinces and of growth, martyrdom, dynamic missionary encouragement and quiet but powerful witness in others," they said in a statement.

The church leaders observed that "as a result of the current demographic shift in the world church, the future of Christianity and the hope for the fulfillment of the Great Commission now lies with them." With an eye to the upcoming Lambeth Conference, they said that they shared "a common experience of life overshadowed by ethnic hatred, political instability and neo-colonialism, social injustice and marginalization, crippling international debt and spiraling inflation, environmental damage and pollution, religious strife and intolerance, unbridled materialism and pervasive corruption."

The church leaders pleaded with the churches of the West "to put pressure on their governments and on the World Bank and the IMF (International Monetary Fund) to respond to the many appeals coming from various quarters worldwide, to make the year 2000 a Year of Jubilee, to remit the two-thirds world debt."

These points, however, do not represent a departure from the positions First World provinces have taken on issues of global economic justice. The divergence surfaced in a section of the statement that assailed Western approaches to scriptural interpretation, making specific reference to sexuality.

With words that would resonate throughout the Anglican Communion, the participants affirmed two key points: (1) "the only sexual expression, as taught in Scriptures which honors God and upholds human dignity, is that between a man and a woman within the sacred ordinance of marriage;" and (2) a belief that "Scripture maintains that any other form of sexual expression is at once sinful, selfish, dishonoring to God and an abuse of human dignity."

The statement concluded, "The Holy Scriptures are clear in teaching that all sexual promiscuity is sin. We are convinced that this includes homosexual practices, between men or women, as well as heterosexual practices outside marriage." It encouraged the church "to care for all those who are trapped in their sexual brokenness" but also support "those who exercise a pastoral ministry in this area."

The church leaders equated the ordination of homosexuals and the blessing of same-sex unions with setting aside biblical teaching, a practice it called "totally unacceptable." To date, no province has authorized either ordination of homosexuals or blessing of same-sex unions, although some, such as the United States, have repeatedly refused to prohibit ordination and to discipline bishops who do it.

The statement called on the whole Anglican Communion to take action and expressed concern about mutual accountability and interdependence. "As provinces and dioceses we need to learn how to seek each other's counsel and wisdom in a spirit of true unity, and to reach a common mind before embarking on radical changes to church discipline and moral teaching."

A few days after the Kuala Lumpur Statement was released, the Standing Committee of the Province of South East Asia passed a resolution that adopted and endorsed the statement and issued a veiled threat that the province intended to support and be in communion "with that part of the Anglican Communion which accepts and endorses the principles...and not otherwise."

The Kuala Lumpur Statement was on its way to becoming the litmus test on sexual morality—at Lambeth and beyond.

The following month, several of the bishops who participated in the Kuala Lumpur meeting brought their concerns to Jerusalem, where the primates of the Anglican Communion were meeting. Often known as presiding bishops or archbishops, primates are those who head a national church or province.

Archbishop Maurice Sinclair of Argentina, an English evangelical who is primate of the Church of the Southern Cone, brought a statement that had emerged from a provincial preparatory meeting for Lambeth in December 1996. The statement charged that the decision of the American church to dismiss heresy charges against Bishop Walter Righter for ordaining a non-celibate gay man to the diaconate was made with an "apparent lack of awareness of implications for the

Communion as a whole in the failure of the majority to identify and affirm church discipline in this area of sexual ethics."
The decision "shakes the unity of the Communion," he
charged, and "has led us to ask questions about the autonomy
of our provinces and the adequacy of our current ways of
relating across the world."

While observing that "Anglican mission has now produced
a totally international and multi-cultural church," Sinclair
asked, "What will hold us together" in attempts to be obedient
to the Gospel? He doubted that "common links in a history
stemming from the British Isles" were "adequate or relevant."
Even "common traditions of worship...have long been diverse
and have further need to be contextualized." Not even the
"moral authority of the Archbishop of Canterbury" could be
expected to "fulfill all the different and sometimes contradic-
tory expectations of his office," he said.

"Common loyalty to Scripture must surely remain but
without a renewal of our best traditions in affirming the
authority of Scripture and applying the balance of its message, this vital bond will be further weakened among us."
Love might work, Sinclair said, "but Christian love requires
discipline as well as emotion."

Dismissing the idea of a "Vatican-style bureaucracy," Sin-
clair wondered, "Is it really Christian to be autonomous? Isn't
Christ's way mutual subjection even in church government?
Long ago we rejected congregationalism at the parish level.
Why should we perpetuate a provincial congregationalism?"
he asked.

"It could be argued that the controversy over homosexual
ordination reflects a sincere (but mistaken) missionary concern in one context which prejudices mission in others, as well
as its own," he said.

The only way forward, Sinclair argued, is for an Archbishop
of Canterbury to "retain his moral authority but not take on a
full-scale global executive role. He would share with the new

Anglican Council and fellow primates in the role of encouragement, direction, and correction. He would be involved in disputed cases only as an exceptional and ultimate source of appeal," he said.

Pointing to Carey's intervention in Rwanda, where he pressed for the resignation of some bishops charged with involvement in the genocide, Sinclair said, "Some light-handed but wise-headed supervision of a collegial nature would do us all good. Authority in the Anglican Communion would continue to be a distributed authority but it would gain the necessary coherence." In facing with realism "the changing world we are called to evangelize and serve," it was apparent to Sinclair that "we clearly cannot afford to be merely a loose federation or a separating family."

At the Primates' Meeting in Jerusalem, Carey set aside an evening for an open discussion on sexuality issues. In what would be a warm-up for Lambeth, one after another of the primates came forward to denounce homosexuality as a sin. The tension hung heavy in the air because everyone knew that the comments were aimed at the Americans and a few sympathizers in other provinces. One African said that, since homosexuals cannot procreate, they are against the will of God. Another said that "we will be written off as heretical in my part of the world if we don't take a clear stand on this issue. We can't afford to hold together truth and error." Pleading for a return to Scripture, he said that "we must not allow false compassion to overcome us—we need tough love."

Only Michael Peers of Canada indicated that he was open-minded on the issue. He used the church's attitudes on divorce as an example of a change in attitude and policy on an issue. "Homosexual people are increasingly visible and audible—and they are asking questions similar to those asked by divorced people in an earlier generation," he said. Canadian bishops have called for "appropriate concern" for those who are living in committed relationships, and the church's synod has overwhelmingly passed resolutions welcoming gays and lesbians into the life of the church...but not in the clergy.

The primates overwhelmingly endorsed the conclusions of the Kuala Lumpur meeting that "the setting aside of biblical teaching in such actions as the ordination of practicing homosexuals and the blessing of same-sex unions calls into question the authority of Holy Scripture. This is totally unacceptable to us."

Presiding Bishop Edmond Browning stood alone in defending the actions of some bishops in the United States. While he was encouraged that the meeting underscored the importance of dealing with economic issues, he was not surprised by the sharp disagreements on sexuality because "we are a long ways from agreeing on sexuality issues."

He told the primates that the church had committed the sin of putting people in a class that is oppressed and rejected. "Our church is not of one mind and I'm sorry to think that some believe we have dealt with the issue lightly. We have been serious about our study."

The primates raised the possibility of a special commission similar to the Eames Commission, which met four times between 1989 and 1993 to discuss the task of maintaining communion when women are admitted to the episcopate. Carey seemed less than enthusiastic but said that he would consider the suggestion.

THE VIRGINIA REPORT

At the same meeting, Irish Archbishop Robin Eames, who chaired the commission, introduced the report of the Inter-Anglican Theological and Doctrinal Commission, known as the Virginia Report because it emerged from meetings at the Virginia Theological Seminary and was supported by the Diocese of Virginia. He was joined in the presentation by Mark

Dyer, former Bishop of Bethlehem, Pennsylvania, who is on the faculty at Virginia Seminary.

As a "further step along the road of self-discovery," Eames said, the report is an attempt to "discover more about what it means to be an Anglican and how we perceive the machinery—the instruments of unity—should inter-relate." The instruments of unity to which he referred included the Archbishop of Canterbury, the Anglican Consultative Council, the Primates' Meeting, and the Lambeth Conference.

The Virginia Report is an intense theological examination of what it means to be a Communion, an exploration of its unity and diversity. "I believe that the next Lambeth Conference will be the most defining Lambeth in history," Eames observed in anticipation of the 1998 meeting. "It will determine what we are and where we are going. It will stand or fall on our sense of unity and vision."

Issues such as lay people presiding at the Eucharist, the sacramental blessing of same-sex unions, and the ordination of sexually active homosexuals "will test the truth of our unity," Dyer said. He expressed his conviction that the Virginia Report, heir to the process used by the Eames Commission, provides a model and theological underpinning for a Communion "held together in the creative tension of provincial autonomy and interdependence."

As a foundation document for Lambeth, the Virginia Report was an attempt to explore the issues of communion addressed by the Eames Commission. During the life of the commission, five women were consecrated as bishops in the Anglican Communion, and the Church of England passed legislation to permit the ordination of women to the priesthood. In addition to the U.S. and Canada, ordinations of women had already occurred in the provinces of Australia, New Zealand/Aotearoa/Polynesia, Brazil, Burundi, Hong Kong and Macao, Ireland, Kenya, the Philippines, Scotland, Southern

Africa, Uganda, and West Africa.

To deepen the discussion, the Archbishop of Canterbury had invited a group of church leaders and theologians, including key ecumenical partners, to meet at Virginia Seminary in December of 1991. This consultation issued a report, "Belonging Together," which was circulated throughout the Communion between 1992 and 1994 with a request for response. The responses were considered by the Inter-Anglican Theological and Doctrinal Commission, formed in the wake of the original consultation, at meetings in December 1994 and in January 1996. The Virginia Report emerged from those meetings.

The report traced the church's struggle to maintain *koinonia* while facing a vast range of social, political, and cultural challenges. "Our response to these issues is conditioned by our particular cultural context, our way of interpreting the Bible, our degree of awareness of being part of a wider human community and our attentiveness to the response of other ecumenical partners, and to the concerns of those of other faiths," the report said in its opening chapter on context.

"When Christians find themselves passionately engaged in the midst of complex and explosive situations, how do they avoid alienation from those who by baptism are their brothers and sisters in Christ, who are embraced in the communion of God the Holy Trinity, but who disagree?" the report asked. "How do they stay in communion with God and each other; how do they behave towards each other in the face of disagreement and conflict? What are the limits of diversity if the Gospel imperative of unity and communion are to be maintained?"

In so clearly identifying the major issues facing the Anglican Communion, the report seemed to sketch the most explosive underlying issue for the Lambeth Conference itself—questions that the conference could not answer, questions that will decide the fate of the Anglican Communion in the years to come. For the goal of the conference, the report argued, "was not simply for strengthening the peace and unity of the Anglican Communion, but also for the faithful and effective engagement of the Communion in God's mission of love and reconciliation in the world."

Despite the intensity of feeling on sexuality issues at Kuala Lumpur and the Primates Meeting, Carey noted that of the nine regional conferences of bishops which met to identify priorities for Lambeth, four of them did not mention sexuality at all. "The rest did not give it high priority. Issues such as international debt and relations with Islam were regarded as far more pressing priorities," he said.

But the impassioned efforts of Americans on both sides of the issue would combine with Carey's subsequent comments to guarantee that sexuality would become the number one controversy at Lambeth '98.

CHAPTER TWO

THE GLOBALIZATION OF SEXUALITY CONCERNS

In many respects, the sexuality issue at Lambeth was an extension of the debate that has dominated the agenda of the Episcopal Church in the United States ever since women began taking their place in the General Convention and in holy orders. In 1970, the very first General Convention in which women were seated in the House of Deputies, the convention authorized the ordination of women to the diaconate. In 1973 similar legislation on the priesthood was approved overwhelmingly by the House of Bishops, but lost on a vote by orders in the House of Deputies, even though a majority of the deputies voted for it.

A vote by orders is a complex weighted voting system in which a measure must win a majority in both the lay order and the clerical order in each diocese. Since each diocese has four lay and four clerical deputies, it is theoretically possible for a diocese to be counted as a "no" vote, even when as many as six deputies vote "yes," if the two negative votes were cast in the same order. A measure can pass only with four and four, four and three, or three and three. Any other combination will result in a "no" vote.

The convention's failure to pass the measure was doubly frustrating to its advocates because there was actually no clear canonical prohibition on ordaining women. The only basis for assuming that it was not permitted was the canons' use of the pronoun "he" in reference to postulants and ordinands. The failed proposal would have amended the canonical language, although many believed it unnecessary, given that bishops have the final say on who may be ordained.

Frustrated by the widespread support and an assumed prohibition based on what they saw as a technicality, three bishops ordained eleven women in Philadelphia in 1974. Their ordinations were followed by another group of ordinations in Washington several months later.

The General Convention of 1976 handed opponents of women's ordination a stunning defeat. Not only did the convention open the priesthood to women, effective January 1, 1977, but it also declared the Philadelphia and Washington ordinations to be valid but "irregular" and took action to "regularize" them. The action amended the canons to make it clear that women could be ordained to the priesthood *and the episcopate* as well as the diaconate.

In two separate actions, the convention also declared that "homosexual persons are children of God with a full and equal claim on the love, acceptance, and pastoral care and concern of the church" and it endorsed civil rights protections for gays and lesbians.

In January, when the canonical amendments took effect, Bishop Paul Moore of New York ordained the Rev. Ellen Marie Barrett to the priesthood. Barrett at the time was vice president of Integrity, the association of gay and lesbian Episcopalians and their supporters. Her lesbian orientation had been known to all involved in her ordination process from the very beginning, but for the opponents of women in the priesthood, Barrett's ordination confirmed their worst fears.

"INAPPROPRIATE AT THIS TIME"

The very next General Convention (1979) would come closer to banning gay and lesbian ordination than any subsequent convention. Acting on the recommendation of the Commission on Human Affairs and Health, which included no gay-identified persons in its membership, the convention passed a resolution advising that ordination of openly gay postulants was "inappropriate at this time."

The action of General Convention in 1979, however, did not halt either the ordination of women or the advancement of gay and lesbian concerns. A group of forty-four bishops at the 1979 convention immediately signed a dissenting statement, saying that they would not be bound by the resolution as a matter of conscience. Lay and clerical deputies from virtually all of the large metropolitan dioceses also signed the statement, and ordinations of openly gay postulants went forward in those dioceses.

The intervening years were spent trying to determine how binding the 1979 resolution was for the church. Attempts at subsequent General Conventions to write a policy into canon law, either prohibiting or condoning the ordination of non-celibate homosexuals, did not succeed, further increasing the frustration level on both sides. Other events only heightened the tension. However, the convention did reaffirm its earlier support for civil rights protections.

In 1989, the high-profile ordination of an avowed, non-celibate gay man to the priesthood in Newark by Bishop John Spong brought strong reaction in the church and led to attempts by some bishops to bring charges against him for violating the spirit of the 1979 resolution. At its 1990 meeting in Washington, the House of Bishops voted 80 to 76 to "dissociate" itself from the ordination. At the same meeting they

Bishops Steven Plummer of Navajoland and Mark MacDonald of Alaska receive Communion from Sr. Rosina, OSH, of Ghana at the opening Lambeth Eucharist. (Photo: Episcopal News Service)

adopted a "Statement on Homosexuality" that called for continuing dialogue.

Less than a month after the House of Bishops meeting, Walter Righter, the retired Bishop of Iowa who was serving as an assistant bishop in Newark, ordained Barry Stopfel to the diaconate. Stopfel was living in a relationship with another man. Spong later ordained him to the priesthood. The next year, Bishop Ronald Haines of Washington, D.C., ordained a lesbian to the priesthood. The news hit the front page of the *Washington Post*.

The tensions fed into the 1991 General Convention in Phoenix. A resolution affirmed that the church's teaching historically has been that "physical sexual expression is appropriate only within a life-long, monogamous" relationship between a man and a woman. Yet it acknowledged that there is a "discontinuity" between that teaching and the experience of some members of the church. An attempt to censure Righter and Haines did not succeed.

The Standing Commission on Human Affairs released its report, based on three years of study and regional hearings, recommending that the decisions on ordinations, including the ordination of openly gay and lesbian candidates, should be left to the local dioceses. Known as the Hunt Report, for Bishop George Hunt of Rhode Island who chaired the commission, it also called on the Standing Liturgical Commission to study the issues and forms for blessing same-sex unions.

The House of Deputies killed a proposal from Bishop William Frey of Colorado proposing a canon that would insist that clergy "abstain from genital sexual relations outside of Holy Matrimony."

Sparks flew in the House of Bishops as heated exchanges by bishops on opposite sides of the issue led to an unprecedented series of six closed sessions aimed at repairing the damaged trust level in the house. The house appointed a task force to prepare a pastoral teaching on sexuality issues, chaired by Bishop Richard Grein of New York. The task force's attempts to do their work in developing drafts in secret failed in a climate of escalating polarization. Leaks of the drafts set the stage for a confrontation at the 1994 General Convention in Indianapolis.

A GAY BISHOP

Two years later, one of the bishops who sat quietly during the debate at the 1991 House of Bishops meeting wrote an open letter to his colleagues announcing that he was gay. The letter went out just before the bishops were scheduled to meet in Panama.

Otis Charles, former Bishop of Utah and recently retired dean of the Episcopal Divinity School in Massachusetts, said that he was "sufficiently troubled by my silence that I subsequently told the Presiding Bishop what I had been carrying silently in my heart for so long...."

Charles said that he could no longer allow himself to be talked about as one of "those" in the House of Bishops. "Sexuality is a part of the richness, the complexity and mystery of God's creation. It is an essential part of our human experience, and it is a part of the experience of priests and bishops," he wrote. "Indeed, it deserves—perhaps even requires—to be dealt with as straightforwardly and sensitively as matters of doctrine and pastoral care." He added that "the choice for me is not whether or not I am a gay man, but whether or not I am honest about who I am with myself and others. It is a choice to take down the wall of silence I have built around an important and vital part of my life, to end the separation and isolation I have imposed on myself all these years. It is a choice to live my life as consistently as I can with my own integrity, a choice to be fully who I am and to be responsible for all that I am."

Charles observed that the issue of racial, sexual, and cultural diversity in the Episcopal Church for the previous twenty years or more had been "controversial, painful and often divisive. Yet something new is being done in our midst, in spite of our reluctance."

The 1991 General Convention had also asked the dioceses to initiate a discussion of sexuality issues at the local level. In presenting the preliminary report to the bishops at their meeting in Panama, Bishop O'Kelley Whitaker, the retired Bishop of Central New York who chaired the committee, said that the study revealed a "willingness to be open." He said that the study also "helped to de-politicize the issue and bridge gaps between people." While acknowledging that some regulations are necessary for the order of the church, he said that he was convinced that "issues of human sexuality will never be solved by legislation."

Whitaker said in his report that more than 18,000 Episcopalians in seventy-seven percent of the dioceses answered a questionnaire. "Almost one hundred percent of the respondents say that one can be a faithful Christian and be divorced or divorced and remarried. Three-quarters report that one can be faithful and live with someone of the opposite sex without marriage. Seventy percent indicate that being sexually active as a gay or lesbian person is not contrary to being a faithful Christian. Respondents are equally divided in affirming or denying that bisexual persons can be faithful Christians," said the report.

Among the other findings, the report said that eighty-one percent agreed that "homosexuality is a genuine sexual orientation for some people," and fifty-three percent thought that "committed relationships between gay and lesbian persons could strengthen the Christian community."

Heading into the General Convention in 1994, it became obvious that sexuality would top the agenda. The bishops tested their collegiality in the wake of the confrontations at the previous convention, drawing on closed annual retreats at the Kanuga Conference Center in the mountains of western North Carolina.

As drafts of the proposed pastoral teaching ricocheted throughout the church, opposing sides girded themselves for battle.

The bishops of the church's Province VII, twelve dioceses in the Southwest, arrived at the convention with protest. Their Affirmation Statement, signed by 101 bishops, charged that the pastoral was advocating a substantial departure from the what it termed the "biblical" understanding of sexuality, and it reaffirmed the teaching that the only appropriate context for sexual intimacy was within life-long, monogamous heterosexual marriage. While saying that the draft had "a good deal of helpful material in it," the Affirmation said it did not provide "the clear guidance wanted and needed by Christian people for faithful living."

"We affirm the teaching of Scripture and tradition that marriage is life-long in intention, sacred in character, and a reflection on the human level of the love relationship between God and the Covenant People in the Old Testament, and that between Christ and the church in the New Testament," the bishops said.

The statement added that "sexual relationships outside of marriage constitute a denial of God's plan for humanity, and they must be met by a call to repentance and amendment of life." It concluded that "neither the church nor its bishops have the authority to compromise in principle, or give approval in practice, to standards less or other than our God has given us."

At convention, in a civil but intense debate, the draft document was amended to strengthen the language on chastity and marriage and then the bishops voted to downgrade its status from a teaching document to a "pastoral study document of the

House of Bishops to the church as the church considers issues of human sexuality." And they attached the Affirmation from Province VII.

Later, Bishop John Spong of Newark dramatically introduced a *Koinonia* Statement, signed by fifty-five bishops present at General Convention, asserting that sexual orientation is "morally neutral," that marriage is an "honorable vocation for some of God's people," and that "faithful, monogamous, committed" relationships of gays and lesbians are worthy of honor. Some bishops sought to attach the *Koinonia* Statement to the study document and, in the end, neither it nor the Affirmation was attached.

A somewhat ambiguous guideline at the end of the pastoral study document said that bishops should ordain "only persons [they] believe to be a wholesome example to their people, according to the standards and norms established by the church." That angered some bishops who charged that the ordination issue could not be a "local option."

Both houses of the General Convention agreed to change the church's canon law to ensure that no one would be barred from access to the ordination process because of "race, color, ethnic origin, sex, national origin, marital status, sexual orientation, disabilities or age, except as otherwise specified by these canons." The bishops blocked a resolution calling for the church to develop rites for blessing same-sex unions, although they agreed to a substitute resolution endorsing a study of the theological and pastoral considerations that would be involved in developing such rites.

A HERESY TRIAL

Clearly frustrated by the church's inability to resolve the issue in favor of their understanding of the tradition, the conservative bishops filed charges against Walter Righter in January 1995. They charged that, in ordaining Barry Stopfel to the diaconate, he broke his vows to uphold the doctrine and teaching of the church and should be tried on the church's so-called "heresy" canon. Before the court could meet, it was necessary for one-quarter of the bishops to agree to proceed with a trial.

Under the leadership of Bishop William Wantland of Eau Claire, the General Convention had changed the requirement for bringing a presentment of charges from the previously required three-quarters of the entire House of Bishops to just ten bishops with jurisdiction, meaning bishops who head dioceses.

After considerable political maneuvering, the necessary consents were received by August 18 and, despite attempts by Presiding Bishop Edmond Browning to head off a confrontation, the Episcopal Church moved towards the second heresy trial in its entire history.

The Court for the Trial of a Bishop held a preliminary hearing in Hartford, Connecticut, and both sides quickly agreed that, before a trial could proceed, the court had to determine what was at stake. They agreed that it would be necessary to determine whether the church had a doctrine on the issue of non-celibate homosexual ordinations.

While Wantland, a trained lawyer who was author of the original presentment, and Hugo Blankingship of Virginia, who served as co-counsel for those bringing charges against Righter, argued for a different approach to the trial, they agreed that "the question of doctrine is the threshold issue that must be decided before you can proceed."

Michael Rehill of Newark, Righter's attorney, went a step further and argued that the court was required to establish that a doctrine exists, that Righter "knew and understood that doctrine, and that he deliberately chose to defy it."

After both sides filed briefs, the court met in Wilmington, Delaware, in May of 1996, and by a seven-to-one vote rendered its judgment that there was "no core doctrine prohibiting the ordination of a non-celibate, homosexual person living in a faithful and committed sexual relationship with a person of the same sex." The court also stated that it did not find "sufficient clarity in the church's teaching at the present time concerning the morality of same-sex relationships" to support the charge that Righter was guilty of "holding and teaching doctrine contrary to that held by this church" or was guilty of violating his ordination vows to uphold the doctrine and discipline of the church.

Without clear General Convention action one way or the other, the court indicated that "this issue will not be resolved and the church unified in its faith and practice by presentments and trials, nor by unilateral acts of bishops and their dioceses, or through the adoption of proclamations by groups of bishops or others expressing positions on the issues."

The court was careful to point out, "We are not deciding whether life-long, committed, same gender sexual relationships are or are not a wholesome example with respect to ordination vows....We are not rendering an opinion on whether a bishop and diocese should or should not ordain persons living in same gender sexual relationships. Rather, we are deciding the narrow issue of whether or not under Title IV [the canons that govern the conduct of bishops] a bishop is restrained from ordaining persons living in committed same gender sexual relationships."

In a dissenting opinion, Bishop Andrew Fairfield of North Dakota argued for a broader interpretation of doctrine, maintaining that the 1979 General Convention resolution embodied authoritative doctrine.

In a statement released the following day, the ten bishops who brought the presentment called the court's decision "stunning" though predictable. "In a single pronouncement it has swept away two millennia of Christian teaching regarding God's purposes in creation, the nature and meaning of marriage and family."

In the ensuing months, the Kuala Lumpur meeting would issue its statement linking the issues of economic justice and sexuality. The following spring, the Episcopal Synod of America (ESA) would endorse it. ESA is an organization within the Episcopal Church formed in 1989 that continues to oppose the ordination of women and what it perceives as liberal trends in sexual morality. The group had not previously been identified with economic justice concerns.

In a letter to Archbishop Moses Tay of South East Asia, the ESA thanked him for his role at the Primates Meeting in making it "abundantly clear to the American primate that you felt his province should be expelled from the worldwide Anglican Communion should the American church fail to reverse its de facto acceptance and endorsement of the ordination of non-celibate homosexuals and the blessing of same-sex unions."

The ESA bishops said that they "celebrate our continued communion with the Province of Southeast Asia and other like-minded provinces." The letter said that they looked forward to meeting with Tay and others at an Evangelism Symposium in September "to explore ways to make our joint witness to biblical Christianity at Lambeth and beyond."

Signing the letter were Bishops Jack Iker of Ft. Worth, William Wantland of Eau Claire, John-David Schofield of San Joaquin, Keith Ackerman of Quincy, and Donald Parsons and Edward McBurney, both retired Bishops of Quincy.

"Ongoing attempts by U.S. Episcopalians to downplay homosexuality as a moral concern have outraged Asian, African and South American members of the worldwide Anglican Communion, to which the Episcopal Church belongs," said a May 6 press release from the ESA. It alleged that the proposal to expel the Episcopal Church from the Communion "for repeated breaches of Christian moral teaching" met with "wide favor" but did not make it on the agenda of the Primates' Meeting because "the church's official teaching remained orthodox."

The ESA release said that the resolution from South East Asia "speeds what many observers view as a coming realignment

of Anglicans which will see traditionalists of different geographical regions standing together morally and spiritually in
defense of principles denied by revisionists who, in many
cases, are their own bishops and fellow communicants." The
ESA has persistently called for a non-geographic province in
the Episcopal Church to protect traditionalists, charging that
there is open discrimination in the ordination process for
those who continue to oppose the ordination of women to the
priesthood. The ESA has also reached out to traditionalists in
the Church of England who also have sought a separate
province to protect their views.

From the conservatives' standpoint, the General Convention of 1997 only made matters worse. Besides electing someone who was perceived as a liberal as Presiding Bishop, the
House of Deputies came within one vote of asking the Standing Commission on Liturgy and Music to prepare a rite for
blessing same-sex unions. Both houses cleared the way for
dioceses to offer health benefits coverage for unmarried
domestic partners, pointing to the example of several major
American corporations. It voted down extending pension benefits to surviving partners of gay and lesbian clergy, however.
On the last day the convention issued an unusual apology to
homosexuals inside and outside the church for what it called
"years of rejection and maltreatment by the church," while
acknowledging "the diversity of opinion...on the morality of
gay and lesbian sexual relationships."

In the wake of the decision not to proceed with the heresy
trial of Righter, the convention attempted clearer definitions of
what constitutes "doctrine" and "discipline" in the church. The
source of church discipline is found in "the Constitution, the
Canons, the Rubrics, and the Ordinal in the Book of Common
Prayer," said one resolution. And another defined doctrine as
"the basic and essential teachings of the church" found in Holy
Scripture as understood in the Apostles' and Nicene creeds, the
sacramental rites, the ordinal, and the catechism of the Book

of Common Prayer.

A resolution that would have endorsed the Kuala Lumpur statement was referred to an interim body. Others dealing with definitions of immorality, the authorizing of same-sex blessings, even one calling for a twenty-one-year moratorium on ordinations of non-celibate gays and lesbians while allowing "local option," were either discharged or rejected.

DEVELOPMENTS OVERSEAS

Meanwhile, the Church of England's General Synod also met in July. At that meeting, Archbishop Carey admitted that "when the primates met in March this year, it is true that a number of differing views about homosexual practice were expressed vigorously, and it was suggested that a number of provinces might feel so strongly about the issue that they would find it difficult to remain in communion with provinces that decided to ordain practicing homosexuals or welcome 'same-sex marriages.'"

Carey added that in his private discussions with some of the primates he discovered that "homosexual practice was simply not on the agenda of over two-thirds of the provinces as a live issue—and even in those provinces which were discussing it, no imminent legal changes were envisaged, whatever more subtle, non-legal changes might be afoot."

Carey also suggested that Archbishop Desmond Tutu of Southern Africa did not speak for the bishops of his province when he endorsed gay rights as a justice issue. "We know that, in the Anglican Communion, there is a strand of opinion challenging the traditional understanding of the church. We know that the great Desmond Tutu, a personal friend of mine, is an eloquent exponent of that opinion. But it remains a minority view," Carey said.

"Let me remind Synod that, under his successor, Archbishop Ndungane, the bishops of the Province of Southern

Africa have agreed to a statement which, though pastorally sensitive, includes this reaffirmation of the church's position that sex is for life-long marriage with a person of the opposite sex, for the purpose of companionship, sexual fulfillment and procreation."

What set off Carey's comments was an earlier press story in which Tutu, the celebrated hero of the struggle against apartheid, had blasted the "reprehensible" statements made by President Robert Mugabe of Zimbabwe who called homosexuals "pigs" and "perverts," describing homosexuality as a "Western perversion" unknown in African culture. He had been asked about the situation as the World Council of Churches laid plans to hold its Assembly in Harare.

Tutu said that he had chosen to speak out when most church leaders had avoided the issue because "it is a matter of ordinary justice. We struggled against apartheid in South Africa because we were being blamed and made to suffer for something we could do nothing about. It is the same with homosexuality. The orientation is a given, not a matter of choice. It would be crazy for someone to choose to be gay, given the homophobia that is present." Tutu said that he could not have fought against the discrimination of apartheid and not also fight against the discrimination which homosexuals endure, even in the church, which he described as "still confused."

"Our Anglican Church says that orientation is okay, but gay sex activity is wrong. That is crazy. We say the expression of love in a monogamous, heterosexual relationship is more than just the physical but includes touching, embracing, kissing, maybe the genital act. The totality of this makes each of us grow to become giving, increasingly godlike and compassionate," Tutu said. "If it is so for the heterosexual, what earthly reason have we to say that it is not the case with the homosexual, provided the relationship is exclusive, not promiscuous?" Tutu asked. "I hope that one day we will have the courage of our theology."

Tutu had joined 300 other international church leaders in sending greetings to the Lesbian and Gay Christian Movement (LGCM) of England on its twentieth anniversary in February 1996. He made his statement in March, in response to questions about his signing an ad that recognized the "valuable contribution made to the continuing debate on sexuality" and calling on the churches to "engage fully with this important question."

In March the bishops of Southern Africa issued a statement, based on a study document issued by the province's theological commission in 1995, that said, "Our church has recognized for some time that the expression of human sexuality is a matter of increasingly urgent pastoral concern...and, as a church we still have a long way to go to come to terms with, and frequently even to discuss, many aspects of human sexuality. Homosexuality is such a concern."

The statement continued, "For many it is a matter of pastoral crisis. Others are scarcely aware of the urgency. Certainly, as bishops, we have no consensus on a number of the problems relating to homosexuality and we are aware that that same lack of consensus exists in our church as a whole."

Yet the statement went on to assert a general agreement that "as a church we have been responsible over the centuries for rejecting many people because of their sexual orientation. The harshness and hostility to homosexual people, still expressed by many within the church, is neither acceptable nor is it in accord with our Lord's love of all people. We repent of this attitude and ask forgiveness of the many homosexual people who have been hurt, rejected and marginalized because of this deep-rooted prejudice."

The bishops affirmed the church's traditional understanding of marriage and said that it had no authority to bless same-sex relationships and "this should remain the case unless the church reaches a different mind on the subject."

It called for further study, especially study dealing with the biblical texts on the subject. "As bishops we are unhappy at the tendency in some quarters to attack homosexuals on the basis of simplistic interpretations of certain scriptural texts."

While the controversy gathered steam, Carey made his own position quite clear. "I do not find any justification, from the Bible or the entire Christian tradition, for sexual activity outside of marriage," he told the General Synod, using comments similar to the ones he made at a convocation at Virginia Seminary in February. "Thus, same-sex relationships in my view cannot be on a par with marriage and the church should resist any diminishing of the fundamental 'sacramentum' of marriage." He added that he did not share the assumption that "it is only a matter of time before the church will change its mind."

In a sermon, Carey described the situation as he saw it. "We face a potential conflict, a paradox which is in danger of becoming a burden. Anglicanism is flourishing. At its heart is the principle of freedom. We are not a monolithic church which dictates to our members precisely what shall and shall not be the package of faith. But nor are we simply a collection of independent churches, doing what we will regardless of the effect we have on others," he said.

Carey said that Anglicanism is "a movement which is confident of its roots in the Gospel, confident in its determination to be a church of the people, wherever the people are, and confident, I hope, in our desire to remain in relationship with one another—to be in communion—because of our relationship with Christ. But that in itself suggests a voluntary curtailment of our freedom."

According to Carey, "The greatest heresy of all is the failure to live and work together as Christians when we disagree and we dare not, must not, should not, allow any issue, however important to us personally, to become a matter that divides the church."

THE DALLAS STATEMENT

That September, on the heels of the General Convention of the American church and the General Synod of the Church of England, fifty bishops from sixteen nations met in Dallas and issued a strong statement linking international debt and sexual morality, echoing the sentiments of Kuala Lumpur.

The Dallas Statement said that "unbridled economic individualism" has led "both to the break-up of families and the escalation of international debt." And it drew a direct tie between "concern for the social good of nations" through debt relief and the promotion of "strong, healthy families through faithful, monogamous heterosexual relationships." The meeting was sponsored by the Oxford Centre for Mission Studies and the Ekklesia Society, an umbrella organization of traditionalists in the Episcopal Church. It was hosted by and received financial support from the Diocese of Dallas.

The bishops, most of them from Africa, expressed gratitude for the Kuala Lumpur Statement, saying that they "share in the affirmation that the biblical sexual norm is clear" and that the "church has no authority to set aside clear biblical teaching by ordaining non-celibate homosexuals or authorizing the blessing of same-sex relationships."

Drawing a distinction between homosexuality as an orientation and the gay agenda as a socio-political identity, the statement concluded, "It is not acceptable for a pro-gay agenda to be smuggled into the church's program or foisted upon our people—and we will not permit it."

The statement called for further reflection in the Anglican Communion on the "centrality of the authority of Scriptures in our understanding and interpretation of the world" and the "ministry of the obedient Christian community...."

In a proposal that would find considerable resonance at Lambeth, the bishops asked the Anglican Communion to use the meeting of primates as "a place of appeal for those Anglican bodies who are oppressed, marginalized or denied faithful episcopal oversight by their own bishops."

The statement warned that "those who choose beliefs and practices outside the boundaries of the historic faith must understand they are separating themselves from communion, and leading others astray," adding that "the reality of broken fellowship can extend to individuals, congregations or even whole dioceses and provinces."

The Rev. Vinay Samuel, executive director of the Oxford Centre, said that the dozen bishops from the Episcopal Church who participated "spoke in terms of near despair at their inability to influence the course of events" in the American church.

While Samuel and Archbishop David Gitari of Kenya, the other chair of the conference, were surprised at the bluntness of the statement, they agreed that the bishops had every right to express their strong convictions. "This is a theological statement, not a political one," Samuel said in an interview.

Both the Dallas Statement and the Kuala Lumpur Statement share "a common spirit that we are going in the wrong direction," Samuel said, and that Anglicans committed to orthodox Christian faith want to "contribute to the shaping of the theological direction of the communion" and ask Western churches to stop making decisions that breed disunity.

The Rev. Bill Atwood, general secretary of Ekklesia, said that he had spent the previous few years establishing links with bishops and dioceses around the world and was encouraged by their "heart, life and vitality." Unlike previous Lambeth Conferences, where the voice of bishops from the two-thirds world was muted, he predicted that the bishops of the

South would have a significant impact on the 1998 Lambeth. It turned out to be a serious understatement.

In January 1998 the diocesan bishops of Rwanda weighed in, after reading the statements from Kuala Lumpur and Dallas. "We are convinced that homosexuality and lesbianism are clearly a deviation from the natural norm and divine order and those who practice homosexuality and lesbianism are in sin," they said. "We know that some Westerners have introduced homosexual practices in the Great Lakes Region of Africa but we, as Africans, repudiate the practice and do not wish it to be seen in our province. We want to promote stable, monogamous marriage between a man and a woman within the love of God." The Rwandans would be very vocal at Lambeth.

In May members of Reform, a group of conservative evangelicals in the Church of England, went so far as to urge Carey to withdraw the invitations sent to Spong and other liberal bishops. Their plea came in the wake of Spong's publishing of *Twelve Theses* in which he rejects the church's understanding of "theism" and says that Christianity is facing bankruptcy.

Among his theses, Spong says that:
- Christ's death as a sacrifice for the sins of the world is a "barbarian idea" that "must be dismissed."
- The bodily Resurrection "cannot be" because it defies what we now know about physics and space.
- "There is no external, objective, revealed standard writ in Scripture or on tablets of stone that will govern our ethical behavior for all time."
- Prayer "cannot be a request made to a theistic deity to act in human history in a particular way."
- The story of the Ascension "assumed a three-tiered universe and is therefore not capable of being translated into the concepts of a post-Copernican space age."
- The story of the fall of Adam and Eve and the concept of original sin are "nonsense."

"What I'm trying to do is separate the human 'experience' of God from the official 'explanation' of God that churches have been offering for nearly 2,000 years," Spong said.

The English evangelicals were not alone in the criticism of the Newark bishop. American conservatives also challenged Spong on his *Twelve Theses* and his book, *Why Christianity Must Change or Die* (Harper San Francisco). Morehouse Publishing issued a collection of essays, *Can a Bishop Be Wrong? Ten Scholars Challenge John Shelby Spong.* The book's editor, Dean Peter Moore of Trinity School for Ministry in Pennsylvania, said that the timing was coincidental, that the book "has been in the works for years." He charged that "the God Spong talks about is a silent God that in no way communicates with the created order. In the end, he offers us an inarticulate being about whom nothing really can be said with any clarity."

Bishop James Stanton of Dallas, one of the contributors to the book, said that Spong is "painting himself as a heroic rescuer of the downtrodden, or a sort of Galileo who suffers persecution bravely for the sake of truth" when he is really "a bishop fighting a holy war to make the church safe for atheism." He accused Spong of preaching "provocative blasphemies."

In response, Spong said that he chose "to stay and wrestle with my Christianity, to try to understand ideas of Trinity and Incarnation, not in the way people did in the third century."

Other American bishops, however, lined up to oppose Spong's approach. The bishops of West Texas, for example, in their diocesan newspaper blasted the *Twelve Theses* as a "call for not so much a new reformation as for an abandonment of the Christian faith and its rearticulation in terms which are foreign to sacred Scripture and the catholic faith." Bishops James Folts and Robert Hibbs accused Spong of "pressing the envelope of faith and morals for the sake of an enhanced relevance in an increasingly post-Christian culture." They said that "of late he seems to have fallen out of the boat."

In June a group of fifty bishops from the Episcopal Church signed a statement saying that they "publicly disassociate ourselves" from Spong's *Twelve Theses*. "In no way do they represent the doctrine, discipline or worship of the Episcopal Church, or any other branch of orthodox Christianity," they said. "We respect John Spong's right to his personal opinions, but we declare they are clearly outside the realm of Christian discourse, and we deplore his use of the office of bishop to propound them." Alleging that it was a contradiction for him, as a bishop, to confirm and ordain people to a faith he no longer confesses, it said such an action was "morally fraudulent and spiritually bankrupt."

AFRICANS ENRAGED

Despite this criticism, Spong pressed his concerns further. In an extraordinary exchange of letters in the year before Lambeth, Carey and Spong increased the intensity of the debate on how Lambeth would handle the sexuality issue to a surprisingly confrontational level.

Spong sent a "white paper" on homosexuality to all Anglican bishops, accusing Carey of showing "no moral credibility" and "disappointing those who expect more of his leadership role." He demanded that the issue be "openly and authentically" discussed at Lambeth.

Spong's letter, made public in London in the fall of 1997, outlined his "deep concern for a significant part of both our communion and the human race, namely the gay and lesbian population of the world." He said that his nine-page paper was in response to recent statements that had been openly critical of the progressive attitudes among some Episcopal bishops, referring to Kuala Lumpur and Dallas.

"I am fearful that when we meet at the Lambeth Conference in 1998, we will act out of our long-standing ignorance and fears, instead of out of the Gospel imperative and thus deal one more violent blow to these victims of our traditional prejudices," Spong wrote, adding that he intended to "challenge the prejudice and ignorance that I believe has been inflicted upon this Communion."

Spong argued that the "scientific evidence is overwhelmingly accepted by the medical and scientific community" but continues to be rejected "by uninformed religious people who buttress their attitude with appeals to a literal understanding of the Bible. This same mentality has marked every debate about every new insight that has arisen in the Western world over the last 600 years. It is a tired, threadbare argument that has become one of embarrassment to the cause of Christ."

In personally attacking Carey's leadership, Spong suggested that the Archbishop was acting out of his own prejudices and showed "no moral credibility" in making "ill-informed" statements on homosexuality.

Spong also attacked Archbishop Maurice Sinclair, whose Southern Cone statement, presented to the primates at their Jerusalem meeting, had expressed concerns similar to Kuala Lumpur. Spong accused him of misusing the Bible as "a weapon of repression" to condemn homosexuals. He likened Sinclair's statements to the church's use of biblical passages to condemn Copernicus and Galileo in the seventeenth century for their discoveries, as well as justifications for slavery in the eighteenth century or the twentieth century distortions of the Bible to undergird segregation, apartheid, and the second-class status of women. "The Bible must never be used to give moral justification to prejudice of any kind," Spong said.

Carey quickly responded, accusing Spong of using a "hectoring and intemperate tone" and inflaming an already difficult situation. Carey's letter, also sent to all Anglican bishops, said that he feared that the Lambeth Conference would be jeopardized by a "showdown" on sexuality issues, and he warned of the "divisive potential of this, not just for the Communion, but for people more generally." Carey predicted a "very negative and destructive conflict" if bishops came to Lambeth expecting a showdown on the issue.

"I assure you that there will be open and honest debate on all issues that concern our Communion," Carey told Spong. "I understand that you feel passionately about this, and that you have the support of a significant number of bishops. However, I ask you in turn to recognize that a very large number of bishops from all over the world disagree with you with equal passion."

Holding out the possibility of appointing a commission to deal with sexuality issues, similar to the Eames Commission appointed in 1988 to deal with holding together the Communion while it faced the likelihood of women in the episcopate, Carey said that such an outcome would be less likely "if you, or indeed, others on the opposite side of the argument intend to split the conference open on this matter."

Carey urged Spong and other bishops, "Do come in peace, do come to learn, do come to share—and leave behind the campaigning tactics which are inappropriate and unproductive, whoever employs them."

Spong fired back another response, charging that Carey had not been so quick to accuse other bishops of being intemperate when they issued statements like Kuala Lumpur or Dallas. "Those statements made assertions about gay and lesbian people that were not just intemperate, but offensive, rude and hostile," Spong wrote. "Those statements went so far as to threaten schism if their point of view did not prevail or to break off communion with provinces of our Communion who disagreed with them."

Spong also contended that the statements "threatened to withdraw financial support from the work of the church unless the church's leadership endorses their point of view.

That strikes me as a form of ecclesiastical blackmail. By your silence in the face of these affronts, you reveal quite clearly where your own convictions lie. That makes it quite difficult to have confidence in your willingness to handle this debate in an even-handed way."

Charging that Carey and other English bishops were more concerned with church unity than with the truth, Spong said that he was convinced that "the church can live with divisions. Church unity is important to me, but it is not an ultimate value. Truth and justice are." He promised "to stand between the gay and lesbian people I am privileged to serve and the negativity and abuse of one more insensitive statement issued on this subject by those who, while quite sincere, are not well-informed." And he said that he would be guided at Lambeth by the motto of his alma mater, Virginia Theological Seminary, "to seek the truth of God whence it may, cost what it will."

"CATECHESIS ON HOMOSEXUALITY"

In May of 1998, Spong and Bishop Peter John Lee of South Africa issued "A Catechesis on Homosexuality," a study paper on the issue. The two bishops, who came at the issue from opposing points of view, identified three areas where they believe there is general consensus and three areas where there are deep divisions, proposing that the Archbishop of Canterbury appoint a commission to study the divisions over the next ten years and report to the next Lambeth Conference.

"We call all bishops to listen to the divergent voices on this issue and to see each other, no matter how deeply divided on this issue, as we really are—faithful Christians seeking God's will....We ask no one to compromise his or her convictions as many fear they might be asked to do," they said in a covering letter.

The bishops contended that the points of agreement included the belief that "homosexual people are God's children who with the entire human family share in God's love and they must therefore be treated with fairness, justice and equality before the law; Second, we stand together in upholding the sacredness of marriage and the importance of the family unit in every society; Third, we believe that the vast majority of the bishops of this Communion are ready to declare that any sexual activity that is predatory and unwelcome, any pattern of sexual behavior that seeks to impose upon a weaker person the will of a stronger person is wrong and should be condemned...."

Among the areas where disagreement is still strong, the bishops cited the blessing of same-sex couples, ordination to the priesthood of gays and lesbians living in relationship, and the authority of the Bible.

Spong and Lee urged Lambeth not to take a vote that "would imply that one side has won or the other side has lost this debate. The church is, in our opinion, too divided and the divisions are so deep that victory for either side would be narrow and those who felt defeated would not take the defeat passively....The result would be that the body of Christ would be wounded and our common witness weakened."

On the eve of Lambeth's opening, Moses Tay and six other bishops from South East Asia expressed their own concern to Carey on how the sexuality issue would be handled. But they also raised another issue—how the Anglican Communion Office (ACO) was being administered. They deplored the dismissal of the Rev. Cyril Okorocha of Nigeria, who headed the ACO's evangelism office and was the staff at the Kuala Lumpur meeting.

(At Lambeth Tay would issue a rebuke to Carey, describing the dismissal as "dishonest and displeasing to God," calling on him to consider the abolition of the Anglican Consultative Council. The British press pounced on the story and said that the dismissal was an example of a high-handed action, taken without consultation. Eames of Ireland said that allegations that the dismissal had been racist were "absolute nonsense.")

The bishops actually questioned the continued existence of the Anglican Consultative Council, at least in its present form, and asked for a review to determine "if it is now outliving its usefulness." They also strongly criticized Spong's *Twelve Theses* and the catechesis prepared by Spong and Lee and concluded that the Anglican Communion was "at the crossroad and crisis of faith and mission."

This sensitive state of affairs would be further aggravated by an interview Spong gave to Andrew Carey, son of the Archbishop of Canterbury and deputy editor of the *Church of England Newspaper*, wherein Spong made some comments that would further anger the Africans and seriously damage his credibility at Lambeth.

Spong said in the interview that much of the African church had only recently "moved out of animism into a very superstitious kind of Christianity," and that they had not "faced the intellectual revolution" of the West, that the influences of thinkers like Copernicus and Einstein were therefore not on their "radar screen." He said that "scientific advances have given us a new way of understanding homosexual people," a "knowledge that hasn't percolated down" to the developing world.

When Carey pressed him on how he thought those comments would sound to Africans, Spong added, "If they feel patronized that's too bad. I am not going to cease to be a twentieth century person for fear of offending somebody in the Third World." Unfortunately, the headline read, "Africans one step up from witchcraft," a term Spong had not used in the interview but which was picked up carelessly by some of the media and became a caricature of his views.

For the Africans, already furious over Spong's position on

homosexuality, the comments were incendiary. Archbishop Njongonkulu Ndungane of South Africa admitted publicly that many had been hurt by the comments. He and Presiding Bishop Frank T. Griswold of the Episcopal Church U.S.A. stepped in and called a meeting of Spong and some African bishops in an attempt to prevent any further damage.

In an interview with David Skidmore of the Lambeth news team, who was writing an article on the situation, Spong admitted that he had "unintentionally alienated" the Africans but did not revise any of his original comments nor was he prepared to make a public apology.

"I do not know how we can ever get around the fact that we come from completely different cultures," Spong said in his interview with Skidmore. "I don't know what to do about that," he admitted. "Religion is a deeply emotional thing. It gets into the fiber of our soul. It is part of our security system."

He said that his criticism of attitudes in the developing world was not intended to denigrate the personal faith commitments of the bishops nor their churches but that cultural differences required the church to communicate the Gospel in its own setting, using different language and symbols. He admitted that using the word "superstitious" was "unfortunate and I think it communicated an unfortunate message."

As a bishop in the New York metropolitan area, Spong said that he had been trying for years to reach the unchurched "post-modern" community who are deeply skeptical of traditional church practices and symbols.

On two trips to Africa, Spong said that he had been impressed with the vitality of the witness and ministry of the churches, particularly in light of the economic hardships and the human rights abuses. But these supportive remarks would not be appease the rising African fury.

CHAPTER THREE

APPEALING TO LAMBETH

With women bishops making their first appearance and Third World bishops hurt over the perceived arrogance of First World liberals, the bishops gathered at Lambeth to work out the future of the Anglican Communion or, in the more apocalyptic view of some bishops, to preside over its potential death and burial.

Carey knew that the stakes were high. In the presidential address at the official opening of the thirteenth Lambeth Conference on July 19, he called for "a more radical discipleship shaped by God's transforming power."

In his hour-long address to bishops and their spouses in a sports center made to look like a tent, Carey stressed the need for renewal in the Anglican Communion's vision, its faith and order, its mission, and in the way that bishops understand their vocation as church leaders. To tepid applause, he also extended words of welcome to the eleven women bishops in attendance.

Carey pointed to both the blessings and disappointments since the last Lambeth. Among the blessings he cited the "toppling of the Berlin Wall," the elimination of apartheid in South Africa, prospects for peace in Northern Ireland, and the success in some provinces of the Decade of Evangelism.

Among the disappointments, the genocide in Rwanda was at the top of his list. He also pointed to the continuing war in the Sudan. "Poverty and starvation stalk too many of the lands where Anglicans serve; the AIDS virus is a curse in too many countries and blights the lives of millions. Ignorance and lack of educational opportunities hold back millions of young people," Carey said.

"Even when evil seems to prevail in so many places and in so many ways, the challenge before us is to bring to the world an authoritative version of the God of love and justice who is the beginning and end of all things," he continued.

The first task of the conference is "to be a place of transformation and of renewed vision, for the sake both of God's church and, still more importantly, of the world," Carey told the hushed assembly. "Here in this conference we have the opportunity to bring and share with each other all the distresses, as well as the joys, of the cultures from which we come—all the different understandings and divisions of the Anglican Communion, as well as what unites us," he added. Carey expressed the hope that "we too will talk about our theology as much as the issues that confront us because solutions will only emerge from a real encounter in gratitude with our living God."

In stressing the need for renewal, Carey quoted Brian Davis, the Archbishop of New Zealand who had died a few weeks before Lambeth. "The Anglican *via media*, or middle way, has encouraged the growth of tolerance, freedom and generosity of spirit," Davis wrote in his book, *The Way Ahead*. Anglicanism is "not a coercive institution but depends on friendly persuasion. Within our decision-making structures we know, most of the time, how to argue and fight fairly. We are also an inclusive church, welcoming those whose faith is fragile and uncertain, as well as those whose faith is strong and heroic."

Brushing aside the image of "some kind of Anglican comprehensiveness that is vague or wooly or is uncertain about the foundations of our faith," Carey had something else in mind. "We have a firm hold on a historic creedal faith, earthed in Holy Scripture. This is primary and pivotal—and there are boundaries to our faith and morals which we cross at our peril," he warned.

Citing the Virginia Report, the pre-conference paper on Anglican theology and structure, Carey said that Anglicans "affirm the sovereign authority of the Holy Scriptures as the medium through which God by the Holy Spirit communicates his word in the church and thus enables people to respond with understanding and faith." The Virginia Report, he noted, also says that the Scriptures "must be translated, read and understood, and their meaning grasped through a continuing process of interpretation," understood by the application of the "twin contexts of tradition and reason."

Going directly to the heart of the underlying issue of Anglican unity and identity, Carey asked the question, "If the Anglican Communion is a family of interdependent churches, and the Lambeth Conference has no binding doctrinal force, in what sense can we speak of the Anglican Communion?"

The question evokes "both the strength and weakness of our form of ecclesial structure," Carey said. "In the absence of any universal structures of collegiality that could determine how each province should act, there are those consequently who want to give the Archbishop of Canterbury a more monarchical role." In its wisdom the church and his predecessors, Carey observed, has "rejected this option firmly."

In shying away from that option, it is too easy to do the same with "the other bonds of unity—the Anglican Consultative

Council and the Primates' Meeting and the Lambeth Conference," he said. "Thus, if we meet as a fellowship of self-governing, national churches, in what realistic form can we claim to be a Communion?"

Carey said the answer lies in "what we share and hold in common. A common heritage of doctrine, faith, liturgy and spirituality, an understanding of authority as expressed through a 'dispersed' rather than centralized authority; episcopal leadership exercised in conjunction with synodical government."

Warming to his subject, Carey went on to assert, "To be in communion means that the local church both expresses and encompasses the faith of the universal church....And for dioceses, provinces, and the Communion itself, it means to keep in step, to maintain unity at all times." Carey took the next step, asking, "How may we stay together when difficult decisions threaten to divide us? How may we be more effective leaders of our provinces, dioceses, and churches?" The answer, he contended, lies in the Virginia Report's description of how Anglicanism works, how it can stay together in the face of substantial disagreements.

"With so many threatening divisions in our world and the anger, hatred, distrust, and cynicism which erodes our real community, let us enjoy our fellowship and life as a gift from the gracious and generous God we worship," Carey concluded.

The bishops and their spouses responded with a standing ovation. "I found it to be a gracious reminder of what the Anglican Communion is and needs to continue to be, and of what we need to recover," said Bishop Clark Grew of Ohio.

Bishop Catherine Waynick of Indianapolis found Carey's emphasis on diversity the strong point of the address. "That is one of the best gifts of the Anglican Communion. When we are doing that well, we are offering the world a particular kind of witness it otherwise might not get."

Despite this good beginning, many of the emotional pre-conference tensions manifested themselves immediately. The Spong interview with Andrew Carey had reinforced the suspicion of many conservatives that the liberals were arrogant. Eager to sidetrack the confrontation, South Africa's Ndungane told a press briefing, "Spong has apologized out of good will. That's it. I think it ends there."

Many of the Africans were not mollified. Bishop Wilson Mutebi of Uganda described the attempt at an apology as "superficial" and called on Spong to repent to God and to the other bishops for going "astray." Archbishop Kolini of Rwanda said that the potential racism in the remarks was "a minor thing." He added, "What hurt me is theological. That's the real me. My skin is part of me, but my theology is the real me. That's my hope, that's my destiny."

"He looks down upon Africans," Kolini contended. "He thinks I am a naïve person who has not been educated enough to know Scripture. I do not accept his apology." Bishop Sam Valliya Theotthil of India agreed, saying that the problem would only get worse because the apology had not "come from the heart."

In a letter distributed to all primates at the conference, Bishop John Rucyahana of Rwanda called for Spong and seventy-five other American bishops who signed the 1994 *Koinonia* Statement to be declared out of communion, according to an article in *The Anglican Way,* the publication of the Prayer Book Societies Worldwide.

The futility of efforts to repair the rift would become clear as the section charged with speaking to sexual issues prepared its report and the matter was put to a vote in plenary session.

On the morning when the section reports were released, Archbishop Robin Eames of Ireland, who chaired the Lambeth communications team, warned in a press briefing, "In some areas we will find agreement, and it won't surprise you that in some areas we will not find agreement." He urged the press contingent to approach the plenary debates with special sensitivity. "It's easy to go for shallow stories of various disagreements," he said. And he reminded them that Lambeth is not a legislative assembly, that draft resolutions are subject to change. "They are not carved in stone, they are in plasticine," he said. Eames admitted that cultural differences could complicate the plenary sessions since Anglicans make decisions in some very different styles.

Bishop Michael Nutall of South Africa, chair of the resolutions committee, said that most of the 108 draft resolutions were not even subject to debate but had been placed on an "agreed" list. As a point of procedure, however, if fifty bishops thought that a resolution on that list might be contentious, it could be moved to the list for debate. "A maximum of thirty will be debated," he said.

"We're not in the business of trying to suppress voices from any quarter of the conference," added Philip Mawer, secretary of the Church of England's General Synod, who served as secretary of the resolutions committee at Lambeth.

Nutall explained to the journalists that votes would be vocal and then, if necessary, by a show of hands. Provision could be made for a secret ballot.

"From its first meeting, our sub-section of about fifty bishops found it impossible to even discuss homosexuality," said Bishop Ronald Haines of Washington, who was a member of the group. "Only when we broke into groups of four did we make any progress. I was in a group with a bishop from a diocese in the South Pacific consisting of small island villages," he wrote later in a report to his diocese. "There is no term in his language for homosexuality and he had never discussed the subject, taboo in his culture. When I asked what happens to individuals who feel or act out on same-sex attractions, he replied, 'The village elders take care of them.' An African bishop told me there are no homosexuals in his diocese, although he later shared privately there were, but the subject is not discussed since Christians are either married or single and celibate."

Haines added, "Only by a monumental struggle did the sub-section cobble together, word by word, a statement and resolution that was, in my opinion, well on the conservative side of center."

The report of Section One, "Called to Full Humanity," dealt with a staggering list of issues, including Human Rights and Human Dignity, the Environment, Human Sexuality, Modern Technology, Euthanasia, and International Debt and Economic Justice.

In its introduction, the section report said that "our contexts and cultures are different, but many of the issues we face in a fast-changing world are similar."

In what sounds in retrospect as a description of the encounters in small groups but not true in plenaries, the introduction added, "The practice of Christian relationship begins with confessing and lamenting our unwillingness to deal lovingly with those who are different....Having seen and been seen, we are moved to hear the story of the other, no matter how much it may differ from our own story or evoke dangerous memories. Truly hearing the story of the other changes one's own story forever. This is the preamble to ongoing conversation, in which differences can be acknowledged and common ground sought."

Under the heading of Human Rights and Dignity, the report called attention to the continued abuse of human beings still so very prevalent on the fiftieth anniversary of the Universal Declaration of Human Rights. "Millions of people across the world are the victims of war and violence, sectarian and racial strife, the abuse of political and economic power and the intolerance of the different faces of religious fundamentalism and exclusions. We have been shocked by the way these attacks on human rights have victimised women and children. The face of poverty and of the pain of abuse is all too often to be seen in the lives of women and children."

The sub-section on human rights offered chilling stories of abuse around the world. One bishop shared a graphic story of inhumanity. When a group of young people from Uganda came to his consecration in the Sudan, he said that "on their return they were arrested and their left ears cut off because they were not 'listening to the words of the Koran.' Before they were released they were forced to eat their own ears."

The report summarized its findings under seven broad headings: "The widening gap between rich and poor; the violation of women and children; the effect of the global economy; war, guns, and landmines; racial and caste discrimination; fundamentalism and nationalism; refugee migration, asylum seekers, and uprooted and displaced people; and indigenous peoples."

"Anglicans have been and are being martyred," the report said. "We think of the martyrdom of the late Ugandan Archbishop Janani Luwum...the faithful witness of Archbishop George Browne at the height of the civil war in Liberia...the prophetic witness of Desmond Tutu in opposition to apartheid in South Africa...the peace efforts of the Anglican bishops in Jerusalem...Bishop Dinis Sengulane in Mozambique."

A sub-section report called for a greater emphasis on environmental concerns, pointing out the damage done by human beings to the created order of God. Its report stressed the relationship between that order and the well-being of humanity, and it highlighted the importance of a Christian contribution in efforts to care for the environment, while not flinching from admitting the church's shortcomings in those efforts.

"The last conference focused on women's ordination, this one on debt and sexuality, human dignity, and human rights. But at the heart of the matter we need to relate to the whole created order. We need to relate to the world that God has made," said Bishop George Brown of Australia, chair of the sub-section.

THE REPORT ON HUMAN SEXUALITY

The sub-section report on human sexuality, the unanimous product of some very stormy sessions over two weeks of closed meetings, was for many participants and observers alike a carefully nuanced statement.

Beginning with a clear statement of the church's traditional teaching on sexual morality, the statement's third paragraph said, "We also recognize that there are among us persons who experience themselves as having a homosexual orientation. Many of these are members of the church and are seeking the pastoral care, moral direction of the church, and God's transforming power for the living of their lives and the ordering of relationships. We wish to assure them that they are loved by God and that all baptised, believing and faithful persons— regardless of sexual orientation—are full members of the body of Christ. We call upon the church and all its members to work to end any discrimination on the basis of sexual orientation and to oppose homophobia."

The report went on to admit that the bishops "are not of one mind about homosexuality." It then articulated some of the different understandings, drawing on some of the same distinctions drawn by Spong and Lee in their catechesis.

Some believe that "homosexual orientation is a disorder, but that through the grace of Christ people can be changed, although not without pain and struggle." There are others, the report said, who believe that "relationships between people of the same gender should not include genital expression," based on their reading of the Bible and church tradition, and that "such activity (if unrepented of) is a barrier to the kingdom of God."

Still others believe, the report continued, that "committed homosexual relationships fall short of the biblical norm, but are to be preferred to relationships that are anonymous and transient." Finally, there are those who believe that "the church should accept and support or bless monogamous covenant relationships between homosexual people and that they may be ordained."

Yet the report concluded that there was a clear majority of bishops who were "not prepared to bless same-sex unions or to ordain active homosexuals" and that many believe that there should be a "moratorium on such practices."

After all their prayer, study, and discussion the bishops were ready to concede that they were "unable to reach a common mind on the scriptural, theological, historical, and scientific questions that are raised." And they asked the Anglican Communion for some means of "monitoring work done in the Communion on these issues and to share statements and resources among us." It pleaded for the "sacrifice, trust and charity towards one another" that would be required in dealing openly and honestly with the issues of sexuality.

Gay and lesbian activists had not been permitted to speak to the sub-section on human sexuality, but a week after they were rebuffed, Bishops Ronald Haines and Jane Holmes Dixon of Washington hosted the activist group Changing Attitude and its U.S. counterpart, Integrity, at an open session on "Lesbian and Gay Anglican Experience."

The participants presented their testimonies. "What I really want is a good, long talk about the only question that matters: What is the Gospel?" said the Rev. Michael Hopkins, president-elect of Integrity and an accredited member of the press corps. That discussion would revolve around questions such as "What is grace? How has it freed us from the law? What is the message that we send to the world?" he said. "The Good News, in fact, is liberation from fear. It is amazing to me what happens to the people of God when they stop being afraid."

Otis Charles, the openly gay retired Bishop of Utah, said that the abomination and sin of his life was not homosexuality but his refusal to answer the call of God. "Otis, you are beloved. Come out." He expressed a hope that the bishops at Lambeth would embrace "the rainbow diversity of human sexuality."

Earlier, an attempt to launch a "Rainbow Ribbon Day" in support of homosexuals in the church drew only a small crowd. "We have had many messages of support from other bishops but it was impossible to find a spot on the crowded agenda when everyone could attend," said the Rev. Richard Kirker, president of the Lesbian and Gay Christian Movement in England.

Bishop Richard Holloway of Scotland read a prepared statement, contending that it was time to "add a few colors that were missing from yesterday's photograph" of all the bishops and other participants at Lambeth, "the colors of gay and lesbian Christians. There are those in our Communion who would like to see these colors permanently excluded from the Anglican rainbow."

He added, "If the church is to be true to the all-embracing nature of Christ's love it will one day have to accept with joy the fact that among God's cherished children are gay and lesbian people," whom he described as "God's hidden people, misunderstood, maligned, persecuted, and killed."

Holloway said that he had "no doubt that chaste partnerships among homosexual priests are theologically appropriate, and that the same ethic should apply to them as applies to heterosexual priests." Growing up an Anglo-Catholic, he said that "there probably never was a time when I haven't known gay priests."

Holloway decried the decision the day before by the House of Lords (by a vote of 336 to 129) to challenge a decision by a vote of seventy-two percent of the House of Commons to lower the age of consent for homosexual acts to sixteen. Carey had spoken very publicly against lowering the age. In an article in the London *Times*, he pointed out that the Church of England's House of Bishops, in a statement before the Commons vote, "stressed the need for legislation to be rooted in sound moral values." While there was some disagreement among the bishops over the issue of decriminalization, "all of us agreed that the criminal law affecting sexual relationships should offer protection for people who are vulnerable or at risk of exploitation."

Carey stressed in his comments that "welcoming adequate protection from exploitation is not the same as accepting that homosexual acts for adolescent boys should in some way be endorsed by society. That is not part of the morally healthy society I would like to see."

He concluded his remarks by acknowledging how difficult it is to deal with "these passionate disagreements that divide us as a Communion. But the thing I love most about this rainbow Communion is the way it has always lived with disagreement without breaking apart, because it has always known that we need one another to correct our partial visions of the truth....I believe that the Anglican Communion, at its best, can model for the world a way of living with, rather than dying from, disagreement."

Carey's position was criticized by some columnists in the British press. Writing in the *Independent*, David Aaronovitch said that Carey "has allied himself with the forces of intolerance and reaction, and is using his power as a leader of the established church to assist an unelected group of backwoodspersons to frustrate the decisions of the elected chamber, and to keep sexual relationships for men between sixteen and eighteen criminalized."

Noting that twenty-six "Lords Spiritual" sit in the House of Lords, Aaronovitch expressed sympathy for attempts to "out" the bishops "and then let's chuck them out. For we liberals now know the truth: the House of Lords must go in its present form as soon as possible, and the bishops of this one church, raised by tyrants to pontificate over us, must go too. We should thank the archbishop for at last letting the scales fall from our eyes."

The conservative bishops called a closed meeting at the Franciscan Study Centre at the edge of the Kent University campus because, in the words of a letter of invitation, "there needs to be a consolidation of the orthodox position," one that would "provide both a vision for the future of the Anglican Communion as well as a review of the key resolutions we will be voting on this week." The twenty-seven bishops signing the invitation included many of the Africans who had taken leadership on the issues, joined by some American, British, and Australian bishops.

A "midpoint letter," signed by eight primates, outlined the basic strategy. It said that bishops saw the conference "as a turning point in our history," and described the need for an "injection of greater coherence into the affairs of the Anglican Communion."

The letter once again raised the issue of cultural differences that seemed to infuse the conference. "A crucial question is how we relate to the modern globalizing culture, which, though originating in the West, in one way or another powerfully impinges on us all. While recognizing its benefits, we must ask whether we are in danger of allowing this culture with its philosophical assumptions, economic system, sexual alternatives and hidden idols to determine what we become."

Citing the Eames Commission report's recognition that, in the wake of the ordination of women, "our communion is already impaired," the letter added, "Lack of decision on first order moral issues would further threaten our unity. Then too, responsible love requires a more consistent witness to biblical truth. In this way the world may hear an intelligible message, and our ecumenical partners regain the confidence that we believe what our formularies say we believe."

Among the goals set by the letter were "a commitment to biblical renewal," but also a "call for a suspension of both the ordination of practicing homosexuals and the blessing of same-sex relationships," and a way of "strengthening our instruments of unity so that our provinces may effectively be accountable to each other."

CALLS FOR REPENTANCE

As the sexuality issue was headed for a plenary, bishops from Uganda and Nigeria angrily demanded that bishops who are pushing for equal rights for homosexuals either repent or leave the Anglican Communion. The bishops said that it was an "abuse" to impose the Western concern with homosexuality on the Third World. Bishop Benjamin Kwashi of Nigeria said that many Africans felt "oppressed with this Western problem." He added, "We know that homosexuality is not the will of God."

Bishop Wilson Mutebi of Uganda added, "Homosexuality is a sin and any bishop who teaches otherwise is committing a sin. He must repent in order to be in communion with us. If he does not, we cannot be in the same church as him."

Archbishop Robert Okine, Primate of the Province of West Africa, described the tension between the South African bishops and their African brothers. In an interview with David Virtue of *Christian Challenge*, a conservative independent magazine, he implied that western support for the South Africans had an impact on their attitudes on sexuality issues. "You don't bite the hand that feeds you," he said. "The South African churches have been given millions of dollars from U.S. dioceses and the national church to fight apartheid and support women's ordination. They were easily manipulated to support liberal values because of American money." Then the issue of discrimination towards women was "linked with the homosexual agenda of the western provinces," he alleged.

"We Africans have a sense of appreciation even when we disagree with a person," Okine added. "South Africa's decision to go along with western values is not unconnected with the kindness Bishop Tutu received at their hands." The Rev. Timothy Kujero of Nigeria, who worked with the *Church of England Newspaper* at Lambeth, said that Tutu got money from the homosexual lobby in the United States to pay for his cancer operation. "He has never forgotten their kindness and has repaid them by buying into the homosexual positions of the West," he said.

Okine also charged that the South Africans were in a position to manipulate the process at the conference on the sexuality issue. Ndungane chaired Section One, which dealt with the issue. Duncan Buchanan of Johannesburg had chaired the subsection on sexuality, and Michael Nutall chaired the resolutions committee.

"We got a feeling of manipulation. We could sense it. They controlled the whole resolutions process," Okine charged. "I am inclined to feel there was something going on."

The Lesbian and Gay Christian Movement was heartened when Carey showed up at a reception the organization sponsored in a downtown hotel. "Every year since he became Archbishop we have asked for a meeting," said Richard Kirker. "Our efforts to meet were always unsuccessful. This made us very frustrated and called into doubt his often stated position that he was prepared to talk to lesbians and gay people," he said. "I think he has now reached the point that it is untenable to keep his distance from us and he can see the merit in a face-to-face meeting."

Carey and several dozen bishops mingled at the reception, listening to "personal stories of hurt and the rejection they've experienced in the church and the difficulty of proclaiming the Christian message in the gay and lesbian community because of all the hostility expressed towards them by the church—not least by the Archbishop himself," Kirker said.

Bishop Jason Dharmaraj of South India said he was "unhappy" with Carey's willingness to listen to the gay lobby, according to an article in the *Independent*. "Homosexuality is the outcome of the modern world. It's against the will of God," he said, accusing Carey of being "political." He said that the

Archbishop "must take a religious stand."

Bishop Emmanuel Gbonigi of Nigeria said that he could never follow Carey's example. "I won't listen to them because it would be a sheer waste of time. It's not because I'm a bigot but, as far as I'm concerned, it is against the word of God. Nothing can make us [African bishops] budge because we view what God says as firm."

After two weeks of stress-filled sessions behind closed doors, the report from the sub-section dealing with sexuality issues finally emerged, igniting a fresh controversy over the form of the resolution going to the plenary.

In briefing the press on the progress of the sub-section charged with bringing a resolution to the plenary on sexuality, Buchanan of Johannesburg said that it was clear that its participants came to Lambeth with "vastly different agendas." He said that "for some the issue is crucial and urgent while for others it simply doesn't exist." He pointed out that, at the last Lambeth Conference, "the issue of homosexuality couldn't get on the agenda."

The sub-section had overruled his decision to invite homosexuals to address the group. "The task is to hold together in spite of widely divergent views," admitting that "nobody is listening" at this point in the deliberations. He expressed a deep concern that the issue would "hijack the agenda on other issues." In a moment of clear exasperation he said, "The strength of anger has left me pretty shocked and traumatized." Yet he insisted that he was "a prisoner of hope."

While polygamy was not on the official agenda, there were some reports that western bishops had agreed not to raise the issue provided that African bishops did not speak out about the rapidly rising divorce rate among western Christians.

Five bishops who played key roles in the discussion of sexuality issues at Lambeth confirmed that a resolution from the 1988 conference was still in effect, condoning the practice of some African men with more than one wife to retain them, even after baptism, provided that they do not take any additional wives.

Yet a journalist from the *Tablet*, a Roman Catholic magazine in England, raised the issue in the briefing, asking how Lambeth could condone polygamy but refuse to accept same-sex relationships, especially since Lambeth seemed to be in the business of advocating tolerance for different cultural practices.

"Same-sex unions are not acceptable to Africans, either culturally, theologically or scripturally," said Bishop Zebidee Masereka of Uganda.

Bishop Paul Barnett of Sydney warned that, if liberal bishops continue to ordain non-celibate homosexuals and bless same-sex relationships, they would cause "disruption if not division of the Anglican Communion."

Bishop Otis Charles said that, when Utah was trying to earn statehood, the local Episcopal bishop was among those leaders who campaigned to force Mormons to abandon polygamy. He said that he found it "ironic" that today's church could not make the connection between its change of attitude toward polygamy, at the urging of African bishops, and a call to revise its attitude toward homosexuals.

Charles said that it was not safe to assume that gays and lesbians in the West were Christian, even though they had a deep spirituality. "One of the richest opportunities for evangelism in the church in the United States is among gays and lesbians because these are people who have rejected what they see as an oppressive institution," he said.

ATTEMPTED EXORCISM

An incident outside the plenary hall the day of the debate confirmed Spong's observation that the issue was a highly emotional one. Bishop Emmanuel Chukwuma of Nigeria was

Bishop Emmanuel Chukwuma of Nigeria attempts to perform an unwanted exorcism on the Rev. Richard Kirker of England's Lesbian and Gay Christian Movement. (Photo: Ed Mulholland)

being interviewed by a reporter and, as a small crowd gathered, he declared that Leviticus calls for a death penalty for anyone engaging in homosexual acts. And other biblical sources also clearly condemn homosexuality, the bishop argued.

"Would you be prepared to stone us to death?" asked Richard Kirker of the Lesbian and Gay Christian Movement who was passing out literature to bishops as they entered the steamy sports center for the showdown on sexuality.

The bishop tried to lay his hands on Kirker to "deliver" him from his homosexuality. "In the name of Jesus, I deliver him out of homosexuality," he said as he attempted to grab Kirker. "I pray for God to forgive you, for God to deliver you out of your sinful act, out of your carnality," the bishop shouted as a crowd gathered. Kirker responded, "May God bless you, sir, and deliver you from your prejudice against homosexual people."

"You have no inheritance in the kingdom of God. You are going to hell. You have made yourself homosexual because of your carnality," the bishop said.

With sweat pouring from his face, the bishop screamed again and again for repentance while his wife stood nearby murmuring, "Alleluia." The bishop said, "We have overcome carnality just as the light will overcome darkness....God did not create you as a homosexual. That is our stand. That is why your church is dying in Europe—because it is condoning immorality. You are killing the church. This is the voice of God talking. Yes, I am violent against sin."

When Bishop David Russell of South Africa tried to intercede, pointing out that Archbishop Desmond Tutu "supports the inclusion of homosexuals in the church," Chukwuma marched off muttering, "Desmond Tutu is spiritually dead."

In an ironic twist, Kirker said that he was born in Nigeria and lived there until the age of eighteen. "I had my first sexual experience there," he added.

The encounters were featured prominently on the evening television news programs and on the front page of daily newspapers the next day, contributing to the dismay of the bishops who were trying to deal with the issue dispassionately.

But Kirker was not the only one caught in the wave of vitriol that occasionally spilled over during the early weeks of the Lambeth Conference.

The Rev. Elizabeth Kaeton of the Diocese of Newark, a lesbian mother of six, celebrated the Eucharist in the chapel of King's College in London, as a guest of the Lesbian and Gay Christian Movement. Her license to celebrate as a priest from outside the Church of England was granted by the Diocese of London which was apparently not aware of her background or intentions.

"I'm a missionary for gay and lesbian people to the Lambeth Conference," she told the press after the service. "Some bishops don't even know any gay priests. They are scared of what they don't know, like when we first met people of color. Gay and lesbian priests are not two-headed monsters." According to Richard Kirker, there are no lesbian priests living openly in the Church of England.

Kaeton said in an interview that she had experienced open hostility during the days she spent in Canterbury and said later in a "Love Letter from Lambeth" that it took time to slowly heal from what she called the "surprising brutality and unexpected betrayal I experienced at Lambeth."

Kaeton said that she was "absolutely convinced that in future Lambeth Conferences, our children and grandchildren will look back on the 1998 Lambeth Conference with the same sense of humiliation and shame with which we now view the racism and sexism of previous Lambeth Conferences."

"In some parts of the church I am regarded as an oddity, even an abomination," Kaeton said. "Some bishops won't give me the time of day, but change will happen slowly."

When she was at Lambeth, Kaeton drew an analogy from

the *Wizard of Oz*, to describe the actions of the bishops. "More and more bishops began to bear striking resemblances to rigid men of tin with no hearts, floppy men of straw with no brains, and magnificently coifed and loudly roaring, but otherwise decidedly cowardly, lions." And she said that she was "personally astounded and deeply saddened by the silence from the Lambeth Eleven, the Anglican bishops who are women," pointing out that "not one of them would wear the Rainbow Ribbon and stand in solidarity with us." (Bishop Mary Adelia McLeod of Vermont later said that she wore the ribbon the whole time she was at Lambeth.)

Kaeton repeated a rumor that the women had been convinced not to "rock the boat," although "it is obvious that several women are chafing at the bit." Catherine Roskam of New York and Jane Holmes Dixon of Washington, D.C., she said, broke ranks by appearing at a reception of the Lesbian and Gay Christian Movement, and Dixon, as noted earlier, moderated the unofficial conversation with gays and lesbians where they were able to tell their stories.

In her letter, written when she returned home before Lambeth concluded, Kaeton told of an encounter with a Church of England bishop who said to her, "There isn't a bishop in all of Western Christendom who could lay his hands on your head and remove the stain and stench of your homosexual sin and make you a wholesome example to lead the flock of Christ." She wrote, "We have to help people make the connection that all of the issues of justice are rooted in the same dynamic of fear. Fear has a color, and a shape, and sexuality."

ANVIL OF PAIN

After several closed sessions the sub-section issued its report and proposed a resolution for the plenary, "hammered out on an anvil of pain," according to Ndungane of Southern Africa.

During a rather tense press briefing on the work of the sixty bishops in his sub-section, Buchanan was asked by an African journalist whether the bishop was concerned about "preserving the innocence" of those parts of Africa where homosexuality was not practiced nor even heard of. He quickly responded, "Many people say that homosexuality is the white man's importation, but the evidence is that it is widely practiced throughout Africa."

Bishop Paul Barnett of Australia, a member of the subsection, told the press that their deliberations had been eleven days of the most intense emotional struggle he had ever experienced. At one point the impasse was so apparent that outside help was sought, producing "a totally different report" that attempted to steer a path between opposing points of view, Buchanan said. This had been "substantially, not unanimously, accepted."

The group had been so focused on the report itself that it had not written the resolutions when time ran out so it was referred to the whole section. Buchanan himself tried to draft three resolutions which he hoped "reflected where we were." That was the draft originally given to the press.

Essentially, the Buchanan resolutions affirmed the traditional understanding of marriage "between one man and one woman in life-long union, and believes that celibacy is right for those who are not called to marriage." A second point "calls on all our people to minister pastorally and sensitively to others irrespective of their sexual orientation and to condemn homophobia, violence within marriage and any trivialization and commercialization of sex." He also asked the conference to seek some kind of monitoring on the subject by the Primates Meeting and the Anglican Consultative Council, asking them to "share statements and resources among us."

The conservative members of the sub-section were not satisfied and made some adjustments to strengthen the resolution, including a statement calling on the conference to say it "cannot advise the legitimizing or blessing or ordaining of those involved in same-gender unions."

Barnett said that he considered the resolutions to be "pastoral, caring, and softly spoken, but clear on traditional morals."

Archbishop David Crawley of Canada was less convinced. "The report is more open-ended than the resolutions," he said. "The resolutions are on the conservative side and no one is entirely happy with them. I am very sad that gays and lesbians will have to pay the price of them."

When asked about even stronger amendments coming out of the regions, Buchanan expressed his frustration. "We have worked intensively for two and one-half weeks with much pain and anger. People who have not been through that process are producing resolutions."

THE SEXUALITY RESOLUTION

The thankless, even dangerous, task of chairing the plenary session that would consider the resolution fell to Eames who needed all his skills as a lawyer and participant in the peace process in Northern Ireland to hold things together.

Eames introduced the session, joking that he had tried to find someone else to chair "but in the face of that lack of Christian charity," the job was his. He began with a prayer that the debate might be conducted with "courage and sensitivity." He outlined the procedures, pointing out that six alternative resolutions had been filed so he would let the proposer of each speak for three minutes and then allow time for reflection before proceeding with the vote. "Once we have established the main text, we can then work through the detailed amendments," he said. Voting would be by a show of hands, unless someone called for a paper ballot.

Buchanan then took the podium to say that he took full responsibility for the confusion surrounding the resolution, admitting again that so much time had been spent on the report that he and a small group had tried to write the resolutions. He introduced the rewritten version. (See I.10, p.251) The resolution was not asking anyone to endorse or condone homosexual practice—nor to condemn it. And he pointed out that, since Lambeth was an advisory body without legislative authority, it had to settle for the language advising against blessing or ordaining open homosexuals. Finally, he pleaded for the bishops to allow their differences not to be points of division but of "integrity and graciousness."

Bishop Catherine Waynick of Indianapolis withdrew an amendment she was proposing, reminding the conference that bishops might be tempted to see their role as finding answers to the "many questions to be faced in the messy business of being human" but sometimes the church had thought it was taking a proper stance only to later find it necessary to repent. Bishops are called, not to be correct, but to love, to feed the flock—and help its members love one another. She quoted Archbishop William Temple: "When we choose wisely, God reigns; when we choose foolishly, God reigns."

Bishop Eustace Kamayire of Uganda introduced two hardline resolutions on behalf of the Central and East Africa Region, stressing the traditional teaching on marriage, primacy of Scripture in declaring all promiscuity as sin, and "this includes homosexual practice between persons of the same sex as well as heterosexual relationships outside of marriage." He said that those who "practice homosexuality and live in promiscuity, as well as those bishops who ordain them or encourage these practices, act contrary to the Scriptures and the teaching of the church." The resolution called on them to repent because they were casting doubt on the teaching of Jesus and causing serious damage and scandal.

The bishop contended that the authority of Scripture was under attack by not only those who do not believe but by those who seem to be upholding it. "Those of us who come from the young churches can testify to the transforming power of God," Kamayire said. "This Lambeth Conference must uphold the historic faith."

Bishop Peter Adebiyi of Nigeria introduced an amendment from the West Africa Region, noting that "many parts of the Bible condemn homosexuality as a sin...which could only be adopted by the church if it wanted to commit evangelical suicide." He pointed out that "some African Christians in Uganda were martyred in the nineteenth century for refusing to have homosexual relations with the king because of their faith in the Lord Jesus and their commitment to stand by the Word of God as expressed in the Bible on the subject." He said that the subject was taboo for Africans. The event he described is commemorated in the American version of the Book of Common Prayer as the "Martyrs of Uganda" (June 3). It is also a holy day in the Roman Catholic Church.

Moderator William Moses of the Church of South India raised a point of order, expressing his hope that the chair would establish a time limit on "this trivial business" so that the conference could move on to more important matters. When Eames tested the proposal, he was asked to limit speeches to three minutes.

Archbishop of Sydney Harry Goodhew supported the revised resolution, saying, "I am glad this motion has produced strong feelings, because it is not an incidental matter, but a grave moral issue." He agreed that every mention of homosexuality in the Bible condemned the practice.

Bishop Michael Bourke of England said that it was possible to use the Bible "as a source of inspiration for our faith, and also to oppress people that are different." He offered as an example the use of the Bible to justify racism in South Africa.

The commitment to listen to the experience of homosexuals in the church was at the heart of the Gospel and should not be controversial.

The resolution kept the door open, argued Bishop Richard Harries of Oxford, and it was a unifying resolution while still serving as a strong affirmation of traditional values. While the international debt issue was personally more important, he admitted that he had now come to see that sexuality was a Gospel issue.

Bishop Alexander Malik of Pakistan dismissed the resolution as ambiguous, unclear, and impotent because it did not condemn homosexuality strongly enough for him. He denied the possibility of "gay bashing" in upholding the teaching and authority of Scripture. He was prepared to tell homosexuals that God had created them in his image, as children of God, and that he loved them but that he hated their sins as much as he hated other sins. No one should be excluded from the grace of God or the church but he wondered how someone could remain a bishop while not upholding Scripture.

Bishop John Neill of Ireland rose to support the resolution, contending that it would hold the Anglican Communion together, but he opposed any blatant condemnation of homosexuals saying, "It would divide us." Instead, the church should engage homosexuals in conversation and seek further insights into sexual orientation.

Raising again the martyrdom in Uganda, Bishop Michael Lugor said that "they would laugh at us and say, 'We died for the Gospel, now where are you going?'" The church should say to homosexuals, "Why do you come out and tell us what you do? Go to God and confess your sins."

Archbishop Donald Mtetemela of Tanzania introduced an amendment, seeking to insert the phrase "While rejecting homosexual practice as incompatible with Scripture." Without such an addition the resolution would be too weak, he contended.

Bishop David Russell of South Africa, a member of the sub-section, said that the experience had been a "painful but privileged" one. "It was an amazing coming together," he said. "Please, brothers and sisters, don't crush the achievement made under God. None of us is entirely happy with all the clauses but we have gone a long way together." He urged the bishops to vote against the resolution "if there is something that violates your conscience." He said that he was convinced the "wording of this resolution will enable us to hold together."

Bishop Robert Ihloff of Maryland agreed with Russell about his experience in the sub-section and said that if the rest of the bishops could speak to each other in the same way as the participants in the sub-section, they might reach a similar point. "As someone who used to hold the traditional view, I have witnessed my own change of heart and I now work with priests who are homosexual. I am committed to dialogue."

Bishop Roskam of New York replied to the threat of "evangelical suicide" by warning that condemning homosexuality would be "evangelical suicide in my region" and result in a "divided church."

No one has a problem with homosexual orientation, it was acting on that orientation that was the problem, said Bishop Sehon Goodridge of the Windward Islands.

A vote on the Mtetemela amendment to add the phrase asserting that homosexuality is incompatible with Scripture passed by a vote of 389 to 190, sending a clear signal of the mind of the conference.

In an article he wrote after the conference, Harries of Oxford said that the amendment condemning homosexual activity as contrary to Scripture had not been submitted in time but was allowed "at the discretion of the chairman of the session." He said, "I understand that, if this amendment had not been in and accepted, great numbers of bishops from the African churches would have walked out, and that it was personally brokered by the Archbishop of Canterbury."

The bishops accepted an amendment from Bishop Taita Taveta of Kenya, changing the word "homophobia" to "an irrational fear of homosexuals." And it also accepted an amendment by Bishop John Sentamu of England changing "chastity" to "abstinence," addressing a fear that the interpretation of chastity could include committed homosexual relationships.

An attempt to close debate failed and, when asked by a bishop if there would be time to vote on the amended resolution before time expired, Eames assured him that it would happen.

An amendment calling for conference participants to commit themselves "to listen to the experience of homosexual people," proposed by Bishop Michael Bourke of England, was nearly ignored but, when it was finally introduced, it passed.

Archbishop Moses Tay of Singapore wanted to change the monitoring process on an international level to a provincial level, fearing that it would "allow the promotion of unhealthy literature, which can be quite polluting." He was opposed by Bishop Michael Scott-Joynt of England who asserted, "We listen to each other and assist each other. Why assume the influence would be only one way?" The Tay amendment failed.

Bishop Peter Chiswell of Australia wanted to change the wording to make it clear that the conference would not "approve" the blessing of same-sex unions or the ordination of practicing gays, rather than making it advisory. Bishop Barry Jenks of Canada said that it was not the role of Lambeth to approve or disapprove. He said that the more moderate original resolution had been eroded. "A document whose face, a little conservative, was a face of love and compassion is gradually, bit by bit, step by step, turning into a judgment and condemnation."

CAREY'S POSITION

Before the final vote, Carey made it clear where he stood, endorsing the amended resolution as standing "wholeheartedly with traditional Anglican orthodoxy." He said that he saw "no room in Holy Scripture or the entire Christian tradition for any sexual activity outside matrimony."

Carey said, "I believe that the amended motion is simply saying what we have all held, what Anglican belief and morality stands for." He urged the bishops to honor each other's integrity and not impugn the motives of those with whom they disagreed. He pointed out the other important issues the conference faced. "I fully believe with all my heart that, if this conference is known and named by what we have said about homosexuality, we will have failed."

Acknowledging the potential for the conference to allow "disagreement to become division," Carey said, "What disagreement ought to do is to lead us closer together." He added, "We are aware that we have to go on listening. The dialogue continues." While he was speaking, the time for debate elapsed and a vote was taken—or was it? After some confusion about the possibility of abstaining, a second vote was taken and Eames asked for the result to be accepted in silence. The vote was 526 in favor and 70 opposed, with 45 abstentions.

After the results were announced, Eames said, "I am not saying the problems have diminished, but we have displayed how we can disagree and still love each other."

At a press conference after the vote, Eames, Buchanan, and Bishop Kenneth Fernando of Sri Lanka, vice-chair of the sexuality sub-section, were asked if the resolution now meant that ordained gay priests living openly must leave the church or if their ministry would be limited in any way.

"You cannot invalidate a person's orders or inhibit their ministry," Buchanan said. But he agreed that the decision had

Among the bishops who objected to the vote on the sexuality resolution were (l to r) Holloway of Scotland; Ingham of Canada (partially hidden); and American Bishops Waynick of Indianapolis, Spong of Newark, Jelinek of Minnesota, and Roskam of New York. (Photo: Lynn Ross, *Anglican World*)

sent a kind of cautionary warning to bishops urging them to think carefully about who is ordained. Fernando said that bishops in the United States who ordain homosexuals should take the resolution into account, even though Lambeth is "advisory."

While arguing that "one of the nice things about the Anglican Communion is that you can have both doubt and disagreement," Fernando added that "it does look as though the liberals lost out."

Eames said that he was not surprised by the outcome "for the simple reason that I had been talking and listening among my brother bishops, and I was getting the impression that this was the way it would go. I would draw back from any idea that the liberals rolled over. Looking ahead, I expect we will say that we will monitor this, and I wouldn't be at all surprised if we came out with pastoral guidelines."

Holloway of Scotland later blasted Carey for his intervention, calling it a "pathetic" example of leadership. "He thought that the vote had been taken, so he tried to add a nice fluffy epilogue. It would have been better if he had stayed silent." When asked about Carey's leadership, Holloway asked, "What leadership?"

Holloway said that the vote left him feeling "gutted, shafted, depressed." He said some of the gay youth working as volunteers at the conference "are feeling broken-hearted and wondering if they have a place in this family. It is very difficult to be a lesbian and gay Christian. It takes enormous heroism," he said.

Holloway subsequently said that his criticism of Carey was not meant to be personal. "I was asked what I thought of the speech made by the Archbishop of Canterbury just before the resolution was voted. I replied 'pathetic.' I was referring to the speech and its impact, not to the Archbishop himself. I now acknowledge that the word I used in my pain and frustration was ill-judged and hurtful, and I hereby unreservedly apologize for using it."

He also publicly charged the American conservatives with influencing the Africans. "These Americans have lost the battle in their own Episcopal Church so they have hired a proxy army," he said in a press interview. Observers on both sides of the issue admitted that the climate was more like a political system than a theological debate.

After the conference, Holloway said that he was rethinking his interest in a political career because of the need to challenge "a hardening in church attitudes to certain groups in society, as well as a return to a type of theological conservatism."

In a closing press conference Carey said, "We have to work from theology, and we have to find agreement within that theology so that, as well as listening to the experience of the homosexual community, together we have to listen to authority as it comes to us through Scripture, and through the entire Christian tradition as well." He dismissed the notion that it was largely a cultural divide, with churches in the developed world against the churches of Africa. "On the subject of homosexuality, the rift goes through all the churches," he said.

According to participants, Carey met with conference chaplains shortly after the vote on the sexuality resolution. They threatened to leave the conference and publicly denounce the action. In what was described as an emotional confrontation, several chaplains told Carey that they were homosexuals and that remaining at Lambeth in light of the action was not possible. In an emotional response, Carey pleaded for understanding of his very difficult position in attempting to keep the situation from polarizing any further.

STATEMENT OF APOLOGY

In the wake of the resolution, a statement drafted by Bishop Ronald Haines of Washington, D.C., quickly drew almost 150 signatures. The statement addressed to gays and lesbians said that "within the limitations of this conference it has not been possible to hear adequately your voices and we apologize for any sense of rejection that has occurred because of this reality." The statement committed the signatories "to listen to you and reflect with you theologically and spiritually on your lives and ministries. It is our deep concern that you do not feel abandoned by your church...."

Among the signatories were at least 146 bishops, including the primates of Brazil, Canada, Central Africa, Ireland, New Zealand, Scotland, Southern Africa, and Wales. Initially sixty-five bishops from the United States signed. (Ecumenical News International later reported growing support for the statement, with "at least 179 signing, a number that already far exceeds the combined total of 115 bishops who voted against the conference motion declaring that homosexual practice was incompatible with Scripture. It is clear that some bishops who voted for the motion's hard-line stance on homosexuality have now signed the pastoral statement, which is far more conciliatory, although it does not express any approval for same-sex unions or for the ordination" of homosexuals.)

In a speech at an Integrity conference in Little Rock after Lambeth, Christine Spong said that opponents of her husband squelched his efforts to forge a compromise between liberal bishops of the West and conservative bishops from the global South. She criticized liberal bishops for spurning an attempt by John Spong to write a minority report in the face of an inevitable vote condemning homosexuality, even though he claimed that eighty-eight bishops had expressed interest in such a report.

The day before the vote on the sexuality resolution, Mrs. Spong said, they backed off, making it clear that "they did not want to be associated in any way with anything that Jack did." While a few expressed interest in the immediate wake of the vote, the statement by Haines of Washington seemed more appealing. The day after the vote, "there was no minority statement given to the press, so the only reports in the national newspapers were a total rout," she said. In fact, the Haines statement drew substantial support and substantial press coverage.

Spong issued a personal statement "to my homosexual brothers and sisters in Christ the world over." He reminded them that "no resolution can ever diminish the fact that you are created in God's image, loved by Jesus Christ just as you are and called to the fullness of your humanity by the Holy Spirit." He took some consolation in the fact that "this debate has placed the issue of homosexuality on the agenda of every province of the worldwide Anglican Communion. Once prejudice is examined publicly it is never able to be suppressed or denied again, and homophobia and destructive stereotypes about gay and lesbian people are doomed. Please rejoice in that." He said that "the resolution sought to justify its prejudice by appeals to the authority of Holy Scripture. That tactic was employed in the church's attempt to justify slavery, segregation, and apartheid. It failed then. It will surely fail on this issue."

In his article for *The Tablet*, Harries of Oxford said, "Most of the American bishops were bitterly disappointed, and the question arises as to why their voice was heard so little. One reason," he observed, "was the Spong factor." Because the Bishop of Newark was identified with rights for gays and lesbians, but also known for challenging some Christian doctrines—coupled with his remarks about the African bishops—he speculated that the Americans "were chary about voicing their opinions."

As chair of the House of Bishops Working Party on Human Sexuality for the Church of England, Harries said that he went to Lambeth to listen carefully to what was happening in the Anglican world. "But experiencing the full flood of conservative opinion organized in ways which could be extremely damaging not only to gay people but to the unity of the Communion, I quickly gave myself over to damage limitation."

Harries said that "the worst damage was avoided and that the resultant resolution is one that Anglicans can live with," yet he expressed "real sorrow" that so many of the bishops "had made up their minds before they went to Lambeth and were unwilling to listen to other positions."

Traditionalists from the Episcopal Church were delighted and relieved with the vote. "Lambeth has spoken clearly and forthrightly," they said in a statement. "The Anglican Communion upholds biblical Christian teaching on sexuality. This is good news for the American church and for our ministry in American society," said Bishop James Stanton of Dallas, president of the American Anglican Council (AAC), which describes itself as "a network of individuals, parishes, specialized ministries, and a council of Episcopal bishops who affirm biblical authority and Anglican orthodoxy within the Episcopal Church."

"The Western churches, and particularly the American church, have much to answer for," Stanton added. "The willingness of so many American church leaders to try to legitimize homosexual behavior has foisted this difficult decision on the worldwide church. It has sapped our energy from urgent tasks such as evangelism and justice for the poorest of the poor. It is time for those bishops and others who seek to revise orthodox Christian teaching to submit to the mind of the whole church and the teaching of Scripture."

Bishop Stephen Jecko of Florida, in a column in his diocesan newspaper, said that "it is clear that recent decisions of the American Episcopal Church have placed it at odds with the mind of the greater Anglican Communion. I believe we are at a crossroads in our life as a church. The Episcopal Church has been acting in blissful isolation from the vast majority of Western Christianity which has endorsed biblical sexual ethics, and an openness to the Holy Spirit in the matter of church order." Jecko said that the most important issue facing the church and American society "is the individualism that results in the autonomous rejections of legitimate authority...."

Picking up on a similar theme, Bishop Bertram Herlong of Tennessee said that, while the resolutions of Lambeth are not legally binding, "they represent the mind and heart of the whole of the church. Any provincial church that ignores or belittles them or disregards them is consciously turning its back on the mainstream of the Anglican Communion and choosing an agenda that will be seen by our sisters and brothers of our Communion as self-centeredness and arrogance."

Bishop John-David Schofield of the Diocese of San Joaquin in California was quoted as saying that the vote could lead to the end of ordination of openly gay and lesbian priests. "If they continue, they do so in contradiction to the voice of the Anglican community and of the Scriptures. There is no more authoritative body than the worldwide Anglican Communion. If a small province were to fly in the face of that, it would put itself on the very edge of a split."

Bishop John Takeda, Primate of Japan, also welcomed the vote and said that it showed overwhelming opposition to the blessing of same-sex relationships. "I think this will send a message to priests in America and other countries who ordain homosexuals and bless homosexual unions that the Anglican Communion is against that."

Some American bishops were upset and defiant. Bishop Frederick Borsch of Los Angeles issued a letter expressing his disappointment and pointed to what he called "a large gap between the pastoral experience of many bishops in our part of the world from that of bishops from other countries." He said that his diocese, which has about thirty openly gay priests, would continue to take a liberal line. "Things will not change. We ordain human beings. We do not discriminate because of sexual orientation," he said.

Waynick of Indianapolis said that she was "saddened" by the debate and the resolution but added, "I think we have chosen foolishly today, but I believe God is still reigning."

A few admitted that they left haunted by Carey's comment that the Lambeth Conference would be a failure if it were known only for its action on the sexuality issue. Others were impressed that sexuality was on the agenda at all and not surprised by the results. Spong even predicted that there would be openly gay bishops at the next Lambeth Conference.

Archbishop Michael Peers, Primate of the Anglican Church of Canada, wrote a letter from Lambeth in an attempt to interpret the action for his province but also place it in the context of wider issues on the agenda.

"The perception of this message varies from those who receive it with joy, as a vindication of traditional Christian teaching, and those who find it a devastating betrayal of the gospel of love," Peers wrote. The Lambeth resolution on sexuality is, "strictly speaking, broadly in accord with the current policy of the Anglican Church of Canada," although the decision of his church's General Synod in 1995 "obviously contains a considerably stronger affirmation of gay and lesbian Christians than the Lambeth text."

Peers said that he must dissociate himself "from any who perceive this action as a victory," and he said that he and many of the Canadian bishops had been "scandalized" by some of the comments during the debate, "marked at times by outright condemnation of homosexual persons, sometimes phrased in viciously prejudicial language" that "is not consistent with the gospel of Jesus Christ as I understand it." He said that he signed the pastoral letter written by Haines of Washington.

In a column in the *Guardian,* Bishop Victoria Matthews of Canada said that "bishops know the anguish of the gay and lesbian community. Many of us know of men and women who have been attacked verbally and physically because of their sexual orientation. These voices are begging the church to take a stand that will affirm them," she wrote.

Yet Matthews and others recognized the difficult position of many bishops who shared stories of "the contempt of Islam extremists who view the Anglican Church as a weak and morally corrupt church. They anticipate going home to increased violence if the Lambeth Conference appears to endorse the gay lifestyle."

PRESS REACTION

The British press had a field day reporting on the decision on homosexuality. The headlines screamed: "Liberal bishops routed in vote on homosexuals," said the London *Times*. "Bishops vote to condemn gay practice," said the *Daily Telegraph*. "Bishops defeat gay activists," said the *Daily Mail*. "Anglicans ban gays," said the *Mirror*. "Church says emphatic No to gay sex," said the *Express*. "Liberal bishops lose the war of words," said another. "Anti-gay bishops crush liberals," said the *Guardian*. "Lambeth Conference condemns gays," said the British Broadcasting Company.

Editorial comment was quite pointed. The London *Times* called it "a surprisingly trenchant verdict." While lauding the obvious diversity of the Communion, the editorial said "that cannot be the same as an easy relativism which accepts the legitimacy in some provinces of the Communion of practices which, in the deep conviction of others, are incompatible with biblical teaching and thus with the Christian faith."

Pointing to what it considered the underlying issue, the editorial said, "In seeking to reflect both biblical truth and the spirit of Christian charity, mere agreement to disagree would have been not only a shirking of Christian duty, but a source of anguish that would, especially although not exclusively within the devout and rapidly expanding African dioceses, have weakened the cohesiveness and integrity of Anglicanism." It said that the final results were "not an intolerant document," even if "liberals may feel that Lambeth has erred on the side of a fundamentalist theological outlook."

While some British press commented on what looked like a survival decision, others thought the decision was forged in the face of some new realities. In an effort to avoid schism, "all but a handful seemed determined to bend as far as they could to accommodate the other side, and to maintain the wide embrace of the Anglican Communion, which has always been its strength and its weakness," said Tom Utley in the *Daily Telegraph*.

"But for Anglicans, the question is how far can a church bend, for the sake of unity and 'inclusiveness' before it makes itself ridiculous and wholly pointless?" Utley asked. "In my view, the Lesbian and Gay Christian Movement is asking the Church of England to bend much too far."

Arguing that "nobody in the church hierarchy is persecuting homosexuals or asking them to bear a heavier cross than the rest of us," Utley wrote, "All the church is saying is that sex is for the procreation of children within marriage, and that buggery, like masturbation and adultery, is wrong."

In fact, Utley was convinced that "the homosexual lobby is persecuting the Church of England, and trying to exploit its weakness for compromise. If homosexual practices are wrong—as the Scriptures and 2,000 years of Christian tradition say they are—then no amount of shouting, or marching, or placard-waving is going to make them right. All that a victory for the homosexual lobby would do would be to turn even more people away from the church."

He concluded, "Thank God for the bishops from Africa and Asia—and give him his due, for the Archbishop of Canterbury himself....They have kept open the arms of the Anglican

Communion to that great majority who would like to believe, but find it hard enough as it is, without having to sanctify buggery."

Also writing in the London *Times*, Simon Jenkins disagreed, arguing that "the Anglican Church, at least in England, has not surrendered its reason but for the time being it has set its door against a group of sincere adherents. If I were a homosexual, I would go elsewhere. I would seek a church that honors a more generous love, that sees in all personal relations the rock on which community is built."

"The pleas of the gay and lesbian Christian movement fell not so much on deaf ears as on ears more tuned into poverty and persecution than preferential lifestyles," said Elaine Storkey in the *Independent*'s Weekend Review.

A colleague at the *Independent*, Catherine Pepinster, said "too often consensus leads to the canker of compromise, to a bland, hybrid society. It's happened repeatedly in the commercial world: do we really want the ethical and spiritual equivalent of the Coca-Cola culture?"

For her, the action by the African bishops would not let that happen, and it is time to abandon our cultural arrogance and our fantasies of a melting pot based on the assumption that "given time the world would be ours," that in a few years "the rest of them would come round to our thinking....West is not necessarily best, but nor is living in the kingdom of the bland. It is time we learnt to live side-by-side with those with different values, and offered them the dignity we feel they owe us."

"The moment has come to find a different way," and that way is not Spong but rather Voltaire, who said that while he may disagree with what someone said, he would defend to the death the person's right to say it, Pepinster said. "Men in purple—like the rest of us—it's time you grew up."

The liberals at Lambeth "are the new imperialists, seeking to change deeply held ideas in Third World countries...and to spread their own peculiar obsessions and moral (or a-moral) agenda throughout the world," said Dr. Theodore Dalrymple in an op-ed piece in the *Sunday Telegraph*. "For in their hearts they do not believe it is possible for people from poor countries to hold conservative convictions as a result of their own thought and experience."

He concluded, "In times of rapid change, people do not want a church that blows with the wind; they go to church for enduring, transcendental truths that help them navigate the change that they otherwise find so disorienting....The very nature of religion, and religious truth, renders the church the prisoner of its past; and if it changes, it must do so slowly, imperceptibly and organically, not by great leaps or complete reversals."

The American press weighed in with its own comments. In an opinion piece distributed by Religion News Service called, "It's time to listen to Third World Christians," Erich Bridges said, "Hurray for the bishops—the Anglican bishops from Africa, Asia and Latin America, that is." He added, "Tired of getting pushed around by modernist theological bullies from North America and Europe, they stood up for biblical morality...and "responded to the modernists' effort to put the church's stamp of approval on homosexual practice...."

Bridges, who works for the Southern Baptists, called the resolution itself "mild," but quickly added that "it constituted a stinging rebuke to liberal clerics and their hopes of winning over pagan Western culture by surrendering to it." He called the perspective provided by the Third World bishops "refreshing."

In an August 14 editorial, *The Wall Street Journal* said that "the setback Lambeth represents for the left wing was not simply the rejection of their sexual agenda. It was that the debate exposes the growing rift between the Old and New World, North and South if you are being politically correct." It used Spong's comments on the African Christians as an illustration of an attitude that shows the "hollowness of the left's commitment to diversity—or, for that matter, the Third World. The increasing participation of African and Asian bishops has traditionally been celebrated as confirmation of the Anglican church's claim to catholicity. But that was only so long as the colonial churches marched in lockstep to the left's agenda."

The editorial concluded "if we have learned anything from Lambeth 1998, it is that Christian orthodoxy is far less parochial than its liberal counterpart."

American Presiding Bishop Frank Griswold responded in a letter to the editor, pointing out that the bishops had committed themselves to a listening process. "The fruits of such listening, particularly in parts of the Anglican world where sexuality is seldom if ever publicly discussed, cannot be predicted, but it is a process to which the bishops of the Anglican Communion have obligated themselves."

LESBIAN AND GAY REACTION

In response to the vote, lesbian and gay activists formed a new inter-Anglican coalition, the Alliance of Lesbian and Gay Anglicans, that said it would work for "the unconditional inclusion and full participation of gay and lesbian people in all facets of the church's life throughout the Anglican Communion," according to a statement. The coalition will include Changing Attitude and the Lesbian and Gay Christian Movement (LGCM), both based in the United Kingdom, and Integrity, based in the United States and Canada.

The stated goal of the coalition would be to seek affirmation that sexuality is a gift of God; that sexual orientation is morally neutral; that lesbians and gay men in "faithful, committed, life-giving and holy" relationships should be honored; that all baptized Christians should have full access to all orders of ministry in the church; that these goals are consistent with Anglican tradition; and that the full inclusion of gay men and lesbians is based ultimately on "the total witness of Holy Scripture."

The LGCM said that an informal survey of bishops taken earlier in the conference indicated more openness on the subject than represented by the vote with two-thirds of those responding indicating support for an inter-Anglican commission on sexuality and the "full participation" of gays and lesbians in the life of the church. More than eighty percent opposed discrimination based on sexual orientation but slightly less than half supported blessing homosexuals living in committed relationships. Just over half said that they would not ordain non-celibate homosexuals. About ten percent of the 739 bishops responded.

Integrity issued a statement, "We're Not Going Back," stating its belief that "the division over this issue has only been exacerbated" by the conference's rejection of "homosexual practice as incompatible with Scripture." It also said that "the chances of this resolution's positive reception by the majority of U.S. Episcopalians is slim to none," adding that the resolution would have "a negative impact on church growth in the United States" because of its exclusionary tone. "The full inclusion of lesbian and gay ministries in the Episcopal Church will continue," as will the ordinations of openly gay and lesbian clergy and the celebrations of gay and lesbian unions.

The Lesbian and Gay Christian Movement held an "After Lambeth" conference at the University of Derby which drew a dozen bishops, representatives of 32 dioceses and almost 300 participants.

Holloway of Scotland, a keynote speaker, acknowledged that the authority and interpretation of Scripture had been an underlying issue at Lambeth, one that had not been adequately addressed. "We are not here to preserve the church from conflict and challenge—not even those of us who are bishops, because we should always be trying, imperfectly and through compromised institutions, to express the absolute unconditionality of God," he said.

Holloway expressed his fears that attitudes in the Church of England have hardened and he sees no prospect for a more tolerant approach. "I am saying to some of my young gay friends that they should think seriously about leaving the Church of England because things have got that bad" and that clergy would continue to face oppression, he said in an Edinburgh lecture called, "Was the Trojan Horse Gay?" "I could stock the Scottish Episcopal Church with sexual refugees from the Church of England. Hardly a week goes by when I don't get a letter from someone, usually with a heartbreaking story."

At its biennial conference at Oxford, the organization "Affirming Catholicism" passed a resolution "by a very substantial majority" charging that the resolution rejecting all homosexual practice as incompatible with Scripture "lacks the customary reflective balance of Scripture, tradition, sound scholarship and pastoral discernment found in classical Anglican approaches to controversy."

Describing itself as "a movement within the Anglican Communion which was launched in 1990 to affirm the intelligent, inclusive catholic tradition," the resolution added, "Our church does not approach other issues, such as the church's treatment of women or of those who remarry after divorce, in this literalist fashion. We believe that the question of homosexual relationships constitutes a similar issue."

The resolution observed that "there has been and remains a longstanding catholic tradition of pastoral dedication and service in some of the most demanding parishes by homosexual priests, both those who are celibate and those who are in a stable relationship," and it is "our duty to support" them.

In a letter to the Archbishop of Canterbury, Affirming Catholicism said it was expressing its "empathy with and support for those of our brothers and sisters in Christ who have been made to feel even more vulnerable by that resolution's tone and content," and to stress a "determination to oppose any further retreat into selective biblical literalism. We were of one mind that remaining silent at this time would effectively be collusion in an apparent attempt to undermine the church's celebration of the insights of the critical study of the Bible."

THE ROLE OF AMERICAN CONSERVATIVES

One of the lingering questions hovering around the edges of the conference was how well organized the conservatives were—and what role the Americans played in shaping the response to the issues that most concerned them.

"There are persistent rumors that the anti-homosexual alliance has been mobilized and is being coordinated by American right-wing evangelicals," wrote Madeleine Bunting in a piece in the *Guardian*. "In return for funding meetings of bishops from the developing world in recent years, they have primed them with the importance of arresting the decline of the church in the West caused by liberal decadence. It is claimed that American evangelical bishops promised to support a tough stand on international debt in return for the developing world bishops taking up the crusade against homosexuality."

She observed that "the passionate anti-homosexuality is also home-grown in both Africa and South East Asia. In Zimbabwe homosexuality is illegal and gay rights activists have been imprisoned." In areas where Christianity is in competition with Islam and also with independent evangelical churches they face a crisis of credibility, she said.

Holloway of Scotland accused the American conservatives of buying votes with "chicken and sausages" at dinners arranged at the Franciscan Centre on the edge of the campus, headquarters of several conservative organizations. While he admitted that he had no evidence that any money had changed hands, he said that the Americans "sent out expensive mailings here."

Andrew Carey, the Archbishop's son, begged to differ. "Up to thirty right-wingers are said to have been based at the centre, and these people were alleged to have been engaged in 'buying' the votes of African and Asian bishops with food, mobile phones, e-mail facilities and free phone calls back to their dioceses," said Carey in an article in the *Church of England Newspaper* after the conference adjourned. He said that the facilities "were intended to resource and network the Third World bishops and provide care, in a way that the official bureaucracy could never have done. The staff also helped those African and Asian bishops make sense of the largely western procedures in the debate, although many of them did not need this service."

Brushing aside the allegations, Carey noted that Archbishop Joseph Adetiloye of Nigeria said that Africans are dying for their faith, paying a far greater price than any alleged dinner, bribery, or inducement. "After three weeks as a journalist at the Lambeth Conference, it is quite clear to me that there is no right-wing conspiracy, merely an honest attempt to enable Third World bishops to have a greater voice in the conference."

Carey repeated allegations by some of the African bishops that financial assistance might be reduced or cut off because of their stand on homosexuality.

It was not the first time the allegations had surfaced. The Rev. Bill Atwood of the Ekklesia Society wrote in June of 1997 to the Rev. Patrick Mauney, director of Anglican and Global Relations for the Episcopal Church, saying, "Over the last few months, I have become increasingly concerned at the perceptions of many leaders in the two-thirds world that they are risking the loss of financial support from the Church Center if they disagree with the agenda for change of some of the leaders in the American church. This is, of course, particularly true concerning issues of human sexuality where liberal advocacy and actions are of the greatest concern across the Communion."

In his diocesan newspaper, Stanton of Dallas said that he had "disturbing information about the up-coming Anglican Life and Witness Conference" in Dallas in the fall of 1997. "We have heard that the national church has told the African bishops coming here…that if they come to Dallas the funds they receive from New York could be in jeopardy," he said. "The national church has no business playing politics with their funding because these bishops, for the most part, disagree with the liberal bias of the U.S. church."

Mauney responded by saying that "the overseas allocations of the General Convention program budget are the largest single items in the budget and are strictly non-partisan. We give to dioceses and provinces that do not ordain women, for example. There is no ideological means test." Pointing out that "no other church in the Anglican Communion gives more from its provincial budget than does ours," he went on to tell Atwood, "What a tragedy it will be if particular groups and dioceses in our church, unhappy with certain actions (or inactions) of General Convention, attempt to circumvent the national program budget in order to direct funding to overseas partners of their own choosing." Mauney was responding to efforts by Ekklesia and other organizations to support mission work overseas by bypassing the General Convention budget.

As the dust was settling in the weeks after the Lambeth Conference, Bishop Geralyn Wolf of Rhode Island made some outright allegations that conservative American bishops had been involved in influencing the votes of bishops who shared their points of view.

According to a story in her diocesan newspaper, the intense lobbying by conservative groups such as the AAC (American Anglican Council), which advocated a hard line on homosexuality, disturbed Wolf. "Under my door every single night was information from this group. Some of it was just obnoxious," she said, calling the intense politicking "indicative of an evil spirit in the church. There's a lot of evil at work here."

Wolf said that it was apparent that many of the non-Western bishops did not really understand the sexuality issue. "One of the bishops in my small group said, 'You know, I don't understand much about this. Is this homosexuality contagious?' It's clear that, for a lot of the African bishops, they don't talk about this, just like we don't talk about polygamy. I think we have to honor the people for whom this was a little new," Wolf said.

Fear was also a factor, according to Wolf. "Some were told by their governments that should they take any kind of conciliatory line on homosexuality, they would risk being imprisoned on their return," she said. "One in my group was petrified even to talk about it. We underestimate the tensions that some of our fellow Christians live under."

Lobbying was not the only use for American dollars at Lambeth, according to the Rev. Ran Chase, a member of the diocesan staff in Rhode Island who was a volunteer at Lambeth. "I was in line at one of the campus banks, and an African bishop turned to me with $500 in crisp new bills in his hands," Chase reported. "He said, 'What do I do with this? Can I use it?' and I said, 'No, you can't use it unless you go in the bank and exchange it for pounds.' I said, 'Where did you get dollars?' He said, 'Oh, I didn't get it. That nice bishop from Texas gave it to me.'"

Wolf said that she heard reports that between $150,000 and $450,000 was spent by the AAC for Lambeth lobbying.

In response Stanton called the allegations "clearly false" and "outrageous," and "an insult to the men of honor who come from Africa and other places." He dismissed any suggestion that bishops from the developing world were susceptible to such bribery as "clearly racist." And he said that AAC spent only $27,000 at Lambeth, costs they shared with the Oxford Centre for Mission Studies.

In responding to the rumors, Jim Rosenthal of the Anglican Communion Office in London said, "If it's true, it's unfortunate—and there have been other reports of this as well. We have reports of money changing hands on both sides of the issues."

Rosenthal said that "there was an obvious need by a group to have its own center—and in retrospect maybe others should have done something similar." He said that the program at the Franciscan Centre was "superb," but even though he accredited more press to the ACC than any other organization, "we received no reports at all about their activities. I don't think it was helpful for them to be separatist."

Despite his pleas that the conference attempt to find a way to deal with sexuality issues "directly and openly," Rosenthal felt that his pleas were "ignored" and that "only the folks at the Franciscan Centre dealt with it directly."

The Rev. George Conger, one of the key organizers at the Franciscan Centre, flatly denied the bribery allegations. "I can say with absolute certainty that this never happened. I handled all the money."

In a column of reflections for *Ruach,* the magazine of the Episcopal Women's Caucus, Lambeth journalist Katie Sherrod of Texas, said, "If liberal money and organization has influenced previous Lambeth Conferences, as many have claimed, then certainly conservative money and organizations influenced this one. The conservatives' on-campus headquarters at the Franciscan Centre was a high-tech model of a U.S. political campaign office. With admirable efficiency and obvious

effectiveness, they hosted meetings, tutored bishops in procedures and rhetoric, and generally made sure they 'owned' the
agenda at Lambeth."

Sherrod, who was a member of the Lambeth communications team, went on to say that "it was the conservatives'
canny marriage of U.S.-style political organization with the
scriptural fundamentalism of many of the African and Asian
bishops that enabled the conservatives to so dominate this
Lambeth Conference. But if the daily liturgies revealed the
emergence of a post-colonial Anglicanism, the conference
deliberations revealed an ideological colonization of Anglicanism driven by the politics of the Episcopal Church U.S.A."

She asserted that "conservative U.S. bishops successfully
planted the flag of their homophobia in the fertile soil of fear
of fundamentalist Islam."

In passing a strong resolution condemning homosexual
activity as contrary to Scripture, Sherrod said, "Emotion verg-
ing on hysteria mixed with a fundamentalist approach to
Scripture and a rejection of scientific and medical evidence
resulted in a session marked by ugly sniggering and a refusal
on the part of many bishops to acknowledge that the subject
they were addressing so hatefully actually concerned real, live
Christian human beings."

Sherrod went on to characterize the attempts by bishops
Waynick of Indianapolis and Roskam of New York to press for
a more compassionate resolution "like throwing flowers in
front of a tank." She said that, following the vote, she saw
bishops leaving the plenary chanting "victory," and slapping
each other on the back. "But the weary, depressed, almost
eerie quiet that descended on the campus the next day
seemed to indicate that some bishops, at least, were aware
that they had participated in an ugly process that had denied
the humanity of brother and sister Christians."

CHAPTER FOUR

COURTESY, CAUTION, AND THE QUESTION OF AUTHORITY

Somewhat depleted after their sexuality debate, the bishops still had some major issues on their agenda, including how to regard ordained women and those who oppose them.

Flush with their victory on sexuality, the traditionalists received more good news on women's ordination, an issue which had threatened unity ten years earlier. The conference approved an amended resolution stating that "there is and should be no compulsion on any bishop in matters concerning the ordination or licensing" of women. The statement was a clear concession to those bishops who maintain that their consciences lead them to oppose the ordination or deployment of women in their dioceses.

The resolution, called "Unity of the Anglican Communion," was hammered out in private meetings of several women bishops and traditionalists. "During our discussions there were deep and real disagreements," said Bishop Penelope Jamieson of New Zealand. "Our small group began by being suspicious of each other. But as trust between us began to grow, it became our prayer that we could agree on an amendment that we would offer to this Communion as a way of deepening our communion in the heart of God" because of our respect for differences.

The original resolution contained stronger language, requesting primates to "oversee compliance with this resolution by the bishops of their province both within and beyond the province." The revised version changed it to a request that the primates "encourage the bishops of their province to consider the implications" of the 1988 resolution. (See III.2, p.260)

Bishop Victoria Matthews of Canada, a member of the small group that drafted the amendment, said, "At this Lambeth Conference I have been received with a gracious and generous spirit...and as one of the first generation of women bishops, I ask that we keep this same spirit of graciousness and generosity as we continue the process of open reception." She said that dissent could be creative for the mind of the church.

Just prior to the plenary session, she said, "I have no idea the number of years the process of reception of women clergy will take. The church grows into fullness of being by prayer and waiting on the Spirit. I would hope that it would be a matter of time before all three orders of women clergy are accepted, but I could be wrong. The possibility of a reversal is there."

At a morning press briefing before the plenary, Bishop Frederick Borsch of Los Angeles said that he believed American bishops would strongly oppose the aspect of the resolution dealing with women's ordination. "We have long recognized the fact of having only one bishop in a diocese," he said. "Anything different would be alien to our tradition."

During the debate in the plenary, Bishop Barbara Harris of Massachusetts, the first woman to be consecrated to the episcopate in the Anglican Communion, voiced her opposition. "While the language seems gracious, it contravenes the canons of the Episcopal Church U.S.A. and the discipline of the church in the provinces of Canada and New Zealand." She pointed out that the "canon concerning ordination of women in my own province was made mandatory last year at our General Convention. The bishop may indeed be conscientiously opposed to the ordination of women but cannot impose his or her conscience on a diocese. The phrase 'appropriate episcopal ministry' also opens the door for interference in the autonomy of dioceses and provinces, which I believe is a very dangerous enterprise," Harris said.

In support of the resolution, Bishop Geoffrey Rowell of England, which has three "flying bishops" to minister to traditionalists opposed to women priests, noted that "it safeguards the position of bishops who find themselves living under pressure and exercising leadership under pressure. The resolution recognizes the traditionalist position as one that is expressive of Anglican loyalty as much as the position that favors ordination of women."

The amended resolution passed by about an eighty-percent majority. Archbishop Michael Peers of Canada, who had sponsored the amendment, said the intention of both resolutions was to create a Communion-wide "collegial" understanding of the inviolability of provincial and diocesan boundaries. "This conference cannot obligate, but it can urge," he said.

The 1988 resolution, which "reaffirms its unity in the historical position of respect for diocesan boundaries and the authority of bishops within those boundaries," was provoked largely because Graham Leonard, who was Bishop of London at the time, had provided oversight of a traditionalist parish in Oklahoma without permission from the diocesan bishop.

The Episcopal Church has provisions for such alternate oversight, with cooperation of diocesan bishops, but the Episcopal Synod of America has tested that provision on several occasions by sending its bishops into dioceses to claim oversight of traditionalist parishes, without the knowledge of diocesan bishops.

In 1997 a bishop from Rwanda announced that he would provide oversight for a traditionalist mission congregation in

Arkansas formed without diocesan support. The priest who was called to serve that congregation had received letters dimissory from the Bishop of South Carolina, placing him under the care of the Rwandan bishop, John Rucyahana. Bishop Larry Maze of Arkansas said that the call was irregular and removed the Rev. Thomas Johnston from "accountability to the American church." In effect, "what had been a national dispute involving the integrity of diocesan boundaries is now an issue transplanted to the larger Anglican Communion," Maze said in a letter to his diocese.

"My simple but clear concern and commitment is to give St. Andrew's and Rev. Johnston spiritual asylum," Rucyahana said in a letter to Maze. "I am saddened even more that you got to a point where church leaders force people into schism. I pray that this congregation remains Anglican up to a time when you resolve your differences or give it a flying bishop who will nurture their faith from your province."

Rucyahana claimed that the congregation had been "pushed to the edge and applied for a refuge and they have it. I hope that you and your province find a solution to this problem."

In a letter to Carey just before the opening of the Lambeth Conference, Rucyahana repeated his allegation that the parish was being formed "because they disagreed doctrinally" with Maze, noting that Maze had signed the *Koinonia* Statement of 1994 that said sexuality was morally neutral and that gays and lesbians living in relationships could be ordained. Rucyahana dismissed the authority of Lambeth resolutions on diocesan boundaries, saying that "the issue of boundaries and collegiality cannot hold when the central unity in Jesus is damaged."

American Presiding Bishop Griswold and Maze met at Lambeth with Archbishop Emmanuel Kolini, Primate of Rwanda, and Rucyahana in an effort to head off any further confrontations—and to ask the Rwandan bishop to call off his intended visit to Little Rock for confirmations right after

Lambeth. Griswold said such a visitation would be "most unwise and harmful." The visit was called off, at least for the time being.

"It's clear to me that St. Andrew's has become a cause for conservative groups in this country," Maze said in an interview. "And the sad thing is that well-intentioned local Episcopalians are getting caught up in that cause, one that doesn't have anything to do with our life as a diocese. There is no conversation on the local level in an attempt to resolve the issue," he said.

The American bishops on both sides of the issue had strong reactions. Catherine Roskam of New York said that the resolution "doesn't mean anything in terms of our own polity" in the Episcopal Church U.S.A. She pointed to the difficulty of "a kind of arrogance among bishops here that forgets there is the rest of the church. And I doubt that the House of Deputies in the American church is going to take that one sitting down."

In her column in the diocesan newspaper later, Harris of Massachusetts called it "an odious amendment" and predicted "that our U.S. 'selective traditionalist' bishops will seek to use it as a club to prove their affirmation by the wider church."

Bishop Chilton Knudsen of Maine said that the amendment was internally inconsistent "because reception requires exposure and this limits exposure of people to the ministry of women."

Bishop Jack Iker of Ft. Worth, one of the four U.S. bishops who opposes the ordination of women, said that the decision was reassuring. "It made me feel that I'm not on the extreme right-wing side, but stand with most bishops." He thinks the mandatory nature of the 1997 action of General Convention was contrary to the open process of reception. "That's painful on both sides, but there have to be ways worked out of living together in tension so that neither side claims to be the victor," he said.

A historic first: female bishops at Lambeth. Standing (l to r): Victoria Matthews of Edmonton (Canada); Penelope Jamieson of Dunedin (New Zealand); Catherine Waynick of Indianapolis; Mary Adelia McLeod of Vermont; Geralyn Wolf of Rhode Island; Ann Tottenham of Toronto (Canada). Seated (l to r): Carolyn Tanner Irish of Utah; Catherine Roskam of New York; Barbara Harris of Massachusetts; Chilton Knudsen of Maine; and Jane Holmes Dixon of Washington, DC. (Photo: Episcopal News Service)

Many observers were convinced that the resolution would provide grounds for traditionalists to dig in their heels in opposing the action of the General Convention asking them to open the process for women in their dioceses.

The ordination of women, and other "liberal" practices, could reduce the Anglican Communion to a mere "federation" of churches, said one of the Church of England's bishops who provides oversight to those who continue to oppose women in the priesthood.

"One thing destroyed by the ordination of women is the interchangeability of ministry," said Bishop John Broadhurst of the Diocese of London, president of Forward in Faith, an organization that promotes what it calls orthodox Anglicanism. He contended that it would now be "illegal" for a woman bishop from another Anglican province, or for a male priest ordained by a female bishop, to function in England. "This has turned the church into a federation," he said, adding that he did not know how the issue could be resolved.

Broadhurst said that some of those who are opposed to women priests, "which was the view of the church until twenty years ago," are now subject to deep intolerance. "The liberals have tried to exterminate those who disagree," he said in a press interview, citing the Episcopal Church in the U.S.A. and the Anglican Church of Canada. "If liberalism becomes tyrannical, it is the duty of orthodox bishops to protect the faith," he said when asked about the situation in the Diocese of Arkansas where a Rwandan bishop has offered oversight of a traditionalist parish that was formed without the permission of the diocesan bishop.

Instead of traditionalists being on the fringe, Broadhurst said that orthodoxy was experiencing a resurgence. "I suspect you will see a move internationally back to orthodoxy," he said. "I don't see us as a ghetto. I believe we are right on the basic issues, and in the end we will triumph." In the Church of England, he estimated that 500 priests had left to join the

Roman Catholic Church because of the ordination issue, leaving "an enormous wound" in the church.

WARM WELCOME

Despite continuing disagreement over their role in the Anglican Communion, the eleven women bishops reported experiencing a surprisingly warm welcome. They were objects of curiosity for some, approached by many participants requesting a photo opportunity or an autograph.

"People from all over have been introducing themselves," said Harris of Massachusetts. And some of the encounters were particularly moving. "One African bishop introduced himself and told me that he was at Virginia Seminary when I was elected. He remembered how joyous it was and how they had rung the bells and how exciting it was for him to be there at that moment," she said. The wives of some bishops even sought her out to tell her how important her election had been to them personally.

Bishop Ann Tottenham of Canada related an encounter with three teenaged stewards from Tanzania who met her as she was returning from a photo op with the other women bishops. "They all wanted their photo taken with me in all my gear. So I had my photo taken with each of them, and then with all three of them. By the time we finished I felt like a national monument," she said

"It has been a good, stretching, almost overwhelming experience," said Bishop Mary Adelia McLeod of Vermont, the first woman to be elected as a diocesan bishop in the American church. "Overwhelming in listening to all the voices from all over the world—the sense of our connectedness, regardless of culture, of theology, that sense of worshiping the same God."

While a few detractors made comments in radio talk shows prior to Lambeth, the women experienced almost no overt hostility. "I have had no bad moments," said Bishop

Catherine Waynick of Indianapolis. "I have felt very welcome. I was not sure how we would be received here, but I was determined to have fun."

Waynick's photo was splashed all over the press, especially during the opening Eucharist, leading some to suggest that she should win the prize as Lambeth's most photogenic bishop.

"The people who are unappreciative of our presence here are probably just avoiding us," said Harris. She moved around the campus on a motorized cart because of an ankle problem but "people have been very solicitous and kind."

Tottenham admitted that she came to Lambeth "very nervous. I wasn't sure what to expect. I thought Lambeth would be something good to look back on, but I'm enjoying it thoroughly. It's an incredible privilege to be here."

As part of the first generation of women to serve as priests, the bishops often shared similar experiences. "I have often thought of my ministry as a wedge plowing a field that is hard, leaving behind something softer that is ready for new life," said Wolf of Rhode Island, who was the first woman to be elected the dean of a cathedral, Christ Church in Louisville, Kentucky.

"One thing that hasn't really come out yet is how different we all are," added Roskam. Bishop Mark Santer of Birmingham did notice the difference. He told the London *Times*, "I'm sure I am not the only person who has not been surprised at how we have hardly noticed the women bishops here at Lambeth, not because they have been ignored, but because they have been accepted naturally. Like male bishops, they are a mixed bunch and some of them are very impressive indeed."

Several of the women bishops cited encounters with women from other parts of the Communion where the ministry of women is denied or frustrated. About half the provinces of the Anglican Communion ordain women to the priesthood, but only the United States, Canada, and New Zealand have elected women to the episcopate.

"I have a tendency, after nine years of moving into the routine of the episcopacy and with the company of the other women, to forget I was the first, because it feels so natural," Harris said. "But again and again I have been reminded of some aspects of what that meant—and still means."

Harries of Oxford said the participation and influence of the women bishops had helped the cause of their advocates in the Church of England but that legislation opening the episcopate to women was unlikely for eight to ten years. He said the church does not want to drive into a corner, or drive out completely, those who continue to oppose women in the priesthood or episcopate.

All the women bishops pointed to their joining the procession of hundreds of bishops into Canterbury Cathedral for the opening Eucharist as the moment when the historic nature of their presence was driven home most powerfully.

"I was tingling, walking over the threshold, remembering my first visit at the age of twenty-three, never being able to imagine that one day I would be walking in as a bishop in a beautiful purple cassock," said Wolf. Just as she entered, one of the male bishops from the Episcopal Church "turned, took my hand, and said, 'Bishop Wolf, welcome to Canterbury Cathedral.' I'll never forget it."

Jamieson, the first female to be elected diocesan bishop in the Anglican Communion, said that she was "sure I was just gaping as we went in. I was just overwhelmed" at the beauty and significance of the moment, she said.

Waynick agreed that "the sense of the moment of history we represent was almost overwhelming," adding, "At the same time it felt so natural to be there."

Dixon of Washington, who spoke and participated in services at Durham Cathedral before Lambeth, related an encounter at a dinner party afterward with the woman who is the diocesan linkage with companion dioceses in Africa. When asked if she were the first woman bishop, "I said no, that the first is an African-American woman named Barbara Harris. She said, 'Are you telling me that the first woman bishop in the church is a black woman?' I say yes, and her face broke into the most radiant smile, and she said, 'Isn't that pretty.'" Dixon described it as an incarnation moment as this black woman joyously embraced the reality of a black female bishop.

Like all of the bishops at Lambeth, the women bishops participated in daily Bible study groups, and they agreed that it had been the single most powerful aspect of their experience.

"My Bible study group is the most profound happening," Dixon said. "Here we all are, literally from around the world. I'm sure it is the grace of God that has entered in. From the very first day, we have been able to talk in a very deep, intimate way. I wouldn't miss it for anything."

Knudsen said that she had not been treated "any differently from anyone else," adding, "The leadership gifts of the female bishops are beginning to be evident. Gerry Wolf has given one of the Bible study videos. Ann was the preacher at the Canadian evening prayer. Victoria moderated the plenary on making moral decisions....There's been a gentle kind of acknowledgment of our gifts."

She said that the women bishops "have been uniformly well-received," with "not one bit of discomfort by any..." She added that "it has been very good for this Lambeth to break through the gender barrier as it has. I have had more invitations than I can count to come overseas to this or that place to provide people a chance to meet a bishop who is a woman." She said she declined these invitations because she was still settling in with her diocesan family.

Jamieson added, "People have been accepting us in the spirit of the Eames Report, that we are accepted as bishops in our own churches and that we are not telling them what they should be doing in their churches."

Tottenham said that "the thing that is never written about is the fact that most bishops in the Communion are reconciled to the fact that there are going to be women bishops." In an encounter with a bishop from Namibia, he related that something in the culture that oppresses someone could not be accepted into Christianity. "He said that as they considered this, they realized that if they applied this guideline to the ordination of women, then opposition to that would be oppressive of women," she said.

Prayers for the presence of the women bishops were offered daily, under an oak tree on the campus that held a banner inviting passersby to "Meet to pray for our sister bishops." The Rev. Cynthia Black, president of the Episcopal Women's Caucus (EWC) which helped sponsor the prayer spot, said, "We know that any conference is stressful and that any bishop would like to have someone who can ease that stress." The caucus also organized the women for the historic photo of the bishops on a hilltop overlooking Canterbury Cathedral.

"The support of the Episcopal Women's Caucus was remarkable," said Dixon in her report to the diocese. "They ran our errands, treated us to dinner, and prayed constantly for the well-being of the conference. Roman Catholic women from the United Kingdom came to celebrate our presence outside the cathedral on the opening day, and women clergy from England hosted a luncheon and discussion for the female bishops. We, the Lambeth Eleven, were assured by many that our presence brought hope and new life for the Anglican Communion and for others."

In an article in *Ruach,* the magazine of EWC, Black pointed out that there were petty examples that the presence of the women bishops was not celebrated by everyone. Bishops were still referred to by masculine pronouns, even occasionally by the Archbishop of Canterbury, "and volunteers handing out documents to the bishops entering plenary sessions would refuse to give one to the women, saying, 'These are just for bishops.'"

Jamieson warned against unrealistic expectations of women bishops in a pre-Lambeth lecture arranged by Women and the Church (WATCH), another sponsor of the prayer post.

"You will not find in me a very powerful advocate of women as bishops," she said. "For I cannot recommend the job, and I cannot think that anyone would want it or seek it."

While many in her audience might have been expecting a different story, Jamieson said that she had suffered "deep hurt" and "destructive abuse" as the first woman diocesan bishop. I want to tell you that I have found the job no more difficult than my [male] colleagues, and that my failures have been no more marked than theirs. The truth is that the job of a bishop is very hard."

Jamieson said that the expectations of a bishop were "impossibly high," that she had difficulty convincing people that she was neither "a saint, sent to serve" nor a "devil out of hell." On the contrary, she said that she was "simply a woman who has been called of God to be a bishop at this point in the history of our church."

Her rural diocese has moved to a pattern of what is known as "mutual ministry," an attempt at "partnership rather than privilege" among clergy and laity. She said that it was a style "that I warm to" because it is one that "engages, consults, and doesn't move alone or in authoritative isolation. It is right on target for what I would have wished to develop from my experience in both the church and feminism prior to becoming a bishop."

Yet that leadership style means a certain amount of vulnerability. "I have been deeply hurt, punished even, for such leadership, and I am not always sure that I have the courage to risk it again," she said. "For to be vulnerable is to be wounded. It is to know what it is to be broken, to lose complete confidence in vocation and in the ability to even survive."

Noting that her male colleagues were experiencing many of the same problems, Jamieson said that "change is very difficult for some people. It is disorientating, and a bishop bears responsibility for that."

Women in Anglican churches that do not yet consecrate women to the episcopate, such as the Church of England, tend to "oversimplify" the issue, Jamieson said, perhaps even glamorizing the presence of women bishops at Lambeth.

When asked by the press to speculate on which other provinces might choose women bishops, she said that Australia was likely, and perhaps Southern Africa. On the other hand, she said, the Church of England "could surprise us."

BISHOPS OR PATRIARCHS?

Lambeth's cautious acceptance of women in the episcopate was accompanied by a subtle questioning of the nature of episcopal authority. If *de facto* patriarchy could no longer be taken for granted, was there a need for *de jure* definition? Was the concept of *primus inter pares*, first among equals, strong enough for the Archbishop of Canterbury, or did the authority of the office need to be upgraded?

While none went so far as Donald Reeves, who wrote in the Roman Catholic weekly *Tablet* of the emergence of a Patriarchate of Canterbury, the Archbishop's role and George Carey's execution of it became an open issue at several key points in the conference.

In an interview with Paul Handley, editor of the *Church Times*, prior to the opening of the conference, Carey said that he would like to see a yearly meeting of all the primates. "I personally don't want to be elevated into another pope, that's not the way we do our business. I see my role as a servant of the Anglican Communion. But it may well be that we have to put things in position, if we are to be a stronger Communion." He pointed out that the Inter-Anglican Doctrinal Commission, even though an advisory group, could deal with the larger issues.

He said that he had used his moral authority to intervene in Rwanda, "where mistakes were made when Rwanda was set up as an independent province. We never tidied up the constitution of the church, so that when the problems happened, the constitution was still that of the body before it." Carey said that he visited the province, sent delegations and "I think they were partially successful, to the degree that we now have a stable church there...."

But Reeves of the *Tablet* saw it differently.

"It is inevitable that it should be the Archbishop of Canterbury who is the focus and chief representative of the Anglican Communion. He presides at the Lambeth Conference. He is the one, single, constant factor in keeping the Anglican Communion together," he wrote.

Reeves speculated that "what is happening is the birth of a Patriarchate of Canterbury, for the Archbishop's job has grown well beyond the role that was traditional. This ministry is daunting, not just because of its increasing international dimension, but because alongside the ACC and the Primates' Meeting, the Archbishop has no authority except what he is able to offer by way of insight and spiritual wisdom. Symbol, focus of unity, he may be, but at the end of the day it is his demeanor and what he says that counts," Reeves said.

Speculating about the possibility of an Archbishop of Canterbury who is not English, Reeves said that "a way will have to be found to free the Archbishop of Canterbury, whether English or not, to be the Patriarch of the Anglican Communion, if the Anglican Communion is to be taken seriously." He cited Archbishop Robert Runcie's address to the 1988 Lambeth Conference and his suggestion that the choice was between unity or gradual fragmentation. The issue is to "free whoever is Archbishop of Canterbury to give unhurried time to the development of the Anglican Communion. The Archbishop is no Pope," Reeves observed, but "he will not undertake his ministry alone. But unless a future archbishop recognizes the heart of his ministry as service to this global fellowship and gives it priority, then the days of the Anglican Communion are numbered."

In his opening address to the conference, Carey specifically eschewed any kind of "hierarchical, monarchical form of top-down authority" and praised "dispersed rather than centralized authority."

A draft resolution, emerging from Section Four, recommended that a commission be set up to examine under what circumstances the Archbishop and his successors might intervene in the life of a province of the Anglican Communion.

The conference approved a resolution that "notes with gratitude the ministry of support which the Archbishop of Canterbury has been able to give in Sudan and Rwanda, and recognizes that he is called upon to render assistance from time to time in a variety of situations." Another part of the resolution, citing "the very grave difficulties encountered in the internal affairs of some provinces," invited the Archbishop of Canterbury to appoint a commission. Its purpose would be to make recommendations to the Primates and the Anglican Consultative Council concerning when and how it might be appropriate for him to "exercise an extraordinary ministry of *episcope* (pastoral oversight), support and reconciliation..."

"The church in Rwanda lost an opportunity to be prophetic during the genocide," Carey said after a visit to the country in the spring of 1995. "The church should have been calling out for justice but by and large its voice was silent." During the visit, protestors waved placards naming bishops, including the country's Anglican archbishop, who they claimed were involved in the genocide. Fearing reprisals, the bishops have refused to return to the country. The Anglican Consultative Council, meeting in Panama in October of 1996, declared those dioceses vacant and urged the church "to set in motion legal procedures to elect bishops to those four vacant sees." Bishop David Birney, who was sent by Carey to Rwanda, warned that the church was in danger of losing its credibility among its own people and with the government of Rwanda, as a result of the continuing crisis in leadership.

On a similar tack, a resolution from Section Three sought to expand the responsibilities of the Primates' Meeting. It included the possibility of intervention in cases of exceptional emergency which are incapable of internal resolution within provinces. It also called for providing guidelines on the limits of Anglican diversity in submission to the "sovereign authority of Holy Scripture and in loyalty to our Anglican tradition and formularies."

The resolution affirmed the role of the Archbishop of Canterbury and the Lambeth Conference, "together with inter-provincial gatherings and cross-provincial diocesan partnerships, as collegial and communal signs of the unity of our Communion."

After the conference concluded, the British press speculated about how much Carey's leadership authority had eroded as he attempted to hold things together. Christopher Morgan in the *Sunday Times* said that one bishop told him that confidence in Carey was "dented," and another expressed "disappointment" over his leadership.

A few cited his intervention in the sexuality debate as an example of how "his leadership was very much undermined." Liberal bishops said the vote was evidence of a creeping "fundamentalism" within the church and proof that there were serious divisions. Bishop Rowan Williams of Wales said, "A gulf has opened up which can't be quickly bridged."

Carey dismissed the criticism, while acknowledging that some bishops were not happy. "It has come from a very tiny group. We can disagree. I welcome dialogue," he said. He said that he intervened in the homosexuality debate to unite the church. "The vast majority of the conference knew that I intervened to calm things down."

DEFENDING CAREY

Some bishops leapt to his defense. "To have held together such a disparate conference is a great achievement," said Bishop Michael Nazir-Ali of England in the London *Times.*

Stanton of Dallas applauded Carey's "forthright, centrist and orthodox" leadership, saying that "he played a central role, as well he should, in all the deliberations. After the attack against him by some before the conference, and some afterward, his generosity of spirit and calm but clear exercise of leadership made this conference the unifying force it became." And he said that, whether or not this Lambeth was a historic watershed, as some have argued, "George Carey's emphasis on renewal and transformation will be responsible for what lasting effect this conference will come to have."

In an article for the *Catholic Herald,* Ruth Gledhill of the London *Times* said that she was "one among many who have seriously underestimated the Archbishop of Canterbury." She said that there was "an element of subconscious snobbery involved" because he did not quite fit the mold, growing up in public housing. But he "had a real-life spiritual experience of God." And he actually prefers soccer to cricket or rugby. As far as the establishment was concerned, "he was most definitely an outsider."

Gledhill said that the Lambeth Conference made it clear that "rather than change himself to fit in, Dr. Carey changed the church to fit him." She said that his wide travels, especially in the developing world, had gained him a high degree of respect in those countries. "Lambeth illustrated the extent to which the axis of Anglicanism is changing, and Dr. Carey is pivotal in this process."

Instead of trying to fit into the "old boy network" so prevalent in the Church of England, he "has broken the mold and forged a new one for himself and his successors," Gledhill asserted. "At Lambeth it was at times heartening and wonderful to see the more extreme liberals, whose politically correct agendas have been immune from all challenge and criticism, on the run for the first time." Yet she quickly added, "There was also, on the other hand, something slightly scary about the way well-organized teams of conservative evangelicals seized the ball with such relish, and ran with it to score goal after winning goal, completely outpacing the hopeless, crumbling defense of the opposition."

"Dr. Carey does not care whether he is popular or not. What he cares about is God and Jesus Christ," Gledhill concluded. "None of us can again make the mistake of underestimating his ability, a strength and determination close to stubbornness when he believes he is doing God's will. The liberals might protest, argue, and rationalize. But a real, deep and fundamental belief in God, Christ, and the Word is a strange thing in an Anglican bishop."

Some of the strengths Gledhill cited were apparent in an interview Carey gave in *Hello!* magazine just prior to Lambeth. Carey pointed out that he had been to sixty-four countries since assuming his office. When asked about what he enjoyed about being the Archbishop of Canterbury, he said, "Serving people and seeking to use my role to change things for the better." The most poignant moment for him was "going into a Roman Catholic church in Rwanda three years ago, where I saw the remains of 5,000 women and children butchered to death in the terrible genocide. Words cannot sum up the feelings of desolation and sadness that arose in those of us who were there."

Paying a touching tribute to his wife Eileen as his partner, calling her "my best friend," Carey admitted that being parents in the public eye had its difficulties. "In the early days it was difficult, because people were inevitably interested in my children and the failure of two of their marriages, but thankfully everything has gone right for them since. The pain of their lives being upset by that kind of intrusive journalism has mercifully faded away."

When asked how he would like to be remembered, Carey said, "I do not do my work to please others. I shall be satisfied if I have been faithful to my calling and have been a man of principle and integrity, passionately committed to the cause of Jesus Christ and wholeheartedly desiring his church to be more like him."

"George Carey is a plain man, but not illiberal," said a profile in the *Independent* just days before Lambeth opened. "Though he takes a traditional line on homosexuality...he is, when dealing with individuals, a man of pastoral breadth and more liberal than supposed."

The profile said that his speeches and sermons in the last two years have revealed more consistency and sureness. "If not scintillating, they are serious-minded and sound." Even the gaffes that seemed to mark his early years have given way to a more calculated approach—including remarks he made in the spring of 1998 at Luxembourg's Roman Catholic cathedral reminding the Pope that the Eucharist does not belong to any one denomination. "We do not own it, rather, it is a gracious gift from God," Carey said, asking the Vatican to be more generous in interpreting its own position. "He took a hard line because he was getting nowhere with the present Pope," one senior Third World bishop told the author, Paul Vallely. "He is preparing for the post-John Paul II agenda."

"If his lack of a patrician manner has lost him points at home, it does the opposite abroad," the *Independent* article said, noting that Carey seems adept at understanding and relating to people in less sophisticated cultures.

In an interview with a church paper in Melbourne during a visit to Australia in 1997, Carey expressed interest in creating an Anglican Congress of lay people, an idea he subsequently floated at the Lambeth Conference. "I hope people will recognize that, if I can actually strengthen leadership in the Anglican Communion, that's going to lead to mission. It's going to lead to deeper unity."

He also addressed an issue that would become somewhat of a controversy later—hospitality at the Eucharist. "Although I can understand theologically the argument against inter-communion, I would like to see Rome relaxing its rules from time to time, and have a rule of hospitality, as we have in the Anglican Church, where we welcome baptized Christians of other faith traditions," he said in the interview. "I think there may be times when that ought to be allowable—and that's something maybe that would change the climate overnight. It really would."

In discussing the joys and disappointments of his position, Carey cited his attempts to call attention to "those parts of the world where there is extreme victimization of refugees—Rwanda, the Sudan, and elsewhere." But he added, "I have also been delighted to take a strong lead on morals in my own country, and to be recognized for that. Also to take our church through the ordination of women, and to face some of the financial questions at hand."

On the negative side, he has not enjoyed being "the target." He said, "It has been painful when I've been picked off personally. Of course, one can develop another skin. These days it doesn't trouble me as much as four or five years ago. So whatever lies ahead in that direction, it won't hurt me as much as it once did. I can cope with that spiritually."

In an article in the *Independent* just before Lambeth convened, Paul Handley credited Carey with "a strong theology of leadership," pointing out that he has "worked hard to revamp the central power structures of his own Church of England to make them more effective." Handley speculated that there are "others who wish that the Anglican Communion, too, had a stronger center, one that could free the church from the paralyzing effect of endless speculation, lobbying, maneuvering, and debate, and also bring into line any dioceses or provinces that stray from orthodox practice."

While some Anglicans cast a wistful eye at the authority structures in Roman Catholicism, Handley concluded that Carey "is pragmatic enough to realize that few people" believe that authoritarianism works anymore.

The 1948 Lambeth Conference attempted to define authority. "Authority as inherited by the Anglican Communion is derived from the undivided church of the early centuries of the Christian era. It is single, in that it is derived from a divine source and reflects within itself the richness and historicity of the divine Revelation the authority of the eternal Father, the incarnate Son, and the life-giving Spirit." The definition said that it is "a dispersed rather than a centralized authority, having many elements which combine, interact with, and check each other." As such, "It is distributed among the Scripture, Tradition, Creeds, the Ministry of the Word and Sacraments, the witness of the saints and the 'consensus *fidelium*,' which is the continuing experience of the Spirit through the church."

While that kind of authority can be imprecise and often messy, it has saved Anglicanism from hasty or suspect decisions, according to some observers at Lambeth. And it will certainly be called on to do so again.

While it had its difficult moments, no one had walked out of the Lambeth Conference. It had affirmed the traditional biblical sexual morality that is close to Carey's heart as an evangelical. For him, the center of the faith had held.

In a visit to Christ Church in Greenwich, Connecticut, following Lambeth, Carey seemed more relaxed. Interrupting his vacation in North Carolina, Carey participated in a fundraiser for the Anglican Investment Agency and preached at the morning Eucharist at Christ Church. Carey's sermon was based on the encounter of Jesus with the woman taken in adultery. "It is so important for us to learn the lesson of being that kind of church which maintains its principles but in a non-judgmental way as we wrestle with the complex issues in our day," he said.

Acknowledging that members of Integrity were in the congregation, Carey said, "I know that there are some here today who feel that I am on the opposite side from them on the issue of practicing homosexuality. That may well be the case. My integrity too calls me to stand out for what I believe to be orthodox sexual morality. But is it not possible for us to show the way in our divided societies how strong positions can be held in tension without demonizing one another?" Carey assured his audience that he was committed to listen.

In a sensitive personal letter to Integrity founder Louie Crew, a persistent critic of Carey's hesitation to listen to the church's gays and lesbians, the Archbishop said he welcomed the letters he received from gays and lesbians in Connecticut who shared their stories. He said he recognized their pain and invited them to recognize the "positive elements" of the resolution on sexuality at Lambeth.

In the letter, which Crew posted on the Internet, Carey added, "To be truly the church, we must stay together and wrestle with the issues over which we disagree. In the process, pain is likely to be experienced by us all. Each one of us is challenged by new insights and new experiences to confront deeply held beliefs and test them, and that is painful." Carey concluded with his hope for a conversation in the future "when we shall be able to meet and talk about these issues which are so important to us both."

Honoring the pledge he made at Lambeth, Carey met with members of Lesbian and Gay Christian Movement on October of 1998 at Lambeth Palace in London. In a press release after the meeting, the gay participants issued a statement that said, "In a very constructive and positive environment it was stressed on both sides that transcending hostility was the central purpose of the meeting. It was acknowledged that difficulties which had strained relationships, in particular, between the Church of England and lesbian and gay Christians, were serious and required sensitive handling if they were to be overcome."

LGCM officials said "steps were discussed to achieve these objectives, by working cooperatively, while both sides respected the differences which still remain between them. Possibilities for sustaining the debate and discussion will be kept under review."

In a pastoral letter "to the clergy and people of the Anglican Communion" which he hoped would be read in all the churches on Sunday, September 28, the Archbishop of Canterbury offered his own assessment of the Lambeth Conference.

Stressing that the daily Bible studies were "at the heart of our conference," Carey said that "we have been transformed by being together over these three weeks." Listening to the stories "and sharing common concerns we have also seen the face of the world in its agony and confusions. We have taken time together to study carefully some of the profound and perplexing problems which the provinces had requested for our agenda." He said he hoped that "the fruit of our discussions will, I hope, become evident in the days to come."

Carey admitted there were times when the encounter had "been difficult and potentially divisive." Citing the discussions of human sexuality, he said "the issue was debated hotly and we found that our diversity of theology and culture, often a source of blessing, was becoming a 'differing' that could so easily have resulted in bitter confrontation."

"For the vast majority of us involved in that debate, the friendships that had been established, coupled with a desire to listen to each other, enabled us to transcend our differences," Carey added. "Nevertheless, I recognize that for some parts of the church, there was considerable pain to be endured both in the debate itself and its outcome and so the listening must go on, not only to Scripture but also to one another."

Carey urged facing the divisions in the world and the church "with courage and faith. So much energy goes into maintaining divisions instead of working for unity, it is my strong belief that one of the greatest benefits of this conference will be our experience as bishops of pursuing a oneness of aim in the midst of diversity."

The Archbishop said that he was convinced that the participants had gained insights into the meaning of interdependence. "We know now that we must ensure that our structures are more accountable. We know that we must find new ways of supporting the poorest parts of the Communion (often rich in faith and joy). We know that we must become a more outward looking and serving Communion. We know that we must share together our resources in training and biblical scholarship."

CHAPTER FIVE

OCCASIONS OF SHARING

While tensions simmered throughout the conference, there were also moments of joy and celebration as well as occasions of deep sharing, often addressing the sorrowful and painful aspects of Christian faithfulness.

One of the occasions of joy was the Eucharist at Canterbury Cathedral, which opened the conference. Cheering schoolchildren greeted the Prince of Wales and the primates of the Communion's thirty-seven provinces. About 750 bishops participated along with 600 spouses, some more colorful than the bishops in their cassocks. The procession also included two former Archbishops of Canterbury, Lord Donald Coggan and Lord Robert Runcie, along with members of the diplomatic corps, the Anglican Consultative Council, and ecumenical guests.

The liturgy followed a Kenyan text, according to Bishop Roger Herft of Australia who served as Lambeth chaplain. "The Kenyan liturgy has this wonderful flavor of being on a journey," he said. "It is amazingly powerful and anticipatory, and contains some very poignant moments. It also included a dazzling diversity of elements from other churches and other traditions."

The language of the service alternated between Swahili and English and included an African-American spiritual. Lessons were read in Portuguese and Arabic, with Panamanian liturgical dancers filling the chancel before the Gospel reading.

Music from the Taizé Community in France accompanied the intercessions, read in English by Bishop Chilton Knudsen of Maine, the newest of the Communion's eleven female bishops—a first for the cathedral and the Lambeth Conference—and in French by Bishop French Chang Him of the Seychelles. The penitential prayers were led by Archbishop Donald Mtetemela, Primate of Tanzania, and the closing affirmation by Bishop Cornelius Joshua Wilson, the primate of the Communion's newest province in Central America. Bishop John Sentamu, a former Ugandan high court judge, beat a brightly painted wise man's drum as he sang a Kenyan version of the Gloria. And Archbishop David Gitari of Kenya led the prayer of penitence.

Carey welcomed the congregation in Swahili, *Bwana akae nanyi*, "The Lord be with you" and over 2,000 voices responded, *Akae nawe pia*, "And also with you."

Music for the service ranged from the new Lambeth Hymn to songs and hymns from England, Argentina, Korea, and the Russian Orthodox tradition.

In his sermon, Bishop Simon Chiwanga of Tanzania, who chairs the Anglican Consultative Council, acknowledged that "controversial issues and passionate debates do happen, and the Lambeth Conference cannot be an exception." Yet he added, "What is essential for every participant to be aware of is that we have to look for the Christ in each other and to turn the other cheek, particularly when we feel we have been offended."

"Being Christ-like in our differences does not mean having no convictions or clear position of our own. It is a call to interpretive charity in our Christian dialogues," which he defined as "the ability to apply the most loving interpretation to actions and opinions of others...listening to one another in love.

"Interpretive charity calls us to two further things: first, not to disenfranchise or un-church anyone. Hold unswervingly to that which you believe to be of essential truth, but to God leave the final judgment in all matters. Change comes by enlightenment, not by force. Forcing your point of view by excluding from your circle those who disagree with you, or by compelling acceptance, is to usurp the place of God."

He said that God demands the church "to turn itself inside out," to be "primarily a missionary community looking outward."

Yet he warned that "a church that harbors bitterness, anger, and disharmony is distorting its image of a living Gospel and may be on the road to decay. It is in mission in the world that we grow more into Christ's likeness."

Chiwanga concluded by pointing to a golden opportunity for the bishops at Lambeth. "During the next few weeks, as we stand aware of God and the world, we have a tremendous opportunity before us. It is a holy moment, when we can once more demonstrate, through the power of the Holy Spirit, our ability to speak the truth in love, interpretive charity, and to show how truth can triumph over error in a way that is Christ-like."

ELECTRONIC SHARING

As the conference progressed, participants were drawn into diverse conversations at some crucial moments through the effective use of video. The stories poured from several huge screens in the plenary halls.

One video, "Leadership Under Pressure," produced by

Trinity Church, Wall Street, in New York, offered profiles of prominent church leaders around the world, sharing the stories of their struggle with the vital issues facing the Anglican Communion. The fifteen portraits were featured in the daily sessions at Lambeth and used to focus on the Bible study of Paul's Second Letter to the Corinthians.

In a discussion of what he had learned about leadership under pressure in his seven years as Archbishop of Canterbury, Carey said, "The expectation, the amount of work I had to do, was, at the beginning, a horrifying prospect. And I think I was only able to cope by sharing that leadership, by delegation, by accepting willingly the offer of help from other people."

As a parish priest, leader of a theological college, and as a diocesan bishop, "The kind of leadership I'm used to exercising is one that takes risks, that is able to accept challenge, that gets itself dirty and makes mistakes," Carey said. And he said that he believes leadership in the Anglican tradition is one that is "prophetic and bold and compassionate and committed and prepared to travel with risk."

Carey added that "what is going to hold us together is our commitment to historic, biblical, creedal faith, which has always been at the heart of Anglicanism, and a commitment to living in a changing world and not running away from the questions."

Bishop Iraj Mottahedeh of Iran told a harrowing story of survival during the revolution in his country. Placed under arrest, he was sent to the capital. Isolated in his cell, the bishop asked God for tears of release from the tensions of loneliness.

Bishop Mark Dyer told of being in a developing country which was experiencing a major outbreak of leprosy. When a leper asked for a blessing, Dyer admitted that he was afraid "and my fear had imprisoned me in a very significant way." A nun told him he should respond as Jesus would. "So I walked across and bandaged up a few of his wounds on his feet and gave him some sulfur drugs and laid my hands on his head—and we prayed. And there, in a very powerful and overwhelming way, divinity came to dwell with humanity. That was the concelebration of judgment and mercy both of us were celebrating," he said. "In that togetherness and in that touch, Christ came to us in a very, very powerful, converting way....It was a conversion from my fear to a certain security that allows one to be a bit reckless in one's ministry, in a good sense."

Bishop Frank Sargent of Lambeth told of a visit to a diocese in the Solomon Islands, where he experienced people who "understood the communion of saints." That encounter "enabled me to come back to England with a far greater sense of community than I had before."

Holloway, of the Scottish Episcopal Church, urged his colleagues to remember "the impotence of your own human strength." Describing a painting of "Peter the Penitent," he said that Peter was probably intimidated by "a look of absolutely melting forgiveness" from Jesus. "And in my experience that's what does actually change you—when the response to your sin and weakness is absolute grace and forgiveness...that is transforming experience."

When she was diagnosed with breast cancer, a few months after she was consecrated Bishop of Rhode Island, Geralyn Wolf was devastated—but she was "very committed to being absolutely honest and truthful because I felt that truth would lead to freedom" for her and the diocese. "There was a part of me in my leadership that was saying, 'Here I am, vulnerable in your midst, but I'm still in your midst.' I wouldn't choose it any other way because by being here I am strengthened for what comes not only next but for what is happening now. So my leadership was one of presence and openness and receptivity."

Bishop Ben Te Haara of New Zealand said that he "was born on a battlefield—and that battlefield was part of my family history." At the time, the enemy was the British who attacked with a huge cannon, managing to knock down the external palisade, not realizing that there was an interior stockade they couldn't see. The indigenous Maoris won that battle, only to lose when the British attacked on a Sabbath. "Some years later my grandfather reinterred the English soldiers who were buried in a common grave, very hurriedly....And he gave them a Christian burial and put a wall round where the old stockade had been. And then he later built a church on that site, which is called St. Michael's." The lesson for him was that "reconciliation has to be part of my character."

Bishop Dinis Sengulane of Mozambique said that he sees "a very strong connection between peace-making and evangelism." He told the story of going to a new parish in a battle zone "to see some of the things that are happening as the result of the war so that you can help us to heal the wounds which are still bleeding," even though the war had ended five years earlier. During his pastoral visit, the bishop was asked to bless a common grave found when the refugees returned to their homes, to make it a proper cemetery. "The presence of the church has given the people the courage" because they recognized the bones of people who "were made in the image and likeness of God."

Robin Eames, Archbishop and Primate of the Church in Ireland, knows the battlefield personally, recounting how he stood at the grave of a young man who had been blown to pieces by a car bomb. "And when the service was over at the graveside, I felt the tugging at the edge of my robes. I looked down and there was a little face looking up at me," he said. "The question that child asked me will go with me to the end of my life. She said, 'Can you tell me why Daddy will never come home again? And can you tell me why they did it to him?'"

Looking back on his episcopate, Eames said that he was quite aware of his personal shortcomings. "I've made my mistakes.

I've traveled this journey. I've made my pilgrimage. Now, God, forgive its shortcomings, forgive what's been wrong with it. I'm offering it to you. I'm letting go. I get off here. I've done my best. It's over to you."

In moving from a seminary chapel to a ruined downtown church, Bishop Sergio Carranza-Gomez of Mexico said that the poor people of the neighborhood taught him that they had something to contribute. "You always have something to give to the rest of the family, to the rest of the church, the body of Christ. And in the church, everybody's equal....All of us are at the same level and are the same before God," he said.

Bishop Michael Nuttal of Natal in South Africa told of getting caught up "in all the pain and tragedy" of people being murdered in the "political violence of the time." Since he became a bishop in 1975, he expressed gratitude for "the wonderful sense of acceptance and of affirmation...It could so easily have been otherwise in our very divided country because I'm an ordinary white South African who has benefited from the dubious privileges of our race-ridden society. And yet I've experienced nothing but magnanimity, generosity, and acceptance." The culmination was "a memorable partnership" with Desmond Tutu, when Nutall served as dean of the province, acquiring the nickname, "Number Two to Tutu." Beyond the humor was "an icon of loving cooperation between us, which was a gift not only to the two of us and certainly to me, but to our whole church and I think to our country in that important time. It showed what was possible in the community. And it's a sign of grace..."

Jamieson of New Zealand described the "time of strong spiritual energy" surrounding her consecration as the first woman bishop to head a diocese in the Anglican Communion. "I really felt the spirit of God was there and was powerful and was calling all of us into this new future." When the "multitude of expectations became clear," she discovered that she was an icon of what a bishop should be for some people, who expected her to be a "holy woman." She said it took years "to let people know who I was and what I was and to understand that." In that process, she admitted that "there have been some very hurtful times." And some of the quarrels "are profoundly bruising for a lone woman who is in a position of leadership," especially when she was drawn into "advocacy on behalf of women with my male colleagues. And that has not always been heard and has not always been welcomed, although they try hard."

A week after he was consecrated as the Bishop of Bor in the Sudan, Nathaniel Garang was cut off from his diocese—for six years. With a single shirt to his name, he moved among the people of Juba, training pastors and opening about 150 churches.

One of the most difficult situations for Bishop John Austin of Birmingham in the Church of England has been a situation where there is "a collapse of leadership of one sort or another in a parish" and finding a way to deal with that failure. "How do you exercise authority with an appropriate severity but with an appropriate mercy?" he wondered.

"Pulling together, sharing our stories, listening to one another's pain and victories, triumphs and tragedies, has been very, very special for each one of us," said Carey in concluding remarks. Expressing his admiration for Christians who keep their faith in areas of persecution, he said, "I hope people from the developing countries can learn something of the pain of living in heavily secularized cultures where our situations are different—we have to cope with apathy."

The first major plenary of the Lambeth Conference on "The Bible, the World, and the Church" also used the tools of modern communication to show how the Bible has been interpreted through the ages.

The plenary began with "A Living Letter," a video by Angela Tilby, featuring interviews with Anglican bishops and

their spouses from five nations. The video explored the difficult points where Scripture intersects with the world—
through power, poverty, sexuality, and war.

Bishop Roger Herft of Australia, the conference chaplain,
also pointed out that Scripture guides the church in the ministry of reconciliation, a point that was dramatically underscored by the testimony of Bishop Macleord Ochola of Uganda.

"My wife was killed by a landmine last May, and many of
our clergy children have been abducted," he told the plenary.
"They have done bad to us, but we have to forgive in order to
overcome the evil way of the world."

WRESTLING WITH DRAMA

The Riding Lights Theatre Company presented a drama
specially commissioned for Lambeth, *Wrestling with Angels*,
an interpretation of Jacob's encounter with God and with his
brother Esau. The troupe used dramatic music and lighting
on a platform stacked with a dozen six-foot pine coffins and
bathed in an eerie mist.

Dr. David Ford, Regius Professor of Divinity at Cambridge
University who headed the planning committee for the plenary,
said after the play, "We have just been reading a living letter."

Ford said that "there is a division about something apparently non-negotiable between Jacob and Esau," as Jacob grap-
ples with "the mysterious wrestler who knows him only too
well. But even more astonishing is the mysterious complexity
of God's action," he said. "He both challenges Jacob's tangled,
wrongly complex identity and heals it, opening a way for him
and all his people."

While some were moved to tears by the drama, others
were moved to rage. "I must say I felt unhappy to the point of
being sick," said Bishop Riah Abu el-Assal, Bishop Coadjutor
of the Diocese of Jerusalem. He walked out of the plenary.

The source of Riah's anger was the play's approach to the origin of Israel. The play ends with Jacob and Esau embracing, and members of the cast writing "Judah" and "Israel" on two sticks and then joining them to symbolize the creation of the nation of Israel. Riah saw this as an affront to the people of Palestine since Judah to them is the West Bank, the home of more than three million Palestinians and territory occupied by Israel since the Six-Day War of 1967.

"Judah today, in political terms, stands for the West Bank, the occupied West Bank," he said, pointing out that the United Nations and some in the international community support a complete withdrawal of Israel as a condition for lasting peace. The play, in his opinion, gave credence to the contention by Christian fundamentalists who support the efforts of hard-line Orthodox Jews to annex the West Bank and Jerusalem.

If authors of the play had been more sensitive, Riah argued, they would have included Ishmael and his descendents in that scene, thus illustrating that the divine blessing comes to all who worship God, not to Israel alone.

Riah told a news conference that the Old Testament has been misused for more than fifty years by Christian fundamentalists who see the creation of modern Israel as the fulfillment of prophecy.

He considered leaving the conference but, after a discussion and prayer with the Archbishop of Canterbury, he decided to stay and press for dialogue on the Holy Land. The painful snub was not worth risking a major confrontation with conservative evangelicals, he said. "We Palestinians have learned to bury our dead and start again."

Paul Burbridge, who directed and helped write the play, said that he would apologize to Riah. "It is unfortunate that we have discovered a trip wire that we didn't know was there," he said.

Seated on the ancient throne of St. Augustine and flanked by primates of the Anglican Communion, Archbishop of Canterbury George Carey presides at the opening Eucharist in Canterbury Cathedral. (Photo: Jeff Sells, *Anglican World*)

MORAL DILEMMAS

Voices of pain from the developing world also put a plenary on "Making Moral Decisions" into sharp perspective.

Bishop Mano Rumalshah of the Church in Pakistan spoke of the dangers Christians face on a daily basis in a region where Islamic teaching is law. As in his testimony before the U.S. Senate Foreign Relations Committee a few months ago, he recalled the death of his friend, Roman Catholic Bishop John Joseph. He told the hushed audience that his last words were in protest to a blasphemy law "and other black laws, and in the name of my oppressed Christian people, secularism and democracy, I am taking my own life."

While the bishop's suicide stirred debate on the appropriateness of his drastic action, Mano asked if it were "possible to think of Bishop John laying down his life as an act in the same fashion as that of Jesus? Isn't this also in keeping with the call to 'take up your cross and follow me'?"

As examples of the dangerous level of persecution, he told of a fifteen-year-old Christian schoolgirl who was accused of insulting the Prophet Mohammed in her classroom. As a result, 200 local Muslim clerics signed an oath calling for her death. "With the consent of her family and, perhaps, even her religious leaders, she converted to Islam to save her life," Mano said. Two of his parishioners made the difficult choice to convert in order to be accepted as man and wife. Otherwise they would have faced a trial under an adultery ordinance with the possibility of a death sentence.

"In both these cases, there is a deep sense of guilt and remorse, and even spiritual strain," the bishop said. "In these situations of apparent apostasy, what needs to be our moral and pastoral responsibility?" he asked.

Converts to Christianity in Pakistan are legally disinherited of all their possessions and ostracized, according to the bishop. He added that there are even rumors of a proposal to prosecute the converts and anyone who baptizes them under the draconian Blasphemy Law, again raising the possibility of a death sentence. "Should we be encouraging public baptisms of those converting from Islam in such a climate?...As always what we need are new signposts for our generation which are applicable in our respective contexts," he concluded.

A Sudanese bishop's story of how violence invaded his family brought audible gasps from his audience. While he was on a pastoral call, his estranged son-in-law killed his wife and son and then himself. Bishop Daniel Zindo placed his story in the context of a culture of violence resulting from thirty-two years of civil war. "Killing human beings has become a game of interest only" in a society where violence "rises in the human heart, so easily finds a way of becoming violence in our own homes."

Zindo, who would be killed in an automobile accident a few months after Lambeth, asked how it could be possible to "raise children and grandchildren who have witnessed killing and suicide to believe in a God who seeks peace, and our Lord who is our peace? How does one proclaim the good news of God's love to our own families, let alone to a society, who have experienced first-hand a culture of violence?"

In a video prepared by Trinity Church of New York, the stories of ten people illustrated different moral dilemmas.

A Native Canadian told how his culture had been suppressed. "We lost our land and rivers, some say we even lost our souls," he said. "The missionaries said that we must not follow our own spiritual traditions but must worship their God...Our culture vanished, and we were left with nothing. The government has apologized and offered compensation but for many of us the question remains, 'Who am I?'"

The voice of a narrator asks, "As bishops, can we stand alongside cultures within our culture?"

A gay man living in a relationship feels unwelcome in his parish. A priest counsels gay men to "find the courage and discipline to share your love, yet be celibate, faithful to one another and to the church you love." The narrator asks, "As bishops, what message do we want to send to the gay community?"

Another story concerned a former missionary who adopted a Chinese baby girl, knowing that orphanages were filled with unwanted girls; and another, the AIDS crisis in Africa where widows of men who die of the disease are forced to marry their brothers, who may also be infected.

In concluding the plenary, Bishop Rowan Williams of Wales told the bishops that making moral decisions was not like "being faced with a series of clear alternatives, as if we were standing in front of the supermarket shelf."

Christians make moral decisions much the way other people do because "they don't automatically have more information about moral truth," Williams said. "What is different is the relations in which they are involved, relations that shape a particular kind of reaction to their environment and each other."

Christian communities in widely varying cultural contexts "gradually and subtly come to take for granted slightly different things, to speak of God with a marked local accent," he said, yet they all belong to the same body. He challenged the bishops, and the whole Anglican Communion, to "listen when someone says, 'This is what I see, look at me.'"

Williams said that individual personalities and diverse cultures influence moral decision-making, but he urged the bishops to remember their commitment to listen and learn from Christian strangers of the past, present, and future. "I am not sure what or how I can learn from them," he said, admitting that "they frighten me by the difference of their priorities and their discernment. But because of where we all stand at the Lord's Table, in the Body, I have to listen to them and to struggle to make recognizable sense to them." The reflection brought sustained applause, a standing ovation for the former Cambridge professor.

A SPIRITUAL OASIS

After a heavy schedule of sectional meetings, the whole conference came to a virtual halt at mid-point for a prayer vigil. Carey said he hoped it would be "a spiritual oasis" to enable the conference to form its final resolutions "on a spiritual cushion of prayer and meditation."

With the sexuality debate looming, the timing was perfect. And, for most participants, so was the leader—Jean Vanier of Canada, founder and director of the L'Arche Community for people with learning disabilities and other physical challenges.

In his meditation, Vanier addressed what he called "the good shepherds of the Anglican Communion," telling them that he felt humbled to be the voice of those who have no voice. He called those with "mental handicaps, disabilities, amongst the most oppressed people of our world."

"I have visited institutions, asylums which are really places of death—places where these very special people are crushed and hurt, broken, with no voice. And yet they are precious people," he said.

Three bishops responded. Bishop David Andres Alvarez-Velazquez of Puerto Rico described the beginning of an AIDS ministry in his diocese. He said that the vision of Vanier speaks to "our particular ministries—holiness, the life and ministry of a bishop, pastoral care, personal testimony of conversion."

Bishop Barnabas Mondal, moderator of the United Church of Bangladesh, said that Christians in his overwhelmingly Muslim country face "a very difficult spiritual and cultural identity crisis." And he said that he continues to struggle with the issue of how many of the values of the culture can be absorbed before the church's identity is threatened.

"If you asked me all those years ago why I was entering a religious community," said Bishop M. Thomas Shaw of Massachusetts, "I would have told you I wanted more time to pray….A more intense form of community life and a much more simple lifestyle." Expressing appreciation for Vanier's exploration of community and holiness, Shaw added, "I now know there was a deeper reason. I now know that the Spirit was opening me to the abundant presence of God everywhere in the world."

He described how his order, the Society of St. John the Evangelist, has turned its monastery into a place of hospitality, a place of welcome for the pilgrim and the stranger, anyone who is looking for God.

A Service of Light liturgy concluded the meditations. In a homily at the second service, Vanier challenged the bishops to adopt patterns of servant leadership, arguing that Jesus was asking them to exercise their authority "in love, in truth, and forgiveness."

In explaining the biblical account when Jesus washed the feet of his disciples, Vanier warned his congregation that "Jesus is always surprising us. He doesn't like it when we fall into little habits." So the foot-washing experience was "a gesture of communion" but also a lesson, an example of how Jesus "wants us to exercise authority" by being servants of one another. The message is that "we are called to walk the downward path, we are called to be small."

In concluding ceremonies of commitment and discipleship, participants came forward to write on slips of paper what they considered hindrances on their spiritual journey. The notes were then taken outside and ignited.

"Jesus insists upon the washing of the feet because our bodies are precious," Vanier said as the Careys joined him. Beginning with the Archbishop, Vanier washed his feet in a basin and received a blessing. Then the archbishop washed his wife's feet and the ritual spread throughout the hall.

"His simple yet profound addresses on holiness, so clearly modeled in his own life of service, were very powerful," said Archbishop Keith Rayner of Melbourne, Australia. He was particularly moved by the foot washing. The Australians had used a similar ceremony at the church's General Synod when two white bishops and two indigenous bishops washed one another's feet "as a sign of reconciliation."

YOUTH PARTICIPATION

The conference received a welcome infusion of youthful energy in a series of events highlighting the church's relationship with its young people with a goal of encouraging bishops to listen to their voices.

"If 800 bishops go home and meet fifty young people in twelve months, that means 40,000 young people will have had the opportunity to speak to a bishop," said Bishop Lindsay Urwin of England to reporters shortly before the plenary on youth which he helped organize.

"In Western culture, which is a fairly institutional culture, bishops can seem distant figures," Urwin said. And bishops should not "speak at" young people but engage in serious attempts to listen to what they are saying.

The Ascension Eagles, who hold English and European championship titles in cheerleader competitions, charged into the sports arena to the beat of a South African song, "Siyahamba," or "We are Marching in the Light of God," waving red and white pom-poms. The bishops rose to their feet, swaying to the beat and clapping their hands in unison.

The bishops watched a video, "The Connected Generation," which took them on a fast-paced tour of international youth culture. The video's challenge was to encourage the bishops to talk to young people in the language of their culture. Urwin talked with youth workers from the Middle East, the Philippines, and England. A dramatic presentation linked the biblical story of Jesus feeding the multitude to a circle of candles arranged by youth outside the school in Dunblane, Scotland, where sixteen children and their teacher were shot dead in 1996.

"They have constructed their own ritual," observed Pete Ward, youth advisor to the Archbishop of Canterbury. "It's not so different from what we do, but it's theirs."

The plenary ended with a challenge to the bishops to return to their dioceses resolved to meet personally with youth, asking them about their hopes and visions and the way they understand the world but also to pray with them, open the Scriptures and break bread together.

THE SPOUSES' CONFERENCE

Meanwhile, across the campus in a set of light-filled tents erected especially for them, the spouses were holding their own conference.

For the first time, five male spouses joined their female counterparts in what one reporter called "a more subtle, and probably more significant presence" at Lambeth. The spouses' village became a place where they told their own stories, shared their lives and their experiences.

"The diversity and yet common experience and issues for ministry which have emerged are quite remarkably consistent, especially given the range of cultural, ecclesiastical and geographical backgrounds," the spouses said in a report.

According to Eileen Carey, wife of the Archbishop of Canterbury, the program was designed for variety to "enable spouses to learn together, enjoy and encourage one another and, above all, study the Bible and pray together." She said that planning began "as soon as I knew there was going to be a conference in 1998," and involved asking spouses all over the world what they wanted and needed in the program. "We hope the program will help us all in our demanding and sometimes discouraging roles," Mrs. Carey said.

The plenary presentations, aided by similar translation services used at the meeting of bishops, proceeded under four major themes: "For Better, For Worse," a look at the role of the bishop's spouse; "A Healthy World? Strategies for Hope," a look at social issues; "Together in God's Mission: The Vocation of the Anglican Communion in the Twenty-First Century"; and "Go Into All the World," mission and evangelism today and tomorrow.

Dr. Ian Jamieson, husband of New Zealand Bishop Penelope Jamieson, was escorted to the stage by a dozen wives of bishops. He called the other spouses from the Anglican Church of Aotearoa, New Zealand and Polynesia to join him on the stage after his presentation because "they have decided to support me in a way which is very customary in our society and in our church, particularly when our indigenous people are involved," said the first husband of a bishop in the Anglican Communion. The women, most of them barefoot, arranged themselves in rows behind Jamieson and began to sing a Maori song, using the expressive movement and gestures of their culture to express their support and care.

In the plenary six spouses told their stories, the best and the worst they have encountered in their efforts to be partners in ministry with the bishops. They acknowledged the challenges of racism, poverty, gossip, and loneliness but also the times of privilege in shared ministry.

They were joined on the panel by Dr. Elaine Storkey of the Institute for Contemporary Christianity in London. She started her theological discussion with the Genesis account of Adam and Eve, but when she got to the topic of marriage her comments struck a resonance among the spouses.

"Marriage is extraordinary—two people come together

and make reckless pledges to each other," she said. "We image God as we love, sometimes we love against the odds, sometimes we love when we are not loved back, sometimes we love sacrificially."

Elizabeth Appleby, wife of the Bishop of the Northern Territory in the Anglican Church of Australia, described the satisfaction of "caring for clergy spouses and their families, opportunities for leadership in your own right, and sharing with Aboriginal Christians in remote communities." But she added that she was reminded of the comment of a clergy friend who urged her to remember "the miter is also a crown of thorns." As a spouse she also encountered "loneliness at the top, gossip and speculation, expectations and stereotypes," as well as living with the full story behind a decision or action of the bishop while not being able to say anything to protect her spouse. She said that she coped by allowing herself not to cope, involving herself in activities outside the church, and sharing her fears and difficulties with a "soul friend."

"Apartheid is said to be dead but some of us have not yet attended its funeral," said Maggfie Nkwe, wife of the Bishop of Klerksdorp in the Church in the Province of Southern Africa. She shared the difficulties of adjusting after her husband was appointed, moving from Soweto to Klerksdorp "in two cars, into a house we struggled to get because the so-called white church people in Klerksdorp had concluded we would stay in the township and not in the so-called white suburb." The couple "moved into the diocese as if we were moving into the desert—there was no office, no personnel and no infrastructure."

A trained nurse and midwife, she organized the first march of women against the abuse of women "to encourage women to participate in gender issues."

Miriam Ntiruka, wife of the founding Bishop of the Diocese of Tabora in the Church of the Province of Tanzania, told similar stories of hardship. The diocese was formed in an area where there were few Anglicans, in an effort to evangelize the tribes of the area. Since it was formed in 1989, the diocese has grown from 6,000 members and ten pastors to 15,000 members and twenty-eight pastors.

Her role as the wife of the bishop is to be "the mother of the bishop's family," which meant mother to their own three sons as well as five children of relatives, a situation she described as "quite common." At the same time, she tries to encourage her husband with prayer, advice, and support "as he cares for that larger spiritual family that is his diocese." She confided that the bishop's duties often took him away from the family, and that sometimes "brings about a deep wound in the life of the children."

Jamieson confessed that he felt uncomfortable in his early days as the spouse of a priest, before his wife became the first diocesan bishop in the Anglican Communion. "If I had been a woman, wife to a male vicar, there would have been a role indeed—Sunday school teacher, a mower of lawns, a sidesperson [usher] and as the relief organist. But in my case I felt I had the freedom to choose them."

He said that he shared in the privilege of getting to know the people in a large geographical diocese that was thinly populated. He described a visit to a small village and a church dedicated to St. Mark. The service was crowded with many of the farming families. "Some were Anglican, many were Presbyterian, others were from a Pentecostal church in a nearby village," others had no church affiliation. But all had come to express their support for a man and his wife, local farmers, who were to be ordained. "In the whole history of the diocese there had never been a resident Anglican priest," Jamieson said. "It was a huge day for the whole community, affirming its value."

Shamim Malik, wife of the Bishop of Lahore in the Church

of Pakistan, said, "In the beginning I felt inadequate and ill-equipped," wondering how she would balance the roles of mother and wife of a bishop. "I tried my best and whenever I failed I tried harder." The political instability of the country means that church leaders get involved in politics. "The resulting workload is immeasurable, as is the toll it takes mentally, physically, and emotionally."

Eleci Neves, wife of the Bishop of Southwestern Brazil, believes that her role is to protect her husband from becoming "overwhelmed by the bureaucracy of the church." Her ministry focuses on work with abandoned children, the elderly, and those suffering injustice. And she said that one of her most valuable roles as a spouse is to be a listener.

In the spouse's plenary on social issues, Dr. Yuji Kawaguchi of the World Health Organization reported that 28,000 children die every day from diseases that are preventable. And he added that 5.8 million people were newly infected with AIDS and that 2.3 million had died from the disease in 1997. If global warming continues, he warned, mosquitoes carrying malaria and other infectious diseases will spread into new areas.

Sheila Ramalshah, wife of the Bishop of Pakistan, said that only two percent of her nation's income goes to health care. "It seems that the powers that be have decided it is more important to spend about seventy percent of the nation's income on militarism and the related repayment of international debt."

The status of women contributes to their health problems because "their lives become so domesticated and mechanized they are primarily perceived as child-producing machines. As for sexually related disease amongst women, we dare not even guess the true reality." She said that the whole issue of AIDS "is still a taboo subject in our society. We are quite convinced there must be a lot of cases of this nature in our diocese—

especially since homosexuality is rampant there. But there is neither public awareness nor any public debate on these issues."

Juliana Okine, wife of the Bishop of Ghana, attributed her country's growing AIDS problem to "the unlimited matrimonial powers that husbands generally wield over their wives...when it comes to contraception and AIDS protection. The fact that only the male condom is widely available in itself gives a promiscuous man power to sentence a woman to death if he will not use a condom."

Bishop Geralyn Wolf of Rhode Island strongly criticized the American health system in her speech to the spouses, charging that "if you are unemployed or in part-time work in America, health care is difficult to obtain," even in the most technically advanced nation in the world.

Archbishop David Gitari of Kenya said that he has been encouraging simple education programs to deal with a range of diseases that are preventable. "Parish-selected community health workers, after just eight weeks training in the treatment and prevention of our six most common diseases, return to their parishes to conduct seminars. Whenever I preach I also spend a few minutes explaining the importance of boiling water before drinking it."

In a keynote address at the spouses conference on the vocation of the Anglican Communion in the twenty-first century, Archbishop Carey denounced the use of violence to enforce religious beliefs, arguing that "you will not find true believers killing people or blowing up houses or injuring others." The Gospel is about peace, he added. "Anglicans have made a fine contribution to making peace and building bridges between communities."

Carey suggested that the Anglican Church is a rich, international world church on its way to becoming a Communion. "But we shall only become a real Communion when we learn the lessons of sharing the suffering, the pain, and the distress of one another; the poverty and the denial of justice; along with the sharing of our riches and resources," he said.

After his visits to the Sudan, he returned frustrated that there was so little he could offer in immediate help. "I began an appeal and raised £400,000 within a few weeks and sent money to the church. But I should not have had to do that, even though I was glad to do so. If we are really a Communion, we should have structures to assist one another."

He described the initiative, the Anglican Investment Agency, as a simple but imaginative way the Anglican Communion can use the resources of the developed churches to help the developing churches.

Carey also deplored the lack of support among provinces of the church for the Anglican Consultative Council budget, calling it "a scandal" that weakens the whole Communion.

Anglicans, especially those in the West, should be less apologetic about being spiritual, Carey said. "The world wants us to speak of God, to speak of our faith, our love of God, and the meaning of life and death." In addressing the issue of what is distinctive about Anglicans, he said that they are "earthed and anchored in real life," trying to put their faith into practice.

In a tribute to the special role of women, Carey said that "women are the natural 'priests' of the home, they are at the epicenter of family life." But he added that "women can also be natural evangelists and the transformers of society with their gifts of relationships and their connections in the community. I want to encourage these gifts for the sake of the kingdom."

Both the Archbishop and his wife Eileen published books just prior to Lambeth. Her book, written with her son Andrew, was based on interviews with twenty-one spouses of Anglican bishops. In *The Bishop and I,* she says that "one of the most wonderful aspects of the work is the travel to many countries where there are Anglican congregations." In her series of profiles she describes many of the remarkable people she has met on those travels, people whose skills, commitment, and sheer hard work form the backbone of the Anglican Communion.

In his book, *The Canterbury Letters to the Future*, the Archbishop describes how he has experienced God in the world, as well as his own life, "and about what kind of map the Bible and the church have given me to find my way round that experience."

He writes, "We know for ourselves, as communities of believers, the Holy Spirit as the self-distribution of the abundance of God. Is not this something which we should be offering to our world as our own experience of that characteristic life in the Spirit which diverts us from the needless and heedless and destructive life of excess, into the profound and satisfying abundance of life as God has created, redeemed and sanctified it through Christ?" The Christian attributes of love, joy, peace, patience, kindness, goodness, faithfulness, gentleness, and humility could be "prophetic to our culture."

The plenary on mission and evangelism began with some startling observations. "At the turn of the century, over half of all English children attended Sunday school. Today, in Britain's housing developments, only one young person in 1,000 attends an Anglican Church," said the Rev. Wallace Brown. "The younger generation is slipping further away from the church, even though many of them have profound questions and are searching for authentic answers."

Yet Brown reported some signs of hope. His congregation in a housing development in Birmingham had grown "from a small group of elderly ladies to an all-age community of about 250 people."

Growth is more than numbers, argued Jumoke Fashola of the Church Missionary Society—it can also be about "developing creativity, enduring pain, stretching our understanding...trying new things and persistence even when the going is tough."

Fashola told of an encounter with an organization in India that offers basic education to abandoned and homeless children. "Amidst the sadness and deprivation there are signs of growth. It's wonderful to discover a child's creativity and imagination is still there when given a chance to flower."

She challenged the church to seize the opportunities presented by the technological revolution, especially in communications. "The new marketplace is the Internet. We must as a church begin to explore the possibilities of this new medium, or we may find ourselves with nothing to say to a whole new generation."

A group of spouses from differing ethnic groups in Rwanda and Burundi used song and dance to tell their stories of suffering and reconciliation, where cries of fear were replaced by loving embraces.

The spouses were offered a range of pottery, painting, embroidery classes, and even one on how to make and mend a miter. But perhaps the story that intrigued everyone, including the press, was that of Marion McCall, the wife of the Bishop of Willochra in South Australia, whose diocese stretches over an area six times the size of England.

"Spending so much time driving thousands of miles was just killing him," she said of her husband's attempts to minister to his flock. When she announced at a party that she had been thinking of learning to fly, but did not have the money, someone suggested that she ask the people of the diocese to buy shares for $10. She said it was "just extraordinary" how the money poured in.

She told the spouses that "taking off was easy, but landing was a problem...because you are supposed to take the plane down very gently." Unlike driving a car, "there seemed to be no sense in it. You have to steer with your feet, and controls which intuition told me to pull usually required to be pushed, and vice versa," she said. After a week of failed attempts she was ready to quit. "It was more than just not being able to master the basics. I really thought I was going to kill myself each time I tried to land. For the first time in my life I was facing up to real fear, the kind which starts in the pit of the stomach and moves up to the brain.

"It's fear which stops us from doing anything," she concluded. "It's fear which stops us from reaching our true potential." She asked God for strength. When the time came to fly solo, she again relied on God. Flying solo, she realized, "is a bit like having a baby. Anybody can get a plane airborne, but it needs every ounce of strength to land it."

Now an experienced pilot, her request from the Lambeth Conference was for a course in basic airplane repair to help avoid getting stranded in the remote destinations she faces on a regular basis.

Novelist Susan Howatch, whose series of six books about a fictional cathedral city of Starbridge have been very successful, addressed the spouses on the topic of healing, as expressed in her latest book. While the Starbridge novels "explored the great Christian themes of sin, repentance, forgiveness, redemption, resurrection and renewal," she has turned to new questions: How does one explain healing? Can one get beyond any mere description of what happens?

She said it is important to make a distinction between a cure and healing. "Not everyone can be cured of whatever physical and mental illness afflicts them, but spiritual and emotional wounds can be healed so that a better quality of life is obtained," Howatch said. But healing is something that goes on "at some level of consciousness, which we don't yet understand."

She said that the Christian healer is "a servant who seeks to serve God by serving others, just as Jesus did. Jesus wasn't interested in healing people in order to satisfy a craving for power or public acclaim. He was concerned first and foremost with opening himself up to God's will and living with humility—and in this he stands in direct contrast to the wonder-workers, the corrupt healers who are concerned first and foremost with pursuing their own personal aims and living with arrogance."

PHOEBE GRISWOLD'S JOURNEY

Phoebe Griswold, wife of the Presiding Bishop of the Episcopal Church U.S.A., conducted a workshop on "Living the theology of a bishop's spouse: experience, experiment and adventure," an assignment she accepted when her husband was still the Bishop of Chicago.

"I want to take the lived experience of our lives, their experimentation and their adventure, and then reach for God through them," she said after introducing herself. One of the most important characteristics of our time, she said, "is the acceptance and confirmation of women's experience as a contemporary and unique approach to faith, complementary to the experience of men, an approach that can illumine, challenge and edify the church's exploration into the nature of God."

Beginning with "the relationships swirling around me and the stuff of my own gifts," Mrs. Griswold said that she experiments and "then I build a path and a story, an adventure, from what I know. The adventure for me is to live beyond the given, to make choices and to write my own journey. It is both risky and exciting."

She talked about the struggle to shape her own identity, first as the wife of an assistant priest in an affluent suburban congregation. She said she "knew nothing about being a priest's wife." Next they moved to a larger more urban congregation where she was "miserable because I left behind so many of the activities that had previously given me an identity."

She told the group about a dream that became one of the most important signals in her life, a dream in which she learned that "someone had placed a lesson deep within me that was focused on my own growth. An inner voice, caring for my life's wholeness, had spoken while I slept."

With the help of a spiritual director, she learned that "my own voice was different from my husband's, in part because it was a woman's voice." She began to learn about her own "unique identity, to see how I could help build the church and community. I began to understand that I could make choices about how I led my life." She said when her husband was elected Bishop of Chicago, "I experienced a new loss of identity. What I had learned about being the wife of a priest continued to be helpful to others, but I myself was in new territory," experiencing "the sadness that comes from loss of a community."

One of the first things she learned was that the wives of bishops do not have job descriptions, "only an unarticulated assumption that we should be in some kind of relationship to the members of our diocese." In speaking engagements at parishes "I described my own experience, my experiments in finding meaning and purpose in my life, and told where I felt most alive and how best to make a difference."

She chose to work outside the life of the diocese, however, and joined the Heifer Project International, an ecumenical organization that supplies livestock and training to people in the developing world. The international experience exposed her to "the work of keeping life alive—the creation, survival, and the thriving of life [that] is the central meaning of our lives as Christians."

As the wife of the Presiding Bishop, Mrs. Griswold said she feels she has been given "a huge empty plate and the freedom to choose what I want to put on it," that she is being called into "an undefined space full of new experiences and experimentation. I think that the nature of God has a great deal to do with the freedom God gives to us to make choices. It feels like an adventure as I long to move ever closer to the will of God."

In the closing days of the conference, the spouses offered a special musical, "Crowning Glory," the culmination of nearly three weeks of rehearsals. Created by Veronica Bennett, wife of the Bishop of Coventry, and based on stories by Oscar Wilde, the musical brought the standing-room-only crowd to its feet in wild appreciation.

The musical is the story of the transforming power of love in a make-believe kingdom where a dying king confesses that he has a son who was raised by his mother in a cottage in a nearby forest.

The only male in the cast, Phil Roskam, spouse of the Suffragan Bishop of New York, appeared in the segment where the boy is brought to a group of advisors who will prepare him for his role.

As the advisors present the bedazzled boy with the signs of his high office, a sleepy bishop in a tall miter, badly tailored cassock, and mismatched socks slips into the hall and soon begins snoring in his chair. Awakened by the advisors, the ungainly procession moves off the stage and through the audience accompanied by laughter and cheers.

The play takes a serious turn when the boy discovers that his kingdom is a mess. But the advisors dismiss his concerns and proceed with the plans for a coronation. In his dreams the boy learns the depth of exploitation of his people and moves to action, leaving his coronation symbols with the sleeping beggars outside his gate. He shows up for the coronation dressed in the simple robes of a peasant. While the dignitaries jeer him, the people embrace him.

TEA WITH THE QUEEN

As they have at previous Lambeth Conferences, the bishops went off to London to have tea with Britain's Queen Elizabeth II at Buckingham Palace. This time they also had lunch in the gardens of Lambeth Palace, with Prime Minister Tony Blair as guest speaker, and then took a boat trip on the Thames.

After traveling to London in a fleet of more than forty buses, the bishops and their spouses—about 2,000 in all with staff and consultants—filed into the gardens of Lambeth Palace for a splendid lunch in huge tents erected for the event.

Blair told the bishops that "the new global challenges are problems that we solve together as one global community—or not at all." He said that it was clear to him that "the British people do want Britain to provide a lead in the international efforts to eliminate poverty."

Citing international efforts in dealing with the environment, he said a "coordinated global action" is needed, "marrying together the agendas of environment and the agendas of development. We know that developing countries fear that industrialized countries may seek to impose environmental controls, which will prevent their development. It will be impossible, however, to reach effective global agreement on those major environmental challenges unless we commit ourselves at the same time to securing real progress in development for the poorest countries."

Using another example, Blair said war and poverty often go hand-in-hand so "there is a task there for peacekeeping and security, which has again to tie in with the agenda for poverty and development."

In a response on behalf of the bishops, Archbishop Khotso Makhulu of Central Africa said that Lambeth was "trying to address what it is that we can do to realize the best in humanity," seeking the "affirmation of people at every level." He added,

"When you talk of the global, whether it be through trade or in the search for peace and other models of good governance, you are also indirectly reminding us of the global aspect of the grace of God."

Climbing back into their buses, the party drove across the Thames and right through the front gates of Buckingham Palace where they dismounted, clutching their precious invitations. They made their way through to the thirty-acre garden where they attacked tables laden with sandwiches, sweets, coffee, and tea.

After the Yeomen of the Guard, the popular Beefeaters, marched out to clear a space in the crowd of almost 3,000. Queen Elizabeth, Prince Philip, Prince Andrew, and a small party arrived to the sound of "God Save the Queen," played by a military band. Resplendent in a lime green outfit, the Queen moved slowly through the crowd, accompanied by the Archbishop of Canterbury and his wife, pausing to chat with a wide variety of bishops, spouses, and guests from the Church of England.

Among the guests was the four-month-old daughter of Bishop Peter Elbersh Kowa of Sudan and his wife—a considerable bending of protocol since children are not normally welcome at the tea parties because of the potential for disruption of the rather formal occasion.

Bishop Ronald Haines of Washington reported in his diocesan newspaper that the Queen refers to the event as "her purple tea party." But he thought "we looked more like a convention of rainbow people with bishops wearing every conceivable shade of purple, their spouses attired in brilliant array and our skin colors of black, yellow, red, brown, white, and all shapes and hues in between."

The Queen moved to a special pavilion where she took tea with selected guests, including members of the Compass Rose Society, a fundraising project of the Anglican Communion.

After tea and some time touring the gardens, everyone got back on the buses and went to Festival Pier where, as the group climbed aboard for their boat trip, they were greeted by protesters from Outrage, the radical gay rights organization in Britain. Some were dressed in clerical vestments, holding signs that screamed, "Anglicans, stop opposing gay human rights," and, "Stop crucifying queers," and "Carey opposes equal age of consent," and "Lambeth 1998 must support gay equality." In earlier confrontations, Outrage had scaled the walls of Lambeth Palace and interrupted a reception the archbishop was holding for international guests. They also invaded the pulpit of Canterbury Cathedral and interrupted an Easter sermon by Carey.

In public comments before Lambeth, Holloway of Scotland had suggested that the bishops come to the conference prepared to throw their miters into the Thames to symbolize their willingness to eschew the signs of their office. "Anglican bishops are no longer prelates or monarchs who rule the church," he said. "They are now bishops in synod who work collegially with the laity and other clergy of the church." He said that he was convinced that "we need a plainer, people's episcopacy. We work through synods as bishops and yet we still dress like medieval, authoritarian bishops."

In his comments opening Lambeth, Carey sounded as though he agreed with Holloway on his basic point about making bishops more accessible. "I would gladly fling all my miters in the River Thames if it made any difference to our ministry today," he said.

So Carey and Holloway, joined by Spong, Bishop David Cole of New Zealand, Bishop Andrew Cameron of Scotland, and Carey's grandson, Simon Day, took biodegradable miters made of rice paper, supplied by Holloway, and as the boat passed the Millennium Dome, tossed them in.

Although photos were taken, they were not shown to the

press, supposedly because they might catch Carey in an undignified moment. An article by the Lambeth news team that included a description of the miter-tossing event was stifled, and some of the British press were told by members of the communication staff that it never happened.

Ruth Gledhill of the London *Times* said later, "Not only was it made impossible for us to record or photograph this eminently newsworthy event, but none of the communicators could confirm, even after the event had happened and right up until midnight, four hours later, that it had indeed taken place."

The incident underscored a surprisingly adversarial relationship between the press covering the conference—especially the British papers—and the communications team.

A SPECIAL HELL FOR JOURNALISTS

"I had always wondered whether there was a special hell for journalists, and now I know there is—it is the Lambeth Conference..." wrote Gledhill in a piece she called, "My Lambeth Hell." She said that "the psychological torture was the worst." If she were not bound to honor her parents (her father is an Anglican priest), "I would halfway through the conference have left the Anglican Church for good."

Gledhill said that "most of us there to cover the conference arrived with a positive, friendly attitude to the Anglican Church. We were as determined as they were that we should not be sidelined away from important subjects such as international debt and Muslim-Christian relations. But in the end homosexuality was all that most of the bishops seemed to want to talk about." She said that she was "baffled by the defensive attitude towards journalists."

The problem emerged at the very beginning, she said, when journalists were given bright pink identification badges and became known as the "pink pariahs." It soon became clear that bishops had been warned to avoid anyone with a pink badge and, she charged, members of the official communications team would even follow her to make sure that she did not try to interview bishops without making an official application first. She said that she learned that the Rev. Bill Beaver, director of communications for the Church of England, who was in charge of relations with the press, had actually warned the bishops that "pink means danger." It forced her and other journalists to find alternative means of getting interviews. "But it was all so unnecessary, and so avoidable.

"Given the level of disinformation, it was hard not to sink into paranoia," Gledhill said. While the communications team tried its best to accommodate the journalists, "What was objectionable was the sense of control. The lack of trust was almost tangible," she wrote. "Lambeth has changed the Anglican Church, irrevocably. It has also changed me. Whether for better or for worse, as with the church, it is far too early to say."

Jim Rosenthal, director of communications for the Anglican Communion Office in London, responded by pointing out that he had assembled a communications team of seventy people "to enable, first and foremost, communications to our dioceses around the globe on a daily basis." He said that there were no major problems in that effort. "There were no complaints from the *Los Angeles Times* or the *New York Times*. We provided a first-rate facility with modem connections, phone points, an air-conditioned, well-fitted-out briefing hall and, on a good day, coffee or tea."

He pointedly added, "The Church of England, as I know from my nine years in this country, has a unique relationship with the media. Most other Anglican provinces, including the United States, do not find every decision made, problem solved, or perceived news items, covered in the 'secular' press. Thus some bishops coming to Lambeth were, by their own choice, hesitant to comment to press representatives. We did offer to help bishops who had stories to tell the press and did not know how to go about it." He said that he had apologized to Gledhill. "Hellish encounters can be the vehicle for redemptive experiences. May it be so for Ruth Gledhill."

Victoria Combe of the *Daily Telegraph* grudgingly admitted that the attempt at control was working, thanks largely to Beaver, whom she called the "chief spin doctor." Yet she said that "this preoccupation with presenting a harmonious, united church makes me nervous." She said that the church had always been marked by serious disagreements. "An insecure church is tempted to smother the disagreements. A bold church allows its sons to bicker and differ. Perhaps if they did, there would be space for the Holy Spirit to enter."

Madeleine Bunting of the *Guardian* was just as blunt, charging that the conference "implemented what it understands of press relations—a tightly controlled media operation has reduced all stories to banalities, leaving a vacuum happily filled by the opponents and advocates of gay rights....Surely the Lambeth Conference should abandon its pontificating to the world and accept what it is, a theology seminar with a lot of praying, of little interest to anyone except its participants and a few devotees back home."

"With this conference, the media relations of the Church of England have finally caught up with corporate practice," observed Andrew Brown in his media column in the *Church Times*. "We have rival press officers briefing furiously against each other, and a huge media staff devoted to ensuring that bishops are hard to find and their spouses impossible to talk to."

The pink badges also offended Doug LeBlanc of the *United Voice*, a conservative publication in the Episcopal Church U.S.A. "Pink badges mean do not talk to this person without arranging an interview through conference communications; pink badges means conference communications will decide whether the journalist is entitled to talk with a bishop, or whether a bishop has received inordinate attention; pink badges are not as severe as the pink triangles of Nazi Germany but the spirit is similar. They single out certain people, in this case journalists trying to do their job, as fit for lesser treatment. It is difficult to imagine Polly Bond, patron saint of journalists who work within the Episcopal Church, smiling beatifically from Heaven at this chain of events," he wrote in a commentary for his magazine. "Further, those of us who have worked as journalists for a few decades do not require the hand-holding of an office that wants to know whom we would interview, when, where and what about."

The press operation was not entirely bleak, according to LeBlanc. He said that members of the official news teams, most of them Americans, "include some talented, hard-working journalists who also care about truth. Some of them are fighting their own battles, within the system, for candor and openness." He concluded, "The beautiful thing about truth is that it cannot be suppressed forever. Spin doctors, apparatchiks, and PR consultants, whether in governmental politics or church politics, often attempt to lock truth in darkened corners."

Working conditions for the communications teams at Lambeth were far from ideal and sometimes the tensions ran quite high, given the pressure of deadlines. And some staff members described occasional incidents of sexism and haughtiness on the part of some British members of the team, especially towards the Americans. Admitting that some of the tensions in the press operation were "unnecessary," Rosenthal said that tensions in the conference itself crept into the pressroom because of differences in style, approach, and even beliefs on the issues. "We were part and parcel of what was happening in the whole conference," he said.

Addressing criticism about his role in the press operation, Rosenthal said that he intentionally kept a low profile, hewing to his goal of keeping the Anglican Communion informed and leaving relations with the secular press to Bill Beaver. "It was clearly his responsibility, as press officer for the Church of England, to take care of the British press and other secular press."

The ability to use electronic mail to let people know what was happening very quickly "transformed Lambeth," according to Rosenthal. "The ability of people to sit around their computers to follow events, was a new height for us." And it also introduced "the capacity for an endless flow of conversation and comment about Lambeth," he said.

Rosenthal is obviously proud that in his nine years at the Anglican Communion Office he has greatly increased the visibility of the Archbishop of Canterbury and emphasized his "unifying effect" within the Communion.

At the 1988 Lambeth Conference, Rosenthal noted, few bishops even knew who Archbishop of Canterbury Robert Runcie was or what he looked like. "But this time nearly every one felt they knew Carey, where he has been on his international travels, and what he thinks about issues," he said.

THE CLOSING PLENARY

The final plenary took the bishops back to where they began three weeks earlier—"The Bible, the World, and the Church," this time looking to the future.

Professor David Ford of Cambridge, who spoke at the opening plenary, said that the conference had run on the tandem tracks of worship and Bible study. "The worship has never been without the Bible at its center, and the Bible studies have been embraced by worship," he said. "And at the heart of both Bible and worship is what perhaps unites us most strongly— the desire for God, that hunger and thirst for God which is itself a gift from God." Quite beyond the headlines in the press, worship and Bible study helped the bishops deal with sensitive and contentious issues.

The Anglican Church has always been in tension over the ordering of its life, Ford said. While Anglicans avoid authoritarian structures, they also try to avoid an approach where each church is free to interpret the Gospel and the church's teachings according to its own context, one in which "no one is ultimately accountable to anyone else."

He used as his example of the tension between diversity and accountability the struggle in the sub-group dealing with sexuality. "They have given us a sign of our agony but also of hope," Ford said. "Yet it is also clearly unfinished business." He also cited the work of the conference on international debt and Christian-Muslim relations as an example of how the conference had come together in its efforts to relate the Gospel to the church's social witness.

Ford offered four points for the bishops to consider as they headed home. The first was an appreciation for how prayer and worship unites the Anglican Communion, how hearing each other's stories had helped overcome stereotypes and ignorance. If that sharing can continue, he said, then the Communion can look forward to growing even stronger in its witness. "I suspect that this circulation of specific prayer might well be the most important single preparation for the next Lambeth Conference," he said.

Another crucial step, according to Ford, is that the bishops must continue to support the Communion's networks which connect people on a variety of vital issues and ministries, calling them "essential to a dynamic unity" and "perhaps the most significant transformation in the shaping of our Communion life." He cited the networks dealing with the issues of immigration, ecumenism, the environment, peacemaking, and youth.

According to Ford, education is the key arena where these networks can be strengthened for both clergy and laity. "We will fail them if they do not receive a Christian faith which invites them into a mind-stretching and life-long pursuit of truth and wisdom," he said.

Ford said that he was encouraged by the establishment of an inter-Anglican fund for emergency assistance and funding to dioceses and provinces for development, and how they may serve as vehicles for the Jubilee 2000 campaign.

"It may be that the sincerity of our demands that creditor nations should forgive unpayable debts will be judged—and not least by God—by the scale of generosity our Communion practices," he contended.

The session concluded with a panel discussion on the relationship of Scripture, the church, and the world, moderated by Ford and including bishops from Australia, Central Africa, the United States, and South India.

The four panelists emphasized the interdependence of the Bible and the church, though they differed somewhat on the role of the church in developing Scripture. Archbishop Harry Goodhew of Sydney saw the Bible as the genesis of the church, while Bishop Griswold of the U.S. emphasized how the early church gave form to the New Testament, seen most clearly in the Acts of the Apostles.

"Suddenly the early community had to deal with the fact that their world had been expanded," Griswold said. "Their sense of boundaries overleaped by the Spirit."

Carey closed the final plenary with a "Lambeth Call to Prayer" and the release of the new *Anglican Cycle of Prayer*, produced by Forward Movement Publications. Each bishop received a copy of the volume, which was assembled during the conference, with prayer requests provided by each bishop. "The *Anglican Cycle of Prayer* is one of the things that unites us," said Carey.

The participants responded to the call by recommitting themselves to prayer, "following the example of Christ," and dedicating themselves "to lead people to deepen and strengthen their life of prayer."

"We have come to know for our own selves that so to delight in each other's diversity is not, as some commentators sometimes seem to suggest, in any way to 'fudge' the hard questions," Carey said in his sermon at the closing Eucharist. "Quite the opposite. God invites his people to enjoy diversity, to use it, not to weaken but 'for the building up of the body.' So it is not an amiable compromise but a diversity through which we are strengthened to face the hard questions."

As he had at the beginning of the conference, Carey admitted that the bishops had gone through moments of tension and conflict, times when their differences had gathered heat and turned into "a very painful dispute."

The ability to wrestle together with the issues could provide stronger bonds, he suggested. "The kind of unity we want to achieve for the world's sake, is not the facile coming-together of the like-minded or the pretense of agreement where there is none," he said. "It is the profound unity which belongs to a family which has been tried and tested, not just by the diversity of its members and the variety of their lifestyles, but by controversy and profound disagreements encircled by a still deeper love which holds a family together," he said.

Archbishop Keith Rayner of Australia, who presided at the Eucharist, offered the Careys official thanks on behalf of the conference, praising them for their "energy and tremendous enthusiasm" and the special touch they provided. And he presented them with a special bursary fund from conference participants to provide scholarships for students who wanted to study in England.

Noting that recent Lambeth Conferences had ended on a note of doubt that there would be another conference, Rayner said that, thanks largely to the leadership provided by the Careys, "I have not heard that question this time." Future conferences may be different, he added. "We may have to look at how it's done" but he is convinced that Lambeth will continue and "that says a great deal about how we go away from this conference."

A note of festivity marked the formal end of the conference. Bishops, spouses, and staff gathered on the lawn overlooking the city for a barbecue and a magnificent fireworks display. Then they danced to the music of a swing band.

CHAPTER SIX

HOPEFUL SIGNS OF CONSENSUS

The moments of sharing discussed in the previous chapter were not the only points of commonality at the conference. Consensus emerged on a number of issues: the international debt crisis, euthanasia, the promises and dangers of modern technology, the internationalization of Jerusalem, and the formation of a Palestinian state. Common ground was also found on the call for peace in Uganda, a review of UN sanctions against Iraq and Libya, ecumenical issues, and Muslim-Christian relations.

The focus on the international debt crisis was the result of the work of South Africa's Archbishop Ndungane, whose tireless efforts on this issue began several years before the 1998 gathering.

At a keynote speech during a meeting in Scotland prior to a meeting of the heads of Commonwealth nations, Ndungane said that poverty was too big an issue to be tackled by a divided community. He argued that it is time to marshal some of the same forces that were used to fight slavery and apartheid.

In launching the Jubilee 2000 campaign in Ghana, that called for debt cancellation for the world's most impoverished nations, Ndungane told African leaders they should consider setting up an "Economic Union of African States" to ensure growth and development for all people on the continent.

Speaking to African heads of state, as well as leaders from churches, the academic community, trade unions, and non-governmental organizations, Ndungane said that it was time "for the giant of Africa to wake up from its deep sleep and to take its rightful place in the world. We are a people and a continent with a rich heritage, the cradle of humanity," he said.

An African economic union would guarantee that Africa would never again be marginalized or become "the begging bowl of the world," or be exploited. To play a proper role in the next millennium, Africa had to "be freed from the last shackles of oppression that are holding it back—the yoke of international debt." And he said that some debts should be declared "odious" because they were incurred during times of oppression, such as the apartheid era in South Africa.

At a meeting of the International Monetary Fund (IMF) in Washington, D.C., Ndungane said that the world possessed the resources and technology to guarantee every person the basic necessities for life. He argued that new agreements to govern lending and borrowing would "ensure that the relationship developed in such deals between countries is government by a fair set of principles, mutually applicable to all the parties concerned. The adoption of such principles would lead to greater security in our world."

Cancellation of the debt of developing countries, he said, would enable them to start again with a clean financial slate, as well as a fresh understanding of the implications of what it means to be accountable in the world's economy.

Ndungane told the 1997 Primates' Meeting in Jerusalem that poverty is "a decisive issue for the church, a curse that provides one of the greatest threats to society. It is not a debate about money but one about "rights and relationships, it's about powerlessness."

As chair of the section that would deal with international debt—and sexuality—the Archbishop was destined to be one of the busiest bishops at Lambeth, on a permanent hot seat.

The primates agreed with Ndungane that issues of economic justice were uppermost in their minds. Speaking as a member of the design team for Lambeth, Bishop Mark Dyer said that the issue is "not just debt but dehumanization," a contradiction of the belief that all people are children of God. He said that it would be "unfaithful" to watch the systematic destruction of brothers and sisters without making a strong statement at Lambeth.

International debt and economic justice are life-and-death matters for most of the bishops from the developing world, and they infused the conference with a sense of urgency during a crucial plenary on the subject.

"International debt is the new slavery of the twentieth century," said Ndungane in introducing the report of the section dealing with the issue. "The human cost of the international debt burden is intolerable. Its effects are evil and sinful."

The discussion quickly moved beyond abstractions as bishops offered personal testimonies of the effects of the debt trap. A bishop from Zambia said that the rural poor of his country are lucky to have one meal a day. The extended family is breaking down in the struggle to survive and many children take to city streets to beg in an effort to help.

"We are not asking for debt forgiveness, we are asking for justice," said Archbishop Alberto Ramento of the Philippine Independent Church. He said that forty percent of the Filipino budget goes to service the country's $46 million debt. Much of the debt was incurred during the corrupt regime of the late Ferdinand Marcos. "We are paying for the shoes of Imelda Marcos," he said.

Developing countries are "fighting a war," Ramento said. "We are fighting to live with dignity and cannot win this war because we do not have the power to win it on the streets of Manila alone. But it can be won in the streets of London and Washington by those who have the power."

Several bishops pointed to the underlying economic order as a major source of the problem. "Debt cancellation will not change anything long-term. There is a need for a new economic order," argued Bishop Luiz Osorio Prado Pires of Brazil. He is convinced that it will be necessary to change the underlying unjust global structures for people to become fully human. Those who are living a privileged life are not interested in change, he said, and "they support the World Bank and the IMF and share their priorities. But their priorities are not ours....We see in horror the fruits of our work being used just to pay the interest on the debt."

A twenty-minute film by the British relief agency, Christian Aid, introduced the issue at a plenary session and was highly critical of the World Bank. The bank's president, James Wolfensohn, had flown to England especially to address the plenary and expressed his dismay at how the World Bank was portrayed, calling it "difficult to take and very unattractive."

In an emotional response, he said that the film "would have you believe that I rather like children dying, that I have no faith, that my interest is to collect debts, that I have no understanding of education or health, that I know nothing about the impact of payments imposed by governments...."

Wolfensohn said he was "upset" because the film painted "a picture of our institution which is quite simply wrong. I work with 10,000 people in the bank who are committed to poverty eradication. We do not get up every morning and think what we can do to ruin the world." He said that he and the bank's employees "work to try to make the world a better place" because they care.

According to Wolfensohn, the 180 countries that support the bank have cut assistance from $60 billion to $45 billion in the last seven years. He called on the bishops to "give pressure to governments because they are the source of this fund." He warned, based on his travels to eighty countries, "We are losing the battle."

He called on the bishops to move beyond confrontation "because I am doing many of the things that the church wishes to do and should do itself....Let's see what we can do together." He concluded by asking the bishops to work with the bank "to focus on the kids that are dying, and on the children who are not being educated and on the horrors of poverty together."

Some such collaboration has already occurred. In February 1998, the Archbishop of Canterbury convened a meeting between Wolfensohn and the leaders of nine world faiths at Lambeth Palace to discuss ways of working together.

Carey himself has endorsed the idea of a Jubilee Year in 2000, based on the biblical precedent described in Leviticus 25 in which the people of Israel were commanded to return land to its original owners and free slaves every fifty years. He says that the year is especially appropriate because Christians "will be celebrating the two thousandth anniversary of the birth of the one who brought us life, hope, and peace." An international campaign has been spreading through Britain, Austria, Germany and several African nations, including Ghana and Kenya. It is estimated that the unpayable debt is at least $100 billion, although other estimates suggest it is closer to $200 billion.

"Now is the time to pull out all the stops and to harness the energy of a world that, once in a century, seems prepared to use the opportunity of the new millennium to do something that is morally and ethically right—that is the cancellation of the debt," said Ndungane.

During the Lambeth Conference, Carey convened another meeting—this time between bishops and British government leaders. The meeting included Chancellor of the Exchequer Gordon Brown and Secretary of State for International Development Clare Short, as well as diplomats from Canada, Germany, and Russia and senior representatives of the World Bank, the International Monetary Fund, and international banks.

The participants stressed the urgency of the situation in heavily indebted countries and the moral case for change and attempted to identify policies that would link debt reduction with effective long-term policies for economic and social development and the eradication of poverty. According to reports emerging from the closed meeting, it was not a case of morality and economics opposing each other but rather an attempt to establish a moral economics.

Chancellor Brown promised the bishops that Britain would step up its efforts to tackle the "mountain of debt" in response to the pleas and arguments of the churches. "I believe our inescapable duty is to try to ensure by the year 2000 all highly indebted poor countries (HPIC) are embarked on a systematic process of debt reduction," he said. Bishops said that Brown credited the churches with pushing the debt issue to the top of the agenda in a way that would not have happened otherwise.

After Lambeth, Brown, Carey, and Short met at the Prime Minister's residence at Number 10 Downing Street to discuss the government's policy on international debt relief, especially the HPIC initiative, which attempts to cancel part of a country's debt while trying to guarantee repayment of the remainder. The real issue, however, is how the initiative will help fight poverty.

"For us, debt relief should be about reducing poverty," said Matthew Lockwood, head of international policy at Christian Aid. "At the moment it is about accounting. HPIC gets rid of arrears but it doesn't free up resources, and it doesn't offer new ones to meet poverty targets," he said after the meeting.

Lockwood said that some participants like Short had indicated that the government would like to see a clearer tie between the debt relief and the efforts to reduce poverty and may actually be looking beyond the HPIC initiative, which shows that "they understand the limitations" of the initiative, he said.

"There was a clear sign that Britain is prepared to take a lead on this issue," said Adrian Lovett of Jubilee 2000, a coalition which is seeking to eliminate debt in the developing world before the new millennium. Yet she was cautious, saying that "Britain is seen as progressive in the international community, but there is a lot more it can do."

Participants pointed out that Britain is not high on the list of nations who are owed. Jubilee 2000 issued a report that developing countries repaid Britain £73.8 million last year. To completely cancel the debt would cost less than two pounds a year for each taxpayer.

"We thought it critical to put a resolution before you that was not a moral free lunch...not an exhortation to other people to do something but one that affected our lives as churches and as a Communion," said Bishop Peter Selby of England whose sub-section wrote the report and resolution on international debt.

It is "a scandal" that developing nations pay up to ten times as much each year in debt repayment as they receive in aid from wealthier nations, said the report. Much of the problem stems from the "vast expansion" in the power and amount of money and the material and spiritual damage done by the huge increases in borrowing.

The report and its resolution call on church leaders to join political and economic leaders in creditor and debtor nations to monitor the situation, perhaps through a mediation council that would scrutinize both lending and borrowing policies, assess a country's capacity to repay a debt, and challenge corruption.

"We all live in the grip of an economy which encourages over-lending and over-borrowing, an economy which drives us relentlessly into debt," Ndungane told the plenary. "But the poorest, those with very little income to depend on...are enslaved by it. They live in bondage to their creditors."

"To be born in debt and die in even bigger debt is the fate of a third of the world's population," said Archbishop Glauco de Lima of Brazil. He was among those who thought the combined voice of the Lambeth bishops could influence those who run the world's economy.

Bishop Geralyn Wolf of Rhode Island said that listening to the stories from the indebted world "where suffering is so great" moved her to the extent that "my heart has been filled with tears." She pointed out that the United States also has pockets of extreme poverty and a growing gap between rich and poor.

Many bishops left Lambeth with lingering questions of how effective their efforts to address the issues of debt and economic justice could be in such a complex economic context. Yet many bishops from the developing world felt heartened that the issue had been so thoroughly discussed and said they were now able to return to their countries with a glimmer of hope.

The plenary left four bishops from South Asia, however, pleading for a recognition that debt is a worldwide issue, not only an African one. "South Asia, which is 1.2 billion people and classified as the poorest region of the world, even below sub-Saharan Africa, was totally ignored in the platform presentation," said Bishop Mano Rumalshah of the United Church of Pakistan. "Asia is four-fifths of humanity and we had one voice. If within our own family there is this blind spot," he said, "God help us."

Even after Lambeth, Ndungane would continue his relentless campaign to get the issue into the public arena. Delivering the keynote address at a meeting of the Non-Aligned

Movement/Non-Governmental Organization in South Africa he warned that, as the crisis deepened, poor and indebted countries were transferring more and more of their meager financial resources to wealthy nations. That resulted in a situation where the poorest nations were losing their economic independence and were finding themselves "coerced to bow to the whims and demands of Western creditors."

He added, "The children of developing nations find themselves born into debt. No law, domestic or international, exists to save them from the noose of debt enslavement which is their terrifying legacy. Not for them the protection of the bankruptcy court, a mechanism that can be activated by large multinationals when they are in financial difficulties."

Using an argument that proved to be powerful and persuasive at Lambeth, the Archbishop said that cancellation of the debt would "rekindle a flame of new economic hope, not just for the developing countries, but for the world's economy as a whole." The result could be the emergence of a new world community in which resources were shared and poverty eradicated.

OPPOSING EUTHANASIA

The conference also took a strong stand against euthanasia but not before wrestling with some definitions. Arguing that it should not be "permitted in civil legislation," a resolution affirmed the basic theological and ethical principle that "life is God-given and has intrinsic sanctity, significance and worth."

In carefully defining the issue, the resolution distinguished between euthanasia as an intentional act that led to a death and the actions of withholding, withdrawing, declining, or terminating excessive medical treatment of someone in a permanent vegetative state. They said that Christians who want to enable a person to die with dignity might actually embrace these actions. (See I.14, p.253)

"Euthanasia simply means 'a good death,' and everyone wants a good death," said Archbishop Peter Hollingworth of Australia, chair of the sub-section that prepared the report. "Precisely defined, euthanasia means an act by which one person intentionally causes or assists in causing the death of another who is terminally or seriously ill in order to end the other's pain and suffering," he said. He emphasized that the resolution did not call for withdrawal of treatment for a patient in a comatose state.

"Those who advocate euthanasia show little awareness of the Christian experience that people may be redeemed and transfigured through their suffering," said Hollingworth. He said that a key part of his sub-section's work was in drawing a distinction between allowing a terminally ill patient to die and actively causing that death.

Describing modern technology as a "gift with a price," the section report said, "Modern technology can save lives, cure disease, increase productivity, connect people globally...[yet it] can also alienate and isolate people, even kill and dehumanize."

The report described the promises and dangers of technology, using different global perspectives to illustrate the point. "The year 2000 computer bug is an issue for the North. The South is more concerned with technology's effect on feeding people, on war and how technology displaces people," said Bishop Frank Allan of Atlanta in a press briefing.

Despite the pitfalls, the "pervasive presence of information" can be liberating, the report said. "New ideas cannot be kept out, and this has served to promote and extend democratic ideals. Tyrants and dictators cannot carry out their totalitarian rule in secret."

The bishops concluded their report with a theological observation and a practical challenge. "Our dominion over the earth has been at its best a reverent stewardship...at its worst has despoiled the earth...enslaved and destroyed people," it said. Concluding that technology is never neutral, the report said, "From the perspectives of the Gospel, effectiveness is judged by whether the poorest end up with jobs, food and water." In making decisions about the moral use of technology, the bishops said that it is crucial to ask whether the use of power is appropriate, whether it preserves and enhances instead of destabilizing—and whether it can be controlled and is accessible to all, beneficial to all.

JARRING REMINDERS OF SUFFERING

At several points during the conference, participants received jarring reminders that the issues they were addressing were very real.

Archbishop James Ayong of New Guinea asked for prayers for the victims of a tidal wave that struck his nation on July 17. His diocese includes the isolated strip of coastline in the northwest region that bore the brunt of the wave. The remote location made efforts difficult. "It's very isolated and miles from the nearest airstrip," said the archbishop.

Seasonal floods reported in Bangladesh threatened the farms in the Diocese of Kushtia in the United Church. "This is only the beginning," warned Bishop Michael Baroi. Because the floods came at the time of planting, it could spell disaster for the farmers and leave them with nothing. "Once the crop is lost or damaged, they are under debt for life, contributing to the great poverty of the nation."

Near the end of the conference, the bishops were shocked to hear of the bombing of embassies in Nairobi, Kenya, and Dar es Salaam, Tanzania, with heavy destruction and loss of lives. Archbishop David Gitari, the Primate of Kenya, expressed his deep shock. "To hear of bombs exploding in places which are familiar to us is very shocking indeed," he said in a plenary.

The conference also affirmed that Jerusalem should be the capital of both Israel and an independent Palestinian state with free access for all three Abrahamic religions—Christianity, Judaism, and Islam. The resolution came from a regional conference of bishops from the Middle East and South Asia.

Any "meaningful and just peace between Israel and the Palestinians" must include "a right of return to their lands for the Palestinian refugees," said Bishop Riah Abu El-Assal of Jerusalem. And peace must include attempts to "develop a more expansive partnership within the worldwide Body of Christ, between the church communities you represent and us, the indigenous Christians," he said.

Bishop Richard Harries of Oxford, who chairs the Council of Christians and Jews in England, asked that the record note "that there are a good number of Israelis and a good number of Jewish people throughout the world who recognize Palestinians' suffering and are trying to support them in their legitimate goals. And I would not want this resolution simply to go through with any...implication that it is working against Jewish people or Israelis as a whole."

Another resolution pointed to the suffering in Uganda, urging the government to continue to engage in a process towards reconciliation, peace, and justice which "must include the governments of Sudan and the Democratic Republic of Congo, representatives of the main religious bodies and opinion leaders of the areas affected." Bishop Eustace Kamanyire of Uganda proposed a successful amendment that called on the Anglican Consultative Council and the United Nations to "assist in bringing about a quick settlement of this armed conflict." He thanked Carey for his recent visit to Uganda and suggested that the Archbishop might be instrumental in appealing to the UN for dialogue since he is held in high esteem by the Ugandan government.

A proposal from the bishops of East Central Africa and

Presiding Bishop Frank Griswold introduces Roman Catholic observers at Lambeth, including (l to r) -Cardinal Edward Cassidy of the Vatican Secretariat for Promoting Christian Unity, Archbishop Alex Brunett of Seattle, Bishop Philip Pargeter, Bishop Pierre Duprey of the Vatican, and the Rev. Tim Galligan of England. (Photo: Episcopal News Service)

Southeast Asia-Middle East for a Decade for Transformation and Renewal or a Decade of Peace and Reconciliation was not accepted. "I think we need a theme for our efforts, for our thoughts, for our concentration," argued Bishop Bernard Ntahoturi of Burundi. "I cannot believe that this conference wants to be thought to be seeking to limit and define God's gracious work by designating special decades for him for the whole Anglican Communion," countered Bishop Nigel McCulloch of England.

The bishops did pass a resolution calling on the UN Security Council "to urgently review" economic sanctions against Iraq and Libya. The resolution said that the conference was "concerned about the plight of the civilian population of these countries, particularly those who are vulnerable because medicines and food are lacking."

"The sanctions may be to impose or punish these governments, but their victims are always voiceless women, children, and minorities," said Bishop Azad Marshall of the Church of Pakistan.

THE VIEW FROM ROME

In a homily at an ecumenical vespers service, Edward Cardinal Cassidy, president of the Vatican's Pontifical Council for Promoting Christian Unity, affirmed the commitment of the Roman Catholic Church to the search for full visible unity. He warned, however, that local churches should not adopt "a practice or theory" incompatible with the Christian faith.

Some observers concluded that the reference was to the ordination of non-celibate homosexuals but others said that the remarks might also refer to women in the priesthood and episcopate. "The Virginia Report is surely right to argue that 'at all times the theological praxis of the local church must be consistent with the truth of the Gospel which belongs to the universal church,'" Cassidy said. Sometimes the universal church must "say with firmness that a particular local practice or theory is incompatible with Christian faith.

"The theological practice of the local church must be compatible with the theological practice of the universal church," Cassidy insisted. And unless the church addresses the question of authority, theological chaos ensues.

While Cassidy stayed for five days, the other Roman Catholic observers stayed and participated in the whole conference. They included Bishop Pierre Duprey, secretary of the Vatican's Council for the Promotion of Christian Unity; the Rev. Timothy Galligan of England. Galligan handles the council's relations with Anglicans. Bishop Philip Pargeter, Auxiliary Bishop of Birmingham and chair for the English and Welsh bishops' committee for Christian unity, was also present. The group also included Archbishop Alexander Brunett of Seattle, chair of the U.S. bishops' committee for ecumenical and inter-religious affairs and a former member of the official dialogue between Roman Catholics and Anglicans in the United States.

In an interview with *The Tablet*, the English Roman Catholic magazine, Brunett said that "a great bonding" took place at Lambeth. "You are in a Bible study with someone for three weeks and each day you are probing the Word of God. You begin to learn about their lives, their ups and their downs, and they learn about yours, and you go away saying, 'Gee, it's a shame I'm never going to see that person again.'"

When asked what he had learned at Lambeth, Brunett said that "the Episcopal Church in America is not typical of the Anglican Communion. It tends to be more liberal; it tends to be less rooted in the Bible. A lot of the bishops that I was with in my sessions were very 'anti-' the Episcopal Church in America. They thought that they were a group out there doing their own thing. They see it as a reflection of the way Americans are, economically trying to control the world."

Dean William Franklin of Berkeley Divinity School at Yale welcomed Cassidy's remarks as a reaffirmation of Rome's commitment to "the full visible unity of all the baptized." He added, "Cassidy warned that our internal disunity leads to an increasing disunity with the Roman Catholic Church."

Before Lambeth, Franklin had been publicly critical of the Pope's July 1, 1998 apostolic letter, in which the nineteenth-century declaration on the invalidity of Anglican orders was reiterated. Franklin had said, "It shifts the ground of ecumenical dialogue and shuts down the ecumenical method-ology of the last thirty-three years, based on a free scholarly exchange that will no longer be possible." He expressed a deep concern that "from the Vatican point of view, the apostolic let-ter brings to an end a hopeful relationship going back to 1965. We can't avoid looking at this squarely and deciding the consequences for our community."

Yet he found Cassidy's comments at Lambeth that Angli-cans and Catholics are "increasingly bound up with each other" a technical but important description. And the com-ments, according to Franklin, reflected "a level of communion where we need to be realistic with one another."

The Rev. Alyson Barnett-Cowan, director of Faith, Wor-ship and Ministry for the Anglican Church of Canada, found Cassidy's comments "more cautious than enthusiastic."

While Cassidy was not explicit in his references in addressing the need for a universal authority as an instru-ment of unity, he seemed to be "offering the papacy as that authority," Franklin said. "Our bishops may come up with some other forms of universal authority which are not focused on one person or a single office."

Both Barnett-Cowan and Franklin said that the homily offered a "useful context" for the discussions of Anglican-Roman Catholic relations underway in a sub-group of Section Four, chaired by U.S. Presiding Bishop Frank Griswold. "What the cardinal has done is to let us know what their understanding is of what our relationship should be for the next decade—which is real but imperfect communion, with cautions about ways that communion can be improved but also weakened," Franklin said. In the same spirit, "we might want to express, with Christian love, the concerns of the Anglican Communion about the relationship."

Griswold said that the ecumenical participants were at Lambeth "one human being to another in a struggle toward full unity. It is a moment of incarnation." Griswold was later appointed co-chair of the international dialogue between Anglicans and Roman Catholics.

Three Lutheran bishops from Scandinavia were welcomed to the conference. In 1996 the Nordic Lutherans and the Anglicans of the British Isles signed an agreement at Porvoo, Finland, establishing full communion. Archbishop John Vilstrom of Finland called it "one of the most important ecumenical steps of this century...a gift to the whole church." Bishop Andreas Aaflot of Norway added, "There are many things we have learned we can do more effectively together than separately."

John Hind, the Church of England Bishop for Europe, argued that Porvoo forced the ecumenical community to think seriously about apostolic succession, and the "degree of risk worth taking when you agree on the ultimate goal."

"We must not forget the inclusion of the Baltic churches, which have been so isolated through the Cold War," warned Bishop Jonas Jonson of Sweden. "Porvoo lends a dynamic of great significance in our own relationships." He added that the agreement would also be lived out in places like Tanzania and Zimbabwe where the Lutheran churches were established by Swedish mission societies. "The question now is how these churches will relate to the provinces of the Anglican Communion."

In a statement delivered to Lambeth participants, Dr. Ishmael Noko, general secretary of the Lutheran World Federation, proposed a global agreement for full communion between Anglicans and Lutherans. Pointing to the Porvoo Declaration and the growing relationships in other parts of the world—such as Canada, Africa, and the United States—"the natural next step would seem to be a global Anglican-Lutheran agreement on full communion."

The first plenary, dealing with the report and resolutions from Section Four on the theme, "Called to be One," went so smoothly that the bishops were able to move on to reports and resolutions from another section.

Bishop Jabez Bryce of Polynesia introduced the material dealing with ecumenical relations between the Anglican Communion and other churches. He affirmed that "every Lambeth Conference has had a deep concern for unity, both of the church and the unity of the human community." He expressed hope that the provinces of the Communion "will in the next ten years respond with fresh enthusiasm to our ecumenical vocation in a spirit of humility, patience, and loving tolerance."

Bryce sketched three main themes in the section report. The first "reviewed the complex economic scene with its mixture of signs of hope on the one hand and setbacks on the other. Do Anglicans still share a common commitment to visible unity and is there, behind the many ecumenical endeavors, a shared vision of that unity which is God's gift to us and our vocation to play our part in bringing into being?"

The second reviewed "the progress made in bilateral and multilateral conversations at international and national levels and reflected on some of the issues concerning coherence, common vision, response and reception."

The third "took the Conference into uncharted waters with a consideration of the pastoral and ecumenical issues which arise out of Anglican experience of new churches and independent Christian groups."

The themes were tied together, Bryce observed, by an awareness that "our ecumenical vocation is carried out in the context of the encounter with people of other faiths and none. If our witness is to be credible, it requires that Christians are united."

The section report identified "humility, gentleness, patience and loving tolerance" as essential tools for the ecumenical journey.

The report summarized the significant developments in Anglican relationships with churches who are in full communion, local dialogues and regional efforts at cooperation, and discussions with councils of churches, especially the World Council of Churches. The purpose of the search for visible unity, the report said, "is to point to the sort of life God intends for the whole of humanity, a foretaste of God's kingdom. Two resolutions passed by a hand vote, without any debate and no apparent objections. One restated the Anglican commitment to the search for full, visible unity, and the other called for an inter-Anglican standing commission on ecumenical relations.

A third resolution, dealing with unity within the provinces of the Anglican Communion, passed as presented when an amendment that attempted to clarify the role of the Archbishop of Canterbury failed. Bishop Wilson Mutebi of Uganda sought an expanded role for the Anglican Consultative Council, arguing that giving special powers to Canterbury would be a departure from Anglican tradition.

The new ecumenical commission will not only monitor the various dialogues but also intervene "to ensure theological consistency." Under provisions of the resolution, as agreements emerge between Anglicans and other denominations that would affect the whole Communion, the commission would refer the matter to the Primates' Meeting before the new relationship is entered.

All twenty resolutions from the section on the assent list passed without comment or dissent. The resolutions affirmed the 1888 Chicago-Lambeth Quadrilateral as a statement of Anglican identity and unity and welcomed local ecumenical initiatives. They also affirmed the work of the World Council of Churches but asked for consideration of changes so that Roman Catholics might join. Other resolutions commented on conversations with the Lutheran, Baptist, Methodist, Moravian, Orthodox, Reformed, and Roman Catholic churches.

One resolution called attention to what it called "the remarkable progress in Anglican-Lutheran relationships during the last decade in many parts of the world," and expressed a hope that the Concordat between Lutherans and Episcopalians in the United States would move forward, despite a narrow rejection by the Lutherans. It also called attention to a similar decision facing Anglicans and Lutherans in Canada in 2001.

The resolution on relations with Roman Catholics said that the Anglican-Roman Catholic International Commission (ARCIC) would need to address "a number of outstanding issues" and strongly encouraged the continuation of that dialogue. It called for "a high-level consultation" to review the relationship and deal with issues such as the movement of clergy between the two churches and "the experience of Christian solidarity under persecution" in places such as the Sudan, as well as persistent issues surrounding different understandings of the Eucharist and ministry. It urged provinces of the Communion to respond to Pope John Paul II's encyclical *Ut unum sint*, which invited other Christians to "consider the ministry of unity of the Bishop of Rome in the service of the unity of the Universal Church."

The bishops also addressed the phenomenon of the rapidly growing Pentecostal churches, taking seriously for the first time "the vast quantity of Christian people who assemble in new churches and independent Christian groups," said Bishop Stephen Sykes of England, vice-chair of the section dealing with dialogue with other churches. He said that research now estimates "there are 480 million people who belong to Pentecostal churches or are associated with charismatic churches in the world."

Anglicans are finally curious about evaluating "this vast phenomenon" and what it could mean for world Christianity, he said. "They have a lot to teach us. And we have a reason to be penitent for our failure to be more responsive to the needs of men and women across the world." At the same time, "we want to find ways of entering into constructive dialogue without dismantling our heritage," he added.

Moving on to Section Two, "Called to Live and Proclaim the Good News," the plenary received the report and approved four resolutions on the "agreed list," and amended one on mission, urging partnership with Christians of "all traditions."

The conference passed a resolution that "repents of our failures in mission and evangelism." Another urged "that priority be given at every level in our Communion to reaching out to those who have never heard, or never responded to, the Gospel of Christ, and to reawakening those whose love has grown cold...."

MUSLIM-CHRISTIAN RELATIONS

A plenary on "Muslim-Christian Relations and the Anglican Communion," chaired by Bishop Michael Nazir-Ali of England, attempted to look at Islam not in isolation "but rather in the context of our entire attention to interfaith relations here at the Lambeth Conference."

"The one reality is that both Islam and Christianity are missionary religions, both are operating in Africa and East Asia, so the potential for conflict between them is greater—but the need for getting along is greater," said Nazir-Ali, a Pakistani. "When we designed the conference, nearly every province said relations with other faiths was an important topic," he said, so the group designing the conference included interfaith aspects in each section.

Since the media images of Islam are so often stereotypical and intolerant, "We have to ask whether these are the only available images of Islam. What else can we say about a great world faith, which has given rise to so many civilizations?"

Speaking at a press briefing prior to the plenary, Nazir-Ali said it was crucial to the discussion to recognize that Islamic law is not static, that it does have flexibility, and that the bedrock ideals are democratic.

"In Pakistan, the Blasphemy Law is, in fact, profoundly un-Islamic," the bishop observed. "In the Koran there is no punishment on earth for apostasy nor for blasphemy. The Prophet himself forgave those who insulted him," so it is important to "continue to campaign for its repeal."

Some governments *do* use Islamic law as "a way of legitimizing government ambitions," he said, such as the "oppressive, ideologically driven regime in Sudan." And in Iran, Islamic law (*shari'ah*) "was seen as a way of cleansing the country of Western influences after a corrupt regime was deposed."

On the difficulty of living in countries dominated by Islamic principles, Nazir-Ali said that "people should be committed to fundamental freedoms wherever they are. People of all faiths should have equal rights." He expressed dismay that Pakistan had abandoned those principles since "it was founded on the principle that Muslims were an oppressed minority in undivided India."

He expressed a hope that the conference would pass a resolution that "encourages the opening up of Iran, not one that is condemnatory. We want to support those moderate Muslims who are working to open up the country. There is a struggle there that could go either way," he said.

"We have so much more in common with devout Muslims than with our pagan, secular British neighbors," added the Rev. Colin Chapman, a Lambeth consultant who started an organization that promotes dialogue between Christians and Muslims.

The plenary began on a tragic note when Nazir-Ali told a hushed audience that three nuns from the order founded by Mother Teresa had been killed in the Yemen, reportedly by an Islamic extremist.

After a few moments of silence, Nazir-Ali traced the long history of relations between Islam and Christianity. "The Prophet himself had very close relationships with Christians and Jews. Some were among his closest friends and colleagues," he observed. He wondered what had gone wrong given "such a long history of coexistence and cooperation in culture and learning and political life." He attributed much of the problem to the rise of fundamentalism in reaction to colonialism, corrupt leaders, the failure of capitalism, and persistent civil wars.

Presentations by six bishops put the issue into perspective—from the Gambia, where relations are quite good; from Nigeria, where there are some sharp confrontations but also some sharing; from the Middle East, where both religions have struggled for fundamental rights and some autonomy; from Pakistan, where there is very little history of cooperation; and also stories from Britain and North Africa with a mix of good and bad relationships.

Bishop Tilewa Johnson of the Gambia, which is ninety-five percent Muslim and three percent Christian, described a country of tolerance and openness because "freedom of religion is enshrined in the constitution" of a secular state. As a result, "Christians and Muslims attend each other's weddings and funerals" and there is even intermarriage so that "within the extended family there can be both religious communities." Leaders of both offer prayers at all state functions.

Since education has been a priority for the church in the Gambia, "many Muslims have passed through Christian schools, taking part in religion classes and acquiring a knowledge of the Bible and a deep understanding of the Christian tradition," the bishop added.

While conversions are not common, the tradition of rural Muslim children being sent to urban Christian families for education can have "a gradual but profound effect" with hearts being "turned quietly but surely."

In contrast, the situation in Nigeria is quite different, according to Bishop Josiah Idowu-Fearon. The north is almost ninety percent Muslim while the central region, where he lives, is equally balanced. The south, on the other hand, is almost ninety percent Christian. As a result, "Christians have no rights" in the north and central regions with no provision for Christian education in the state schools and prohibitions against using the media to preach the Gospel.

"There is serious enmity or hatred, deep hatred, between Christians and Muslims in Nigeria, especially in the middle part of the country," the bishop reported. "We have lost over 10,000 lives in the name of religion and more thousands have been displaced" with "millions of dollars of property lost in the name of religion."

While the continuing presence of Arab Christians in the Holy Land is "nothing less than an awesome achievement," according to Bishop Riah Abu el-Assal, their dwindling presence means that "our mere physical presence is at stake." He said that today the Arab Christian presence is barely one and a half percent of the population in Israel and the occupied territories. Unless the situation changes, he thought that it was possible that the Holy Land might "become a museum of holy stones."

During the thirteen centuries of what he called "daily living dialogue," Riah admitted that there had been instances of discrimination and persecution but Muslims were learning "to appreciate our presence among them." Part of the reason may be the fact that Muslims in Palestine are historically "more tolerant of religious pluralism than their European counterparts." He added that "our experience of Islam has been one of mutual respect and mutual trust."

In such an atmosphere "we share our faith. We do not impose it. We share it in the spirit of truth and love, and we do not compromise our convictions," he said.

In contrast to the situation in the Middle East, religious pluralism is not a welcome concept in most Muslim circles in Pakistan, reported Bishop Alexander Malik of Lahore. "Islam is not only a religious faith, but a political ideology as well. In Islam, religion and politics are intertwined; they go hand in hand."

He offered as examples, a Muslim man can marry a Christian woman but not the other way around. And a Christian can covert to Islam but Muslims cannot become Christians.

"The Blasphemy Law is like a hanging sword" above the head of religious minorities in Pakistan, Malik said, expressing his concern that those who argue for religious tolerance are silenced. "The most noticeable expression of Islam in the present-day world is the rejection of Western civilization and culture," he said, probably because the West is regarded as too identified with Christianity and yet subject to secularism.

While urging Anglicans to be "open, liberal and flexible," that doesn't mean that "we should accept the ideology of Islam without its critical evaluation, or reject it without reason, or compromise with it at the expense of Christian principles," Malik concluded.

Despite the rise of fundamentalism, other church leaders offered examples that showed cooperation is still possible. Bishop Ghais Malik of Egypt, Primate of the Church in Jerusalem and the Middle East, described the ways that "the Christian minority live among the Muslim majority" in his country and have through the centuries, "during times of joy and times of trouble. They faced wars together, and so they fought together, died together and survived together." People from both religions are "part of the one body of Egypt."

He defined persecution as the official effort by the government to target a minority group and seek its destruction, drawing a distinction between persecution and the kind of troubles that "are started by blinkered individuals or fanatic Islamists with closed minds." In the latter category he put the terrorists who killed Christians and burned their churches in an attempt to "shake the stability of the country, hoping thereby to bring down the government and rule themselves." He said they often argue that they are following the Koran. Seeking converts is illegal in Egypt, Malik said, so Christians "do not impose themselves on others to accept what they believe but rather show them how they live."

Along the same lines, Bishop David Smith of England told how his diocese began a dialogue with Muslims "to develop and foster good relations" by encouraging people "to meet, to build up a sense of trust and respect for those who are different, and to fight against" misrepresentations of Islam.

CHAPTER SEVEN

INTERPRETING LAMBETH

The task of reporting and interpreting the events of the Lambeth Conference did not have to wait until the bishops returned home. For the first time, provisions were made for bishops to communicate what was happening directly to their dioceses—and many bishops availed themselves of the technological possibilities.

For example, a few bishops filed diary-style daily postings on the Internet. Stanton of Dallas gave those with access to the diocesan Web page detailed descriptions of events as they unfolded. He observed, for example, in the Kenyan liturgy at the opening Eucharist "the eager, assertive, and spiritually wise presence of the Africans," adding that he found their leadership "to be enlightening, engaging, and enthusiastic."

Stanton claimed that the Dallas Conference, a meeting of African and American traditionalists prior to Lambeth, "was a real groundbreaker and has been, on the testimony of many, a key event in permitting us to work together almost immediately on hitting the ground. The sense of cooperation and mutuality has been gratifying."

He was particularly encouraged by the unity he experienced among bishops who have been "united in calling for a clear, traditional articulation of the church's teaching" on sexuality. "This is not an uphill battle as it so often seems at the General Convention."

Other bishops used the Internet, provided without charge to all bishops at the conference, to stay in touch with the folks back home. About 300 bishops logged on to send and receive electronic mail during the conference, more than one-quarter of them for the first time.

"It is wonderful to be able to teach these bishops and their response to me is, 'This is so simple.' There are bishops who have never touched a keyboard before who are sending e-mail within twenty minutes," said the Rev. Ron Barnes of Canada, a member of the Inter-Anglican Information Network. A grant from Trinity Church in New York made more than 200 computers, scattered across the university campus, available to the bishops.

Bishop Ed Leidel of Eastern Michigan also kept in touch with his diocese, sharing with them the daily workings of the conference. Like most of his colleagues, he found the daily sharing "extraordinary. One senses that these connections will remain lifelong. Our spiritual friendship becomes the core of our fellowship—our theological differences becomes a clearly secondary concern."

Bishop Frank Gray of Northern Indiana also used the Internet facilities at Lambeth to report back to his diocese. "A most important part of this conference will never be reported in the press or observed in photo opportunities. This part, like the beating of the heart, occurs in quiet ways away from the highly visible places. I speak of the small groups of ten to twelve bishops who meet daily for prayer, Bible study, and discussion."

Gray was in the section, "Called to Proclaim the Good News," a group that included bishops from England, Canada, Peru, the Sudan, South Africa, Papua New Guinea, and Cyprus. In the groups, bishops were able to "share our testimony, including how we were called to ordained ministry, and something about our diocese." Gray said that "the sharing was quite deep and everyone listened attentively as we offered a moment of silent prayer after each witness." In his early reflections, the bishop said that the conference was "quite exhilarating and inspiring."

MOVED TO TEARS

Different provinces of the Anglican Communion offered daily liturgies and Bishop Frank Allan of Atlanta said that he was moved to tears the day the Church in Japan conducted a liturgy on the Feast of the Transfiguration, the anniversary of the atomic bomb dropped on Hiroshima. "I went to the Eucharist expecting to be berated about the bombing. Instead, the Japanese Church apologized for the militarism which led to World War II and for the brutality of the Japanese Imperial Army. I found myself in tears, for this is the first time I have ever heard an apology from the Japanese people."

Gray said he was also deeply moved because his family had been imprisoned by the Japanese during the war. The daughter of the Bishop of Singapore preached the sermon. Her father had been tortured by the Japanese Army, yet he later "went on to baptize one of the persons who had tortured him."

"We U.S. bishops were advised before arriving to keep still and listen, and we did," Allan said in a reflection. Most of the energy of the conference centered on the issues of homosexuality and world debt, he observed. "I believe this focus was symptomatic of a far deeper cultural, economic, religious, and political suspicion." When the bishops moved into plenary to debate and vote on resolutions, "eyes never met. There is much we could have come to understand about our common faith, suffering, and compassion, had we spent more time conversing eyeball to eyeball, as we did in our small groups," he said.

Although Allan was not surprised by the vote on the sexuality resolution, he said, "What surprised and shocked me was the rhetoric of hate and condemnation. A new biblical fundamentalism has taken hold in the Anglican Communion, and this concerns me because it is idolatrous. The issue is not the authority of Scripture, but the interpretation of Scripture.

"I know there is still much that I don't understand, especially about these new Anglican churches in parts of the world I have never visited—the suffering, the poverty, the war, the conflict with Islam, the persecution, the corruption," he wrote. "I want to understand, but I also wish they could understand more of us—that, in spite of our sins, most of the people I know and minister to and with are generous, compassionate, and just. In other words, I wish our eyes could meet."

Bishop Chilton Knudsen of Maine expressed similar excitement about the small group meetings. "The pace of this conference is so intense—the stimulation of so many ideas, conversations, new faces, reading material, press interviews, etc., have forced me to find a few centering points in the days' schedule." She found nourishment in the daily Eucharist where the Lord's Prayer was prayed in the native tongue of each participant, "all making a hum of prayer which rises and falls like a great wave." And there are the stories "filled with the lovely grace of simple human encounter." She added, "In spite of the very strong differences between us, there is a true sense of family here.

"I have had my heart stretched and broken at the stories I hear, and have had my heart warmed at the amazingly warm welcome and affection which continues to surround us who are women, and the genuine spirit of community we have built."

The last week was rough for most of the bishops, including Knudsen, who said that it was "exhausting and painful." When she put up her hand to vote against the amended resolution on sexuality, "I was hissed and verbally harassed by people sitting around me." As she had said during her own election process, she is "prayerfully persuaded that God is calling us to be an inclusive church, in which all people are welcomed, without prejudice or condemnation." She promised that she would "do everything in my power to assure that Maine becomes ever more a safe place for everyone to seek and serve Christ, whatever their opinions or circumstances."

Knudsen's colleague, Barbara Harris of Massachusetts, was even more blunt. In her column in the diocesan newspaper, she expressed relief that the conference was over "and I never have to do this again!"

Even though she knew a number of the bishops, Harris said, "Nonetheless, I was struck by how precious little we really know about each other and the cultural norms and values with which we live, as well as the depth of our divisions." She added, "At times it was difficult to fathom what holds the Communion together beyond our love of the Lord Jesus Christ and Wippell's." The latter is an internationally known firm that provides vestments for bishops.

In trying to explain "the tone of the most contentious resolutions the conference passed," she pointed to "our different understandings and interpretations of Scripture, its place in the life of the church, and the struggle of rapidly growing churches in the hostile environments of many developing nations." Another factor, she said, was the different sharing of authority in parts of the American church. "To put it more bluntly, in many provinces of the church—particularly those in African and Asian countries—diocesan bishops hold absolute sway."

For Harris "the vitriolic, fundamentalist rhetoric of some African, Asian, and other bishops of color, who were in the majority, was in my opinion reflective of the European and North American missionary influence propounded in the Southern Hemisphere nations during the eighteenth, nineteenth, and early twentieth centuries." The hard-line stance on gays and lesbians and the role of women in the church was rooted in what she called "a belief in the inerrancy and primacy of Scripture, which supports a preexisting cultural bias." She said bishops from the developing world brought the same truth "that not only had been handed to their forebears, but had been used to suppress them." And they found allies in "a small contingent of U.S. bishops who had been unable to move their agenda at last summer's General Convention...."

Bishop M. Thomas Shaw of Massachusetts admitted that he was "not prepared" for "the verbal abuse by some of the speakers condemning homosexuals, the hissing and booing at those of us who voted in the minority....It was a very painful time for many of us." He also suggested that the presence of laity, deacons, and priests might have made a difference in the deliberations at Lambeth.

"Our differences will stretch us as a body, as the Anglican Communion," said Bishop James Jelinek of Minnesota in his diocesan newspaper. "We may fall into separate paths in which we hold our truths to be the Truth, in which we may become too fragile and brittle to survive. Yet I hope, I believe, I trust that the Spirit will give us enough elasticity and sufficient grace to grow in loving and honoring one another, even as we seek together to discern God's truth."

On the sexuality resolution, which he opposed, he said, "Some see this as a step forward. If it is, I believe it is only a baby step."

DUELING AGENDAS

Bishop Mark MacDonald of Alaska felt caught between dueling agendas, especially during the plenary debate on sexuality. "It was like being in a dark room and hearing somebody start up a chainsaw, and hearing somebody else start up another chainsaw, and wanting to get out of the room."

He was even more troubled, however, by the angry responses to the conference among Episcopalians in the United States. "The reaction since then has been horrible," MacDonald said. "I have heard so many racist things said about what happened that it's frightening...because some people have said, 'We need to educate those people.' The aftermath has been worse than the experience itself."

In sharing her impressions on Lambeth in her diocesan newspaper, Jane Dixon of Washington said that "whenever the people of God get too close to the mandate of the Gospel regarding the distribution of resources, primarily financial, we create smoke screens or name scapegoats to divert our attention. Women and gay men and lesbians have become those screens and scapegoats."

Dixon said that she remembered the admonition of her mentor, Verna Dozier, who told her "despair is never the response of the faithful Christian." Dixon said that she was comforted by the knowledge that "these resolutions that are exclusive, hurtful, and disrespectful of the dignity of every human being are not the final word, nor are they binding on any province in the church."

Bishop Charles Jenkins of Louisiana, in his column in the diocesan paper, said that he was "taken aback, humbled, and shocked at the stories of persecution, deprivation, and discrimination that many of our fellow Anglicans face around the world. The crucifixion of priests, children being sold into slavery, children being denied an education, pregnant women being cut open to satisfy a bet of soldiers on the sex of the baby, the genocide of people who have been Christians for generations—the stories were appalling."

Christianity living under such dire circumstances "tends to be more biblically literalist, and apparently less willing or able to live with many of the shades of gray with which we in the West have grown comfortable," he added.

As a result of his experience, Jenkins said that "we are challenged to find a new way of being the Anglican Communion. The old way of being church, with a high degree of provincial autonomy and a trust in ways English, is no longer viable. As much as I liked it, it holds nothing for the future. If we try to hold onto this, we will disintegrate from a world-wide, catholic communion into a squabbling mass of little entities. The spiritual implications of such are a disaster! There is nothing more dangerous to a Christian than schism. So we must find a new way of being the Anglican church."

Like many of his colleagues, Jenkins observed that culture "stained" every debate. "I do not take away the theological integrity of any position, but culture informed the faith, and thus the debate, more than I had expected it would. This says something to me about the level of anxiety in the church and the world and the difficulty of moving beyond that anxiety. The reactivity to this Lambeth is also a sign of that anxiety."

In his column entitled, "Christianity caught in a time-warp," Spong blasted the process and results of Lambeth, charging Carey with abandoning his role as a diplomat, throwing his weight "verbally and visually behind resolutions that have in fact left this church polarized. Once more in the name of the God of love, the church has managed to insult gay and lesbian people and to suggest to women everywhere that they are still a problem in the body of Christ."

Calling it "a tense, difficult, and negative experience" for many, Spong added, "No one seemed to recognize that the church in the West had engaged our modern world with its challenging scientific and secular insight far more significantly than has any other part of the Communion." And, he said, "We lived at Lambeth with perceptions of reality so vastly different that the same words simply did not mean the same thing. We became aware that difficult local circumstances so deeply colored one's frame of reference that those outside those circumstances could never understand the words that were being spoken."

Spong pointed out that the issue of homosexuality was barely mentioned at the previous Lambeth but "was destined to take the emotional main seat. We had to unload the stated misperception that it was the United States and Canada which were forcing this debate on the agenda. The fact is that it was the homophobic fears of the Third World seeking to condemn the very mention of homosexuality that made this topic the major item." As he had in his comments prior to Lambeth, Spong said that the failure to recognize "the last 150 years of biblical scholarship that has shaped Western Christianity" made conversation and debate difficult.

"A literalized Bible claiming inerrancy for its words has historically been a source of death far more often than it has been a source of life," Spong argued. "Yet this kind of fundamentalism was clearly once again alive and well in this Communion, making it all but impossible to build in our time a modern and relevant Christianity." He said that Carey's vision of the church was rooted in the past, not the future. "He and I simply do not live in the same world."

Instead of love, "I saw rather pettiness, dishonesty, spinelessness, spin doctors, and absolute distortions of truth as the behavior of those who claimed to be disciples of Jesus. Those who called themselves evangelical journalists were the worst offenders," Spong charged.

"Western leadership was disorganized, inept, incapable of working strategically, and without a common purpose," Spong said. "Their overt refusal to draft a minority statement when it was clear that their point of view had no chance of prevailing and in fact was almost certainly going to be overwhelmed meant that liberal bishops were reduced to making individual responses when the vicious resolutions were passed," statements that he said "lacked both power and persuasiveness and did not provide an effective place behind which opponents of the majority point of view could rally.

"If we cannot reassert the Anglican genius that reason must be an equal factor with Scripture and tradition in shaping the Christian message in every generation, then Christianity as we know it is doomed," Spong concluded. "The Lambeth Conference convinced me completely that my call for a new reformation in the church is right on target, and it showed me exactly why it is that Christianity must change or die."

Spong's wife Christine was even more blunt. In her speech to the Integrity gathering in Little Rock she described a campaign to "take the Bishop of Newark out as a player at Lambeth," beginning with the interview in the *Church of England Newspaper*.

She said that she was "devastated and angry beyond words at the deceit and lack of integrity" when the *Lambeth Daily* printed a story on her husband's "apology" to the Africans, going so far as to suggest that Griswold "was probably part of the editorial team that had decided to humiliate Jack for the apology fiasco."

The complete "rout" of the liberals on the sexuality resolution did not come as a surprise to the Spongs. Yet she said she believed there is a silver lining in the cloud for lesbian and gay people. "I believe that what happened at Lambeth caused a number of Western bishops to finally get off the fence, and they have signed Bishop Haines' letter," including a number of English bishops who had told her that "their careers would go no further if they supported openness to gay and lesbian people."

HISTORIC WATERSHED

Bishop Robert Duncan of Pittsburgh, on the other hand, said he was convinced Lambeth will be seen as a "watershed in Anglican history." He said it succeeded in "outlining matters that cannot be changed, in redefining the nature of the Communion as truly global, and [in] reestablishing the balance (and the means) by which autonomous national churches are sacrificially submitted to one another."

He acknowledged that the conference was "a very difficult one" for the American bishops, who found themselves to be "very marginalized, very far away from the Anglican center." For him the issue is "whether we can be re-centered." In the Bible studies on Paul's Second Letter to the Corinthians, "We are reminded that the apostolic way to re-center a church is to love it, to encourage it, to go to it and, only after all of that, to challenge it. It also demands speaking out of repentance, weakness and the cross, not out of power, wisdom, or pride."

Bishop Joe Morris Doss of New Jersey agreed that the issue was an "ability of ours to hold together a wide variety of opinion and expression," but he concluded that it was "threatened" by Lambeth 1998. "Led by a few conservative bishops in the U.S.A., this conference saw a strong push towards uniformity of teaching and belief. Although the media centered on our discussions regarding human sexuality and the inclusion of women and children, the fact is that this threat to our comprehensiveness goes much deeper than any one topic. There are people in the Anglican Communion, just as there are people in our diocese and in each parish, for whom variety of opinion and the fast pace of change in the modern world are an unbearable burden. They would like to see Anglican tradition and teaching expressed unequivocally, in black and white terms, with no room for dissent, difference of opinions, or theological process."

Doss argued for a return to the "tradition of comprehensiveness" that has been the hallmark of Anglicanism since the seventeenth century. He promised that he was "more committed than ever to defend this treasure of comprehensiveness from those who would reduce it to a single voice and point of view, usually theirs."

Some bishops pointed to what they saw as a contradiction underlying the decisions on sexuality. Bishop Martin Townsend of Easton said that the report coming out of the sub-section represented an honest attempt to find common ground and "from the outset, conservatives were pleased with the statement as affirming their core convictions about human sexuality, marriage, and chastity."

Fully intending to endorse their difficult and painful work, Townsend changed his mind when he saw the changes in the resolution in plenary debate. He became "increasingly saddened by the politicization of the process and the tone of the argument." Even though he was encouraged by the commitment to "listen to the experience of homosexual people," he found himself wondering how that was possible "when our minds are already made up." So he joined the minority voting against the resolution.

"At Lambeth there was an implicit taboo against saying anything critical of the African Church," Townsend said. "Its phenomenal evangelical success in the face of serious persecution has placed it above reproach. Yet one Nigerian bishop in my group, thirty-five years old, conceded that polygamous marriages do happen after people become Christian. He went on to say that the church cannot afford to discipline them because they are usually village leaders. The other Nigerian bishop and the Kenyan bishop in the group agreed that such things happen." He concluded, "Clearly, how the faith gets lived out is culturally influenced."

Townsend echoed the concern for the nature of authority and how Anglicans make decisions. "Biblical scholarship as I

Another Lambeth first: episcopal husbands. L to r: Ian Jamieson of New Zealand, David Dixon of Washington, Larry Waynick of Indianapolis, Mac McLeod of Vermont, and Philip Roskam of New York.
(Photo: Jeff Sells, *Anglican World*)

studied it in seminary and ever since had no place in the debates at Lambeth. Our Anglican basis of authority is in the process of being narrowed in ways that are decidedly un-Anglican. For the moment, at least, Lambeth has said we want uniformity. How this will play out over time and in issues other than sexuality is yet to be known." Describing himself as a centrist, Townsend said that he did not want to lose that "discomforting part of our tradition that comes into our conversations from both the left and the right."

Bishop Gary Gloster of North Carolina, responding to a survey by Louie Crew on how the American bishops voted, watched during the debate on the sexuality resolution as it was reduced to "negative, judgmental, and exclusionary language. This became not a debate on an issue, but an assault on individuals and friends back home who are faithful followers of Jesus Christ. The laughter, the hisses, and the derogatory slurs that accompanied and punctuated the discussion made the plenary hall for me a climate of hostility that wanted victory at all costs." In the conviction that "hostility is not eased by a vote in which winners and losers are created," he said that he abstained. "My abstention was a vote for unity within diversity."

In reaching for the fullness of Christ, "We cannot let ourselves sink to any level of bigotry, intolerance, demonizing or self-righteous exclusion. It must be that we hang in there with the ultimate weapon—love. This is what will change the world."

MORAL UGLINESS

The differences in the interpretation of Scripture also bothered Bishop Clark Grew of Ohio. He characterized the debate on sexuality as "moral ugliness" and said that many conservative American bishops agreed with that characterization. "For the first time, I could really understand the fear with which some gay and lesbian people live every day, and I return to Ohio more deeply committed to having our church be truly inclusive, a church where no person is excluded or oppressed because of a particular biblical interpretation."

"Our experience at Lambeth let us know, at every level, that there is a great variety of biblical and theological understanding in our church that is probably being stretched as much today, and maybe more, than at any other time," observed Bishop Vincent Warner of Olympia. The identity question loomed large and, in his column on Lambeth for the diocesan newspaper, he wrote, "As we face a new millennium, one of the real questions is who will we be as a Communion together..." and "what is the place of the American church in relation to that Communion?"

At an early morning meeting at Lambeth, the bishops from the Episcopal Church met with Presiding Bishop Griswold and his chaplain, the Rev. Martin Smith of the Society of St. John the Evangelist. Smith said that each of the bishops had taken mental pictures of the conference to be put in developing solution, and our picture negatives would need time to be processed." He admitted that, for him, the picture is "still fuzzy."

Bishop Sandy Hampton, the Suffragan Bishop of Olympia, said that he was "not prepared for the anti-United States feeling and attitudes" he encountered. When he raised the issue with his study group, they told him that whoever was on top was likely to be a natural target. The group said there is "much hostility left from the Cold War in developing nations, particularly Africa, when the U.S. supported dictators in the name of anti-communism." And there is some resentment towards the Episcopal Church in the U.S.A. "which seems to think it is ahead on all issues facing the church and it is up to others to catch up."

WHIFF OF RACISM

Bishop Terence Kelshaw of the Rio Grande also picked up whiffs of racism during the debate. "I was there and I heard and saw no hate or condemnation other than the angry outbursts of racism from American bishops who were clearly annoyed that their ideological icon was being ignored," he said.

In an interview with the *Rocky Mountain News*, Bishop Jerry Winterrowd of Colorado said that he made a strictly pragmatic decision in voting for the resolution on sexuality. A long-time supporter of gay rights, he voted with the majority in condemning homosexual activity. "Frankly, the African church needed that vote to take back with them," he said. "They are under a great deal of pressure politically because the Muslims are watching."

Winterrowd rejected the suggestion that his vote was inconsistent with his own reading of Scripture or his position on issues in Colorado, where he chaired a governor's commission recommending legal rights for same-sex unions, according to the newspaper. "I think God intended heterosexual marriage, but the reality we live with is that some people cannot live that way," he said. Arguing that "God speaks with a local accent" and that homosexuality is not a matter of right or wrong, he said, "I don't believe that Scripture necessarily condemns homosexuality." As a step towards reconciliation, he announced that he plans to invite African bishops to Colorado so they can observe for themselves "committed and faithful" gay relationships.

In a letter from Lambeth, Bishop Jack Iker of Ft. Worth said that he and the traditionalists hoped, among their major agenda items, for "some provision for the possible removal from the Anglican Communion of any province whose actions go beyond the acceptable limitations of Anglicanism and thus imperil the unity of the Communion."

Iker and Stanton of Dallas held several open forums to discuss the implications of Lambeth after they returned to their dioceses.

In a gathering at Trinity Church in Ft. Worth following an earlier appearance in Dallas, the bishops said the "arrogance of the Episcopal Church is out of control" and that Lambeth had sent a clear message to the Episcopal Church to repent and "foreswear its foolish ways."

In light of Lambeth Resolution III.2 on the ordination of women, Iker called on Presiding Bishop Frank Griswold to take action. He asked Griswold "to exercise his leadership as chief pastor in front of his church and declare that [the canon requiring all dioceses to open the ordination process to women] is not in keeping with the best of Anglicanism and contrary to the great expressed will of the whole Communion and will not be enforced."

Iker said that "the reasonable thing for the Episcopal Church to do is admit they made a mistake and retract the changes they made." Yet he admitted "that's not going to happen. The arrogance of the Episcopal Church is so beyond control, there's not going to be any reconsideration."

Stanton characterized the Lambeth Conference as a Spirit-filled meeting that gave "joyful, powerful, and unified witness...to what the future holds. It began to define the center and the circumference out of which they [liberals in the church] move at their peril."

Iker said that the conference "is a wake-up call to the Episcopal Church in the U.S.A." For him the question was whether the Episcopal Church is "humble enough to hear what the Communion has appeared to say." He is convinced that the conference "has reminded us that we are answerable to one another, that what we say and teach and preach and legislate in this country affects brother and sister Anglicans all over the world. It is a communion of mutual accountability and we, as the Episcopal Church, must avoid turning our backs on the Communion. If we do, we do so at our own peril."

BUYING VOTES?

Stanton heatedly repudiated what he saw as attempts by liberals in the secular media and the Episcopal Church to downplay the importance of the vote on sexuality. He said that he was "tired of spin" and resented reports that he had bought votes on the sexuality resolution.

"No vote needed to be bought," he said. The overwhelming vote "tells me that there were some people who didn't like this phrase or that, but when it came down to the wire, that house accepted the whole statement." He pointed out that the vote was not a split between north and south—that it carried with majorities in the United States, England, Canada, and Australia. Lambeth made it clear, he said, that "diversity does not mean there are no limits to what provinces can do and still claim to be in communion."

Iker, clearly elated by the experience at Lambeth, said that he came back to his diocese "renewed, reenergized, and enthusiastic" about his ministry. "For the first time in my six years as bishop, I voted with the majority on every issue, even the one resolution dealing with the ordination of women. It was a good feeling." One night when he was out celebrating the unfolding of events at Lambeth, he realized that "this is the way liberals must feel every night at our General Convention. And so now the shoe is on the other foot."

When he heard reports that the American liberal bishops were "hurt, discouraged, despondent, and so forth, I said, 'Yeah, I know exactly where they are because I'm there on a regular basis at the General Convention and at meetings of the House of Bishops.'"

Dismissing some claims in the press that "this is a victory for the conservatives or the traditionalists triumphing over the liberals or whatever," Iker said, "It is nothing more and nothing less than a clear proclamation of biblical truth and the historic faith of the Anglican Church....No longer does the United States or England speak for the Anglican Communion but the church in Africa and Asia does." He returned with a new appreciation for the cultural diversity of Anglicanism but as one rooted in orthodox biblical theology. "For me the Lambeth Conference was a proclamation of Anglican identity."

Iker contended that the Presiding Bishop of the Episcopal Church "is obligated to lead this church in seeing that there is no persecution of orthodox, traditional people and to provide episcopal ministry for congregations in places where they are isolated and ignored and marginalized because of their position on this issue. I think that we'll have flying bishops in the Episcopal Church as the result of the Lambeth resolution." He cited as an example the Suffragan Bishop for the Armed Forces, who "travels all over the United States, across diocesan boundaries, visiting all our military chaplains."

Any kind of presentment or charges against bishops who continue to oppose the ordination of women would result in a "rallying of bishops around the world...to protect him," said Stanton, to loud applause.

"The Africans came determined to speak their minds, and when it was all over, it was clear they had done so," said Bishop John Howe of Central Florida, a leading conservative. The votes at Lambeth will put the debates in the American church into what he called "a very different perspective."

"This Lambeth Conference has demonstrated beyond any possible argument that those of orthodox persuasion are in the very mainstream of Anglicanism, and the extremists are those who have chosen an agenda to the contrary. Should they make good on their vows to continue that agenda, despite the decisions of Lambeth, there is little doubt they will find themselves increasingly isolated and out of communion with many of the other provinces around the world," Howe said.

Archbishop Keith Rayner of Australia would agree with Iker that "this Lambeth will go down as one that called the church back to a stronger biblical basis." Yet he also observed, in a column in the diocesan newspaper, that "for some it was accompanied by a naïve assumption that it is easy to secure agreement on how the Bible is to be interpreted." He said that would be "an urgent task for the coming decade."

At a sermon opening a meeting of his synod following Lambeth, Rayner implied that the church was moving towards more openness to homosexual relationships, using the example of the acceptance of women in the priesthood and a change of policy on divorce. The change came "because human experience leads us to reflect more deeply on the biblical material," leading to a recognition of "real signs of God's blessing of many marriages contracted after a divorce. A similar process occurred in the decision about the ordination of women," he said.

"We recognize among the people whose orientation is homosexual, and who do not believe they are called to celibacy, there are members of the church whose Christian character and pastoral gifts we respect," Rayner said. "All of this raises the question, may it be that God has called us to review the received tradition?"

Any move towards the acceptance of homosexuals must rule out promiscuity, Rayner argued, because "to treat promiscuous relationships as normal and acceptable would be contrary to the Christian ethic and damaging to human society." And he concluded that "any conclusion we come to about homosexual relationships must be consistent with our understanding of heterosexual relationships and be part of a coherent Christian understanding of sexual ethics."

CANADIAN REACTION

In comments after returning to their dioceses, Canadian bishops said in an article in the *Anglican Journal* that they were upset by the tone of the debate on sexuality.

While admitting that the final resolution "reflects pretty much where we are in the guidelines" in the Anglican Church of Canada, Bishop Caleb Lawrence of Moosonee noted that the debate was full of a kind of passion and homophobia that was offensive, even to the conservative Canadian bishops.

"We are at another stage in the journey," said Bishop Terence Finlay of Toronto. In comments the day after the vote, he said that he was "just appalled. I've got lots of anger." He said that gays and lesbians "must be feeling just totally as if they've been written off, totally rejected."

In a diary he sent to his diocesan newspaper, Finlay shared his impression of Lambeth as "an amazing experience, with heart-breaking stories from the persecuted churches in Pakistan and the Sudan," expressing the "wonder of the cultural diversity and inter-connectedness of our global church."

Yet he said "that diversity comes with a price when cultures meet head-to-head in discussions of issues and attitudes."

Finlay said that in the sub-section dealing with homosexuality he encountered "bitter, hate-filled language," arguing that the organizers of the conference "had greatly underestimated the division that occurred." He deplored the encounter between Richard Kirker of the Lesbian and Gay Christian Movement and the Nigerian bishop who tried to exorcise him. He said, "It was disgraceful behavior by bishops who saw gay and lesbian people as less than human."

In addressing the bishops of Section One, he said, "I need to tell you that, in the past few days some will have difficulty with our resolution on human sexuality. But many will be greatly offended by the reported behavior of some of my fellow bishops. The image of a bishop shaking his fist at a young gay Christian and trying to exorcise another, is appalling." He said, "Our Anglican Communion has been wounded by such words—deep offense has been given."

Finlay's diocese, the largest in North America, has a large homosexual population, many of them Anglican. "I'm really sad for the characterization that has taken place of the relationships of gays and lesbians who are members of our congregations. It's a complete travesty." He said that the subsection, where he joined about fifty members of widely varying viewpoints, "stood and sang the doxology" when they were able to unanimously approve the report.

Bishop Victoria Matthews of Edmonton said that the provision for continuing dialogue was especially important. "If followed, we can never have this conversation again," suggesting that the issue will not be the same kind of issue at the next Lambeth.

And Archbishop David Crawley of British Columbia called the debate "disgraceful."

Suffragan Bishop Michael Bedford-Jones of Toronto said he found the debate "emotionally very difficult because friends in and out of the church, and colleagues in the church, were being talked about without their being present." He noted that, in the Canadian House of Bishops, "we try to speak as if gay and lesbian people are present. Our church in Canada has worked very, very hard at listening," he said. "For us, the debate is far from closed."

Bishop Michael Ingham of Vancouver, who accompanied Peers when the Primate walked out of the plenary before the final vote on sexuality but returned later, had a more generous assessment of Lambeth, reporting that what was most striking by the assembly of bishops, theologians, and ecumenical partners from 167 countries was "the air of confidence in the Gospel. While the challenges facing the church were openly stated, and in some ways deepened, there was nevertheless a sense of undiminished confidence in the Christian faith, which for me was unforgettable." And he attributed that to the presence of the Third World bishops and their spouses. Their clear message to the churches of the West is "that we should regain our spiritual nerve, move from a model of survival to one of mission, root ourselves firmly in the biblical and apostolic faith, and believe in miracles."

In describing the work of the conference, Ingham said that "in the area of interfaith dialogue and relations with people of other faiths, this was perhaps the most progressive Lambeth Conference ever," because it "acknowledged the reality of our religiously plural world, affirmed dialogue as the way forward, and rejected proselytism among other faiths."

The convergence and agreement so apparent in much of the conference broke down over the issue of homosexuality. "Lambeth is a mosaic of cultures, languages, histories, and anxieties—and they all surfaced in this subject. It was clear that there is a passionate and intractable conviction among the majority of bishops that homosexual activity is not to be tolerated."

Ingham agreed with others who said they were worried by "a clear tendency toward biblical fundamentalism, a use of Scripture in uncritical and even uncharitable ways that was evident in sermons at the daily Eucharist and in discussions at the daily Bible studies. It was as if the last 150 years of biblical theology and academic research had never happened for many participants."

When asked in an interview what he saw as the long-term ramifications of Lambeth, Ingham was conspicuously more pessimistic. "The religious right triumphed completely, and the next generation belongs to them. Liberalism in the Anglican Communion is dead, and those of us who are liberal will either have to leave or become a remnant witnessing back to the church a dimension of the Gospel that it is not now willing to hear." He said that most liberals are now "powerless and voiceless."

Ingham does not see a resurgence of centrist or liberal tradition any time soon. He said that some of the Canadian bishops even wondered if they could continue in the church—and there are conservatives who would be happy to see them go. "Something central and vital to Anglicanism would be lost," he said.

In a later interview with Ecumenical News International (ENI), Ingham tried to clarify his comments by arguing that Lambeth "rejected the liberal tradition within Anglicanism but I don't think it died—it certainly had a rough time at the Lambeth Conference." He added, "Lambeth is not the whole of Anglicanism. What I was trying to get at was that the fullness of the Anglican tradition was not heard at Lambeth."

As many of his colleagues did in their efforts to interpret Lambeth, Ingham said that "the developing world is very conservative. I distinguish between fundamentalism and conservative evangelicalism. It is clear that at Lambeth, the only Third World voices that were heard were conservative evangelical voices. In fact, many people said that it was the Church Missionary Society (CMS) Lambeth. The Society for Propagating the Gospel (SPG)—the more high church, catholic missionary society that also evangelizes much of the developing world—was largely unheard from," he said.

Ingham told ENI that he considers himself a "post-liberal" Christian because "liberalism has become associated with a sort of secularizing Christianity" that he could not support. As a "progressive Anglican" he expressed annoyance in the way that the religious right uses the term "orthodox." He said, "Many of us who are sympathetic to issues of full inclusion resent the sort of intellectual theft of the word orthodoxy by the religious right," adding that "orthodoxy cannot be equated simply with modern conservative Protestantism." His kind of orthodoxy includes "the centrality of the incarnation of Jesus Christ and its implications for pastoral openness to the world in all its diversity."

WALL OF REALITY

Patrick Mauney, the Episcopal Church's director of Anglican and Global Relations who was a consultant at Lambeth, said that the romantic view many bishops held of the Lambeth

Conference ran into a wall of reality. "They soon found out what kind of a Communion we really are."

Mauney dismissed the notion that the level of theological education would have made a difference in the vote on the sexuality resolution. "Most of these bishops, including those from Africa, are articulate, highly educated bishops who happen to uphold a conservative evangelical view of the Bible. And we must recognize that." He said that it is patronizing and demeaning to say that upgrading theological education will take care of those differences.

When asked whether this is the result of mission efforts of the last few centuries, Mauney, himself a former missionary to Brazil, said, "This is what the Christian Missionary Society hath wrought."

After a few days at a Trappist monastery near Dubuque, Bishop Christopher Epting of Iowa wrote his column for the diocesan newspaper. "It is amazing, but I suppose altogether predictable, that in spite of the incredibly important work done there and the virtual unanimity the bishops found around global issues affecting the world and the church, most attention here at home has been on two resolutions on which there was the least consensus among us—these involved homosexuality and the on-going reception process concerning the ordination of women."

Convinced that "faithful and monogamous, life-long unions, while difficult, provide the best model for responsible sexual activity," Epting said that it was his personal belief that "the church must find a way to offer God's blessing upon Christian people—gay and straight—who seek such a life for the sake of Christ." Yet it is clear to him that the Episcopal Church "while moving in that direction, was a long way from consensus on the matter."

Epting said that he abstained from the vote on the sexuality resolution at Lambeth because "I thought it did not honor the work of those who had struggled so faithfully to produce an original draft and because I could not agree with some of its premises and implications." He said that he signed the pastoral letter to gay and lesbian Anglicans "who I know would be experiencing hurt by some of what was said and done at Lambeth."

Despite his personal convictions, Epting said that as a bishop he would not "teach or authorize officially that which this church does not teach or authorize." As a result, he does not permit the blessing of same-sex relationships, but he said that he would not consider homosexual orientation "an absolute impediment to ordination." In considering the strengths and weaknesses of all candidates for ordination, he and the diocesan committees would seek those who are striving for holiness and righteousness and "doing their best to pattern their lives in accordance with the teachings of Christ" so that they may be wholesome examples.

Telling his diocese that he voted with the majority on the sexual resolution despite being "unhappy with some of the language," Bishop Peter James Lee of Virginia said that though it used "language more strident than we have used in Virginia, [it] nonetheless affirmed our long-standing policy in the Diocese of Virginia...."

While "sexuality captured the headlines," Lee said that several resolutions were "of more lasting significance." He cited those which called on Anglicans "to examine greater roles for the Archbishop of Canterbury and the Primates' Meeting in further strengthening the bonds of unity among the thirty-eight autonomous churches of our Communion." And he said that the Virginia Report made "a significant contribution to the development of theological reflection on our unity in diversity." He also included the attention given to Christian-Muslim relations and international debt as very important for the future of the church.

Bishop Robert Shahan of Arizona said that Lambeth "mirrored our experience of the church in this country as we, in places other than Arizona, work through a series of resolutions that can only express our divisions rather than our unity.

"The debate on the various resolutions was not really a debate, or even a discussion," he said. "It was rather a series of individual speeches standing between the introduction of the resolution and the foregone conclusion that would be the outcome." He is convinced that "resolutions do not convert or convince: they only take inventory of the already held opinions of the participants in the meeting. Lambeth was no different in that regard."

Shahan said that his vote against the final resolution "was as much a protest against the speeches that were made in the debate as on the motion itself. Frankly, I heard comments and statements that afternoon that were embarrassingly disrespectful of other Christians as well as being filled with a kind of self-righteousness that I find it hard to endure."

In an attempt to "speak a word of hope and reconciliation" in his diocese, in February Shahan wrote a pastoral letter. He remembered that, in the time prior to his election, people expressed concern over his position on the ordination of noncelibate homosexuals and blessing of same-sex relationships.

After Lambeth he said that he had "never quite understood why the issue of homosexuality and related matters is of such concern to certain people. It sometimes seems as if one's own salvation is only possible by keeping the church safe from people who differ from us in this way....The politics have come from both sides of the question and both have made reasonable conversation difficult. I have had about enough of it....I tire of the righteousness that is not of God. I tire of a proclamation that is harsh, judgmental and calls forth that same kind of judgmental posture from those who disagree. It creates its own environment in which there is not love, mercy, acceptance, hope, grace or holiness."

He said that he continues to support order and obedience within the church, but that he would, "when given the opportunity, speak and vote in favor of a more inclusive community that more closely reflects what this servant of God believes to be the Gospel teaching of our Savior Jesus Christ....I will seek to move the church to ordain and to call forth those among us whom we deem to be healthy, without regard to sexual orientation or identity...I will not act alone or precipitously but I also will not allow the wholesale condemnation of homosexuality to go unchallenged in Arizona."

But he said that it is not possible to bless same-sex relationships. "That is not to say that same-sex persons cannot live in committed relationships which are a blessing to both persons. I know and have known many such persons who are in long-term relationships. I just believe that 'marriage' is not the right symbol of blessing for them...We should not refuse to bless a relationship of monogamous love and life-long commitment in a church that blesses animals, boats, cars, buildings, candles, pieces of cloth and, basically 'anything whatsoever,' as it says in the *Manual for Priests*." He anticipates a time and a way "to bless those who wish to have a relationship set apart in holiness. Some kind of covenant is appropriate, and I can see this applying to many relationships."

In a letter to the London *Times*, Bishop David Jenkins, the Church of England's most radical bishop when he served at Durham, said that Lambeth voted "to face the moral issues of the twenty-first century on the basis of an unreflective return to the traditions of the sixteenth and seventeenth."

Sounding a lot like Spong, Jenkins said, "Those who are more moved by fear [rather] than full of faith, together with Third World bishops who have not yet faced up to irreversible developments in biblical, historical, and scientific criticism, have prevailed." Yet he added "even the church cannot keep a living God down. We must not allow mistaken fashions for fundamentalisms, whether in Judaism, Christianity, or Islam, to force us to atheism. Jesus is too decisive a clue to the reality, risk, and love of God, and all human beings are potentially worth far too much for that."

Presiding Bishop Frank Griswold said that he abstained from the vote on sexuality "because I found parts of the resolution positive both in tone and content, particularly when considered in relationship to the nuances of the report on which it is based." Yet he objected to other parts and urged the church to "explore more fully the whole question of what is compatible and incompatible with Scripture." He issued a letter to the Episcopal Church on August 14, offering a "pastoral word" on the vote and pledging himself to "do everything I can to foster a climate of frank and respectful conversation which will allow different points of view to address and hear one another...."

Bishop Charles Keyser, Suffragan Bishop for the Armed Forces, said in an interview that he experienced "a great sense of sadness" when he realized "how far we were from each other on significant issues, especially what it means to be fully human." During the debate on the homosexuality resolution "the bottom fell out and I knew that we were in deep trouble." He said that he voted for the amended resolution, as a way of honoring the sub-section process and its report which was more "pastorally sensitive." But he voted against the "unnecessary and imprecise" amendment that said sexual activity is contrary to Scripture, but also signed the open letter written by Bishop Haines as his pledge "to listen, reflect, pray, and work that the church become truly open to all," he said in a letter to all active duty chaplains. "I do not believe that God is finished with his revelation regarding human sexuality to the church, and he certainly isn't finished with me," Keyser wrote.

As the only Caucasian in his Bible study group, Keyser said that he found it difficult to talk about the apathy experienced by Christians in the West. "They didn't understand the pain of being a Christian in the developed world, the secularity, the casual attitudes towards sex, the commercialization, the denigration of the spiritual," he said. "What does the Gospel mean to affluent people who think that they have everything they need?" Keyser asked. Like others, he found it difficult to talk across the cultural divide and mutual understanding took a great deal of common effort. Many bishops, for example, found it difficult to understand a ministry to the military because "they had no understanding of civilian control of the military," he said. "For them the military had a very threatening connotation because they had no concept of a benevolent military—or that a military chaplaincy would be controlled by the church."

Keyser predicted that the blatant political maneuvering at Lambeth could backfire, energizing the moderates. "It could energize those who are centrists, in the middle of the church, who just about reached the end of their patience at Lambeth," he said. "And the base of our collegiality is strong enough to permit disagreements—although Lambeth may be a wake-up call for the American bishops to continue their work on collegiality," he said.

Speaking to his province's synod after Lambeth, Tutu said, "We all left Canterbury aware of a deepened unity precisely because of our diversity. We gloried in a renewed sense of the nature of comprehensiveness....Each province is autonomous and should do what it believes is true and consistent with the Gospel and tradition of the church, and let provinces respect whatever decision other provinces arrived at."

In comments widely shared, Martin Smith of Massachusetts told his religious community on returning from Lambeth, "The Archbishop of Canterbury has made no secret of the threats made by certain bishops from Southeast Asia and Africa in particular not only to walk out of the Lambeth Conference but to break up the Communion unless there was a condemnation of homosexual practice. He saw his role as preventing that split and believes he succeeded. It was blackmail," he charged.

"Homosexuals serve as ideal symbols of what is alien, and this stigmatization was eagerly encouraged by a very active group of American conservative propagandists, with lots of money to spend, who occupied a command center in one of the residences on campus, fomenting and encouraging this movement of collective blackmail," Smith said. "The few bishops who spoke up for the gay and lesbian reality were literally hissed, and denounced in angry whispers as racists and imperialists, for if you supported gays you were opposing the witness of the Third World bishops defending purity and scriptural authority," he added.

"But the main shock of this Lambeth Conference was the discovery that Anglicans are going to find it difficult to pretend that from now on we have a common theological method to arrive at truth together," Smith said.

Bishop Paul Barnett of Australia thinks that the seeds of division are already evident in bishops providing oversight for parishes in other provinces. If that kind of trend continues it could lead to the "unraveling of the Anglican Communion." He said "homosexuality is a diversity we can't live with. There are two integrities in the church. They are both reading biblical texts differently. The two views cannot be held together in one church."

In a reflection, the Rev. Mark Harris of Wilmington, Delaware, expressed his deep concern that the conference "could attempt to determine just who was in communion with the gathered bishops when they met as a group," going so far as to suggest that "certain bishops be called on to repent or leave," giving the Lambeth Conference "a council function that it does not have."

The bishops are invited by the Archbishop of Canterbury "to communion together, to supper," an invitation that does not allow the guests to decide who is acceptable. That would feed persistent fears that "the conference might indeed become a council and might try to determine by whatever means necessary to correct doctrine or discipline." It could even "adapt certain resolutions that would provide a litmus test for future inclusion in the Communion," he added, suggesting that the Kuala Lumpur statement had been offered as one possibility.

Addressing the rumors of a walkout, Harris said, "The idea is that the really successful, growing, and vibrant part of the Communion could leave and take the 'real' church with it, leaving only the empty shell of the degenerate West behind," faced with the prospect that it must "clean up its act and repent."

While arguing that life on the local level would continue no matter what the conference decided, "If bishops in this church come home more hesitant to embrace those who the conference was hesitant to touch, the conference will have been a disaster. If they come home more concerned to regulate right thinking than to embrace new dreams, the conference will have done us a wrong."

The Rev. Jennifer Phillips told her parish in St. Louis, "Only in the local community resides the knowledge to discern how God's faithfulness is being answered in individual lives and households. The Holy Spirit equips us for this work of discipline and blessing. Such discernment cannot be done in the abstract, about whole classes of people, but only in real, particular lives known in the community."

She concluded a sermon encouraging those who disagreed with the Lambeth resolution, "Take heart. Do not be afraid. The church belongs to all of us and we belong to Christ. It is not in the power of bishops to alter that truth nor to tell us how we shall pray about our lives," she said. "The prayer of the Holy Spirit rises up in us, and it will be heard. This congregation will continue to bless God for our lives, gay and straight, black and white, rich and poor, coupled and single, sinners all and all redeemed; and we will not be silent about what God is accomplishing among us."

For an Anglo-Catholic like the Rev. Canon Douglas Williams, "It is no light matter to go against a teaching of the bishops of the church, especially when set forth by such an overwhelming majority. Fortunately, the decisions of the Lambeth Conference, however weighty their influence, are not binding in conscience." Yet for him "it is only with immense pain and distress that I speak as I have in reaction to a teaching of our bishops." Just as the abuse of law was used to suppress blacks and enforce segregation in the South, "In the late 1990s, Scripture is still being used to deny the reality of our gay and lesbian brothers and sisters. Such use of the Scriptures brings the Scriptures into disrepute. Such biblical interpretation by bishops of the church is intolerable," he said in a sermon at Trinity Cathedral in San Jose.

The Rev. David Monteith, curate of St. Martin in the Fields parish in central London, said in the parish's weekly bulletin that "despite all my attempts to dismiss Lambeth as a waste of money or a 'talking shop,' I realized that what bishops said and stood for mattered...because they are physical reminders of the universal and global fellowship of the church..." and "reminders that Anglicanism is based on principles of conciliarity, not collegiality or uniform coherence." He concluded, "We are bound to the real, sharp discipline required to seek the mind of Christ in a church which has to be untidy if it is to be any way related to real human life."

In a letter to his diocesan newspaper, Mark Mammann of Western North Carolina expressed anger and disappointment with what he saw as the "us-versus-them" tone of Carey's statements at the end of the conference. And he asked, "Are our bishops afraid to take a bold stand against hypocrisy and bigotry? Are they afraid to voice disagreement, disappointment and/or questioning to the archbishop?"

He said that he joined the Episcopal Church thirteen years ago because of its efforts to be inclusive but realized that "if the church ever took a stand to divide its children that this would be hypocrisy and I would have to question if this was truly a church of God." He added, "As an individual living on the edge of life with AIDS, God's gift through this illness has been the opening of my eyes to what and who are true and what is false and idol worship."

In a more moderate but no less critical tone, a priest who has worked for reconciliation in some of the most troubled situations in Africa wrote to Carey and said that "the conference's document on homosexuality is an act of aggression towards a defenseless people and will probably haunt you and your leadership for the rest of your life. It will, unfortunately, be the document that your primacy will be remembered by," said the Rev. Albert Ogle, president of The Stones Network, which sponsors international programs for reconciliation and community health, mostly in Africa.

DENIAL AND DEATH

Ogle's letter reminded Carey that at Lambeth in 1988 "a chorus of African bishops," led by Archbishop Yona Okoth of Uganda, "told the Anglican Communion, in no uncertain terms, that they did not have AIDS in Africa. Their denial, in no uncertain terms, was an unfortunate contributing factor to the carnage and pain which would soon wreak havoc in their own households. Yona lost his driver, who committed suicide when he discovered he was HIV positive. He also lost his favorite grandson, his six-month-old great-granddaughter and her mother, countless clergy and friends within five years of speaking so boldly" at Lambeth. Yet the tragedies led to "a kind of conversion experience" and Okoth spent the rest of his tenure in efforts to educate his people.

As one of the few gay priests most African bishops have met, Ogle said that "it was painful to read about the way in which the Anglican bishops talked about me and my gay and lesbian sisters and brothers." He admitted that he was "partly responsible for the ignorance of the Ugandan bishops because I was more concerned about helping them with immediate issues in their dioceses rather than discussing gay issues." He said he was now determined "to enter into a deeper dialogue with them—and I need your support and encouragement.

"We have compromised in Anglicanism on everything from polygamy for Africans to divorce for westerners, and is there no room on the rickety old three-legged stool" of Scripture, tradition, and reason "for gay Christians?" Ogle asked. "The Lambeth Conference was the culmination of a protracted 'philosophical and theological arms deal,'" he said, adding that he had observed African bishops being used "to spread a gospel of homophobia in the U.S.A. at the invitation of some American bishops." And he drew a parallel to the complicity of some Anglican bishops in the tragedy of genocide in Rwanda.

Lambeth has "created a moment in history when the church provided the theological and moral weaponry to those who would destroy us," Ogle charged, warning Carey that the resolution would be used against gay and lesbian Christians. He told of a Rwandan bishop gloating in his comments at a Eucharist that the Africans had kept homosexuals out of the church, not realizing that a lesbian was participating in the leadership of the service with him. "We are undermining our own ability to be agents of reconciliation," Ogle warned, because Lambeth "raised more questions and doubts about our ability to be an agent of reconciliation when we are so bitterly divided and as full of hatred and fear as the tribes we attempt to unite."

In his letter of response, Carey bristled at the genocide reference, telling Ogle that he found the parallel between what happened in Rwanda and "the treatment meted out to homosexuals following the Lambeth Conference resolution quite difficult to take."

Carey said that, during his travels, he had witnessed the valuable ministries by homosexuals, a ministry that "is in no way invalidated by their sexual orientation." Lambeth did not even suggest that there would be any form of persecution or "witch hunt" against homosexuals.

The decision by the bishops at Lambeth was an attempt to "stand back from two particular issues about which there continues to be considerable disagreement within the Anglican Communion—that is the ordination of people in a homosexual relationship and the blessing of same sex unions." The bishops made it clear that their reading of Scripture precludes homosexual practice. "That is a matter of biblical interpretation and one of the strong messages which came out of Lambeth was that this is an area in which the Communion must do more work together."

The Archbishop also argued in his letter that the issue is now clearly on the agenda of the Anglican Communion and the final resolution "is a considerable achievement in the face of alternatives, which were very aggressively anti-homosexual."

The Rev. Jan Nunley, trying to interpret Lambeth to her congregation in Rhode Island, said, "For the sake of unity, bishops kept silent while the lives and loves of people they know, and from whose ministries they have benefited, were dragged through the slime of outrageous assertions and derisive laughter. They failed utterly to interpret the present time in time to prevent the scapegoating of their friends and neighbors and brothers and sisters."

Nunley added a word of encouragement, reminding her congregation that "we are called to endure....If we do not endure, if we give up in despair or anger, we hand the victory over to darkness instead." She said that some "want to quit the Episcopal Church or the Anglican Communion or even Christianity itself over what happened at Lambeth." She said she saw the conference as "the blast of a trumpet" calling on people to work for a church that "is purified of hate and prejudice and fear—starting here, starting now."

A gay man who found a welcome in an Episcopal church in Arizona that provided him with "an open and loving church that made me feel quite secure in my thoughts that I had indeed found the gospel of love within the Anglican Communion" wrote an open letter to the Lambeth bishops. "The events at Lambeth have ripped and shredded that security and that belief," he said, asking "that my name be removed from the membership rolls." He said he was joining a United Church of Christ congregation that welcomes gays and lesbians.

The Rev. Tom Scott of Evanston, Illinois, addressed the matter in a sermon. While admitting that some in his parish welcomed the action of Lambeth, "Many of our lesbian and gay members and friends, on the other hand, are devastated. Some here are like me, straight but not narrow as the saying goes, and we are troubled and heartsick at what has happened in our beloved church," he said. A New York friend suggested that "those of us who feel like the lepers of Lambeth and those who want to show solidarity with them use the medieval leper's bell to signal our presence to the world and each other."

A gay Republican from California wrote to Carey, Griswold, and Spong "to express my gravest concern over the lack of leadership displayed in allowing the passage of the resolution." He said that it would "add fuel to the fires of bigotry that gay and lesbian people face. There is absolutely no reason that a more moderate resolution could not have been issued," said John Chase.

Writing from her parish in Wisconsin, the Rev. Debra Trakel related a difficult encounter with a conservative couple who came to her office after services to ask how the Lambeth resolution would affect efforts to talk their gay son into coming back to church. And while planning the funeral of a prominent member of the church, she tried to coax the man's daughter and her partner into coming to church. "Through her fresh grief she told me that she had really wanted to come back to church. She loved the Episcopal Church. It was the church of her heart. But now, with the vote, she just couldn't and hoped that I would understand. She didn't want to expose her partner to the pain."

RELIGION OF FEAR

The Rev. Robert McCloskey told his parish in Florida that he ran into a "religion of fear, full blast" at Lambeth. He said in his sermon that "this tradition called Anglicanism which we all embrace and cherish—perhaps too much at times—is presently in the grips of a religious fundamentalism" that "finds its support in a biblical literalism which we thought could never be reconciled to mainstream scriptural scholarship and interpretation; and it dominated and pervaded the agenda of the bishops. It is not a pretty picture and like all religion of fear it found its scapegoats...in homosexuals; and it imposed condemnation, ignorance, fear, and anger with a vengeance as spiritually and emotionally murderous and maiming as the physical terrorism of the embassy bombings" in Kenya and Tanzania.

McCloskey, who ran the Marketplace at Lambeth, added, "The antidote to fundamentalism is a clear grasp of the vision which compels and calls us forward. The God revealed in Jesus is too accepting, embracing, and affirming to be reduced to the fear of fundamentalism—be it in the hands of bomb-throwers or purple-shirted prelates exhibiting their own lack of faith and hope."

"For the whole of my ordained life, the growing edge of Anglican Christianity everywhere has been theologically orthodox," noted the Rev. Richard Kew. Speaking as an evangelical, who was in the minority when he was ordained in the Church of England in 1964, he said that the future belongs to evangelicals. "The challenge before the western churches is how we should function as Anglicans in a global family of churches where we are no longer the leader. While not necessarily bowing to the will of the majority, it is reprehensible not to listen to their voice and respect their circumstances." And he said that, in an era of easy communications, "those in the U.S.A. who want to flaunt their individuality should think very carefully about the consequences. Today's foolish ordination, word, or act will probably be used against fellow Anglicans in Nigeria or Sudan tomorrow."

Anticipating what he called "a lot of hiding behind deconstructionist notions of diversities of truths" and the insistence that "our circumstances are different than those elsewhere," Kew concluded, "If this is the way those bent on revising the faith will go in the U.S.A., then they have plotted a course out of Anglicanism. They will also have condemned the rump of the Episcopal Church to being a small and shrinking American sect, a pathetic and compromised aging beauty."

"Maybe this Lambeth Conference has taught us the valuable lesson that Anglican Christianity is not a sub-section of middle-class, middle-England liberalism, but that some parts of the Anglican Church retain the uncomfortable commitment and fire of the New Testament," said David Richards of London in a letter to the *Church Times*.

R. William Franklin, Dean of Berkeley-Yale Divinity School and a consultant to the bishops at Lambeth, commented, "One thing that Lambeth convinced me of is that we are seeing the curtain going up on what may be a more militantly conservative twenty-first century than we expected. A new

Anglican Quadrilateral first seen in outline at Lambeth...proposed a new emphasis in our Communion on (1) growth, (2) freer forms of worship, (3) Scripture study, and (4) clear moral teaching. This new Quadrilateral was articulated by African and Asian bishops who have mastered skills of argument and debate, honed by decades of living in tense, often corrupt political environments, and by dealing with Islam through periods when many of their flock have suffered martyrdom for their faith. This new Quadrilateral is to stand alongside the old Anglican Quadrilateral of the nineteenth century with its four points of Holy Scripture, Catholic Creeds, Sacramental Life, and Historic Episcopate.)

In his syndicated column for Scripps-Howard, Terry Mattingly said there were two ways to look at Lambeth. "Leaders of a powerful new conservative coalition—mostly Africans, Asians, and a few bishops from England and America—were convinced they had prevented a global schism," he wrote. "Leaders of the Anglican establishment were stunned, yet left comforted by the knowledge that Lambeth votes are advisory."

Noting that "tensions between the First World churches and those in the rapidly growing Two-Thirds world—especially between Americans and Africans—touched almost every event here," Mattingly said. "The Americans portrayed themselves as leaders of a living church, one evolving to minister to the modern world. The Africans, they whispered, represent the past, a church chained to traditional views of creeds and Scriptures. The Africans said it is their church that is alive, bringing waves of believers into jam-packed sanctuaries. Trendy Americans, they suggested, are married to the present."

"Africans and Asians stressed that they welcome diversity, especially in culture, worship, and church leadership," he added. "But they clearly consider diversity a bad word, when applied to basic doctrinal issues such as biblical authority, the Resurrection, or defining the sacrament of marriage."

Mattingly said that "it's reasonable for the left to feel threatened right now," pointing to the threat of Third World conservative bishops to provide oversight for traditionalist parishes in places like the United States. He quoted Bishop John Rucyahana of Rwanda, who earlier announced his intention to visit a parish in Little Rock for confirmation, as saying that "we must defend the Bible and the doctrines of our church, above all else. We will find some kind of strategy to do this."

Picking up on the cultural issues, Charles Austin said in his religion column that Lambeth made it obvious that the "conversation has now gone global, and that will not make the discussion any easier. But it will make it more significant as those whose 'pagan' cultures the western churches once evangelized, now step into the discussion as mature Christians, fully responsible for the care of the faith in their countries."

In an op-ed piece for the *New York Times*, Spong decried what he called a trend toward "a narrowly conservative direction" for Anglicans, as illustrated by Lambeth. He pointed out that the church at one time opposed developments in science and supported such institutions as slavery and segregation and "was an agent of the oppression of women, the mentally ill and even left-handed people." The church has made a similar mistake at Lambeth, he said. "Now the Anglican Church, historically dedicated to determining truth through reason as well as through Scripture and tradition, has made an equally egregious error, this time against homosexuals.

"How tragic it is to watch this great force in Western civilization sink into a negative and fearful position," he concluded. "Yet this is what I saw and heard at the Lambeth Conference. It was the sunset of the Anglican Communion."

ANGLICAN RESILIENCE

That kind of gloomy prognosis "sounds similar to voices heard some years ago when the ordination of women was approved by the Episcopal Church," said Presiding Bishop Frank Griswold in a letter to the editor responding to Spong's "ringing indictment."

"The truth is that Anglicanism is far more resilient than any one action would suggest, and Lambeth Conferences, which are advisory, not legislative, have with the passage of time changed their mind on a number of sensitive and controversial subjects," Griswold wrote.

Using an analogy that he employed in a sermon at Canterbury the day after the Lambeth Conference ended, Griswold said. "Just as Canterbury Cathedral, the symbolic center of the Anglican Communion, is a unity made up of a broad diversity of architectural styles representing different historical moments—and the whole building is held together by a dynamic of stress and counterstress—so too is the Anglican Communion: its various distinctive parts press against one another and thereby sustain each other in a creative tension which is integral to its unity."

Griswold argued that, as a part of the larger Anglican Communion, the Episcopal Church in the U.S.A. "does not exist of and to itself. Its own struggles to discern God's authentic desire in the midst of all the stresses and strains which are part of our national life must always be placed in a larger context which includes the more drastic struggles which are confronting our Anglican brothers and sisters in other parts of the world."

He urged a posture of "patience and humility—the willingness to receive from truth of the other—mutual affection and an authentic desire to meet Christ in one another."

Dismissing Spong's allegation that Lambeth represented the sunset of Anglicanism, Griswold quoted from *Murder in the Cathedral* by T. S. Eliot, which was performed several times at the conference. "This is but one moment/ But know that another/ Shall pierce you with a sudden painful joy/ When the figure of God's purpose is made complete."

CHAPTER EIGHT

POST-LAMBETH DEVELOPMENTS

As the dust from Lambeth continued to settle, those who were pleased with the sexuality resolution pressed the Episcopal Church to move toward concurrence, only to be met with a steadfast insistence that dialogue must continue.

Shortly after Lambeth, Stanton of Dallas circulated a proposal for an Anglican Mission and Evangelism Network (AMEN) to build on the "watershed in defining the orthodoxy and commitment to the Scriptures of the Anglican Communion." It was a proposal he first shared with colleagues in the Section Two meetings.

Stanton said that "the conference has developed a momentum for taking evangelism and mission forward. It is important to ensure this momentum is continued and not dissipated when people disperse....There is a need therefore for a global Anglican initiative that will network models and resources and work to advance the mission of God for the next decade." The goal of AMEN is "to promote and support mission and evangelism initiatives throughout the Communion and come to Lambeth 2008 with a wealth of experience and networking in mission to build on and take forward the mission of the church into the third millennium."

The proposal calls for a structure of thirty-seven bishops representing the provinces with a working group made up of four officers and a secretariat with an executive secretary and associates as needed. The founding group included bishops who were politically active on the issues at Lambeth. Among them were Archbishops Adetiloye of Nigeria, Gitari of Kenya, Mtetemela of Tanzania, Moderators William Moses of South India and Samuel Azariah of Pakistan, joined by Bishops Simon Chiwanga of Tanzania, James Stanton of Dallas, Mano Ramulshah of Pakistan, Azad Marshall of Pakistan-Gulf, Rowan Williams of Wales and Peter Lee of Southern Africa. The convenor would be Bishop French Chang Him of the Seychelles.

The Secretariat would be organized with the help of the Oxford Centre for Mission Studies and the American Anglican Council, with Chris Sugden as secretary. Both were part of the conservative mix at the Franciscan Centre at Lambeth.

In another development, the First Promise movement of traditionalists, formed at a meeting of thirty clergy in South Carolina in September 1997, wrote an open letter to Griswold requesting him to "bring yourself, your staff and the stewardship of your office into line with Lambeth." It said it was "not an acceptable position for the primate of this or any church body" to abstain on the issue of traditional sexual morality, as represented in the resolution. "In order to bring yourself in line with what Lambeth has shown to be the faith and order of Anglican Christianity, only two choices exist: repentance or the resignation of your office, for the sake of unity in the Gospel of Jesus Christ as received in the Anglican Communion." It asked Griswold to repent for "knowingly ordaining practicing homosexual persons" and for "refusing to dissociate from Bishop Spong and his teaching, including the *Koinonia* Statement authored by him."

A conservative coalition of laity and clergy, First Promise also wrote to Carey, thanking him for his leadership during the sexuality debate but asking why there was "no formal dissociation from Bishop Spong or his teaching?" And it wondered why there was no call for the Episcopal Church "to renounce and rescind" its recent decisions to develop same-sex blessing rites. In fact, the 1997 General Convention did not endorse such a move. The letter also argued for alternative episcopal oversight, even if it means crossing diocesan boundaries.

First Promise, named for the ordination vow to "be loyal to the doctrine, discipline and worship of Christ as this church has received them," said that it believes "God is bringing judgment upon this church for the repeated and unrepentant disobedience of some of its members and for the failure of its leadership to bring Godly discipline to bear in those situations."

Walter Bruce, president of the Episcopal Synod of America (ESA), also wrote to Griswold, asking him to seek "an immediate halt to the development of any liturgies for the granting of ecclesiastical approval to sexual unions between partners of the same sex..." and "a halt to any current or future initiative to provide same-sex domestic partner benefits for any national church employee."

The letter also asked for "a permanent moratorium on the ordination of any person, whether heterosexual or homosexual, who unrepentantly engages in genital sexual activity outside holy matrimony or teaches others that they may do so," and "an immediate end to the harassment of our ESA parishes in the Diocese of Pennsylvania and the provision of an alternative form of oversight acceptable to them." The ESA also wants "an immediate cessation of the practice of forced visitations by diocesan bishops or their subordinates upon congregations which, on grounds of theological conviction, do not wish to receive them." It was also clear from the letter that the ESA wanted "flying bishops," such as those of the Church of England, who would provide its parishes with a more congenial episcopal oversight.

Writing on the post-Lambeth backlash in *Christian Challenge* magazine, the Rev. Sam Edwards, executive director of ESA, predicted that support from overseas bishops for beleaguered orthodox Episcopalians is likely to increase—but almost certainly is contingent upon traditionalists fulfilling their own responsibility in the American situation. "We must do our own part. We must fight our own battles" and look for allies in that effort but not "rescuers....We're going to have some bleeding. The sooner traditionalists get their minds wrapped around that fact the better off things are going to be."

The Rev. Stephen Noll, who covered the conference for the American Anglican Council, the conservative group headed by Dallas Bishop James Stanton, said in an interview in the *Church Times* that there was no sign that any of the liberal American bishops were rethinking their position. He said that matters would come to a head at the 2000 General Convention if there is a move to approve same-sex blessings or if efforts to block the ordination of non-celibate gays and lesbians is not successful. He predicted that groups such as First Promise or the ESA would be likely to withdraw from the church, appealing to the Anglican Communion, either individually or collectively, for recognition.

"The general feeling is that some of the Third World bishops and archbishops wish to give American bishops the opportunity to respond to the sexuality resolution and would prefer not to go breaking boundaries during that time. But they're not committed to that policy forever."

The situation in Little Rock is just the beginning, Noll suggested, pointing out that a parish in Sewickley, Pennsylvania, is seeking the episcopal oversight of a bishop from Uganda, with the blessing of Bishop Robert Duncan of Pittsburgh.

Christ Church at Grove Farm is not a member of the diocese, although two of its priests are canonically resident in the diocese, the evangelist Dr. John Guest and the Rev. Donald Wilson. With encouragement from Duncan, the parish invited Bishop Wilson Turumanya of the Diocese of Bunyoro-Kitara in Uganda to ordain a third priest, David Valencia, a Chilean who is a graduate of Trinity Episcopal School for Ministry. The independent parish has said that it would "enter into a missionary relationship" with the Ugandan diocese, according to a warden at the parish.

Duncan said, "I'm taking a risk that I think I'm called to take." He hoped that his action was a way to help Christ Church maintain its Anglican links and, if the situation for traditionalists in the Episcopal Church improves, he held out the possibility that it would eventually join the denomination.

"Bishops in Pittsburgh were committed to being gentle with Christ Church as they separated, recognizing that if the American church comes back to its center, as many of us are hoping it will—and working to bring that about, then Christ Church will affiliate with the Diocese of Pittsburgh and, by extension, with ECUSA," Duncan said.

Duncan speculated that the church might be entering an era of reconfigured relationships between parishes and bishops, one that is "not geographic so much as it is affectional or relational."

"I am sure we can establish a history-making arrangement" between the parish and the Sudanese diocese, said Turumanya, "one that may point the way for other churches to remain within the worldwide Anglican Communion without compromising their biblical belief."

In a bold move that drew directly on Lambeth's decisions, conservatives in the Episcopal Church appealed to the world's bishops—and especially the primates of the Anglican Communion—to intervene to protect their orthodox position and to support the possibility of a separate province.

A cover letter to the February 15 petition from the Association of Anglican Congregations on Mission (AACOM), a group of independent congregations which have left the Episcopal Church, said that it was asking the bishops "to put into action their own resolutions." It added, "We are also asking the orthodox bishops to give interim protection and care" to congregations it said were being persecuted.

The petitions also expressed a hope that the bishops would seek the "repentance" of liberal bishops in the American church who have been dismissing some actions of the Lambeth Conference, especially on sexuality. If the 2000 General Convention does not endorse Lambeth, the conservatives want to "separate ECUSA from the Anglican Communion and replace it with an alternative province composed of a continuing Episcopal Church of orthodox-believing Christians who submit to the authority of Scripture."

The petition to the primates was accompanied by a 145-page document that outlines how liberal bishops have supposedly violated the spirit and actions of Lambeth.

"We're in the middle of a major struggle in the American Church," said the Rev. Chuck Murphy of First Promise. He said in an interview with the *Washington Times*, "We've built an international alliance of primates who won't stand for it any longer."

As if on cue, a group of primates issued an open letter to Presiding Bishop Griswold on February 26, reminding him and the Episcopal Church that "each province is accountable to the whole Communion."

The letter expressed "sorrow and disappointment that we have heard from different parts of our Communion statements at variance with what was resolved at Lambeth." It

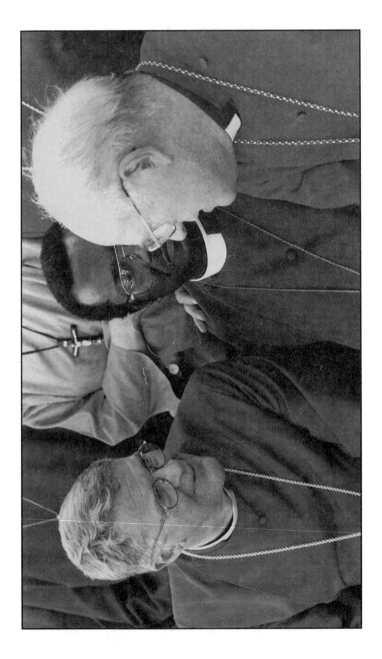

Presiding Bishop Frank Griswold chats with Bishop Daniel Zindo of Sudan and Archbishop of Canterbury George Carey. Zindo was killed in an auto accident three months after Lambeth—and one year after his wife and other family members were murdered in the Sudanese civil war. (Photo: Episcopal News Service)

charged that "there are leaders within your own province who do not wish to follow, and in the past have even broken, the teachings affirmed at Lambeth." It pointed specifically to the resolutions affirming "faithfulness in marriage between a man and a woman in life-long union" and the advice against "legitimizing or blessing of same-sex unions nor ordaining of those involved."

Deploring "the continuance of action at variance with the Lambeth resolutions, within your own or any other province," the letter said that "would be a grievous wrong and a matter over which we could not be indifferent." It asked Griswold "to examine the directions apparently proposed by some in your province and take whatever steps may be necessary to uphold the moral teaching and Christian faith the Anglican Communion has received." It concluded by asserting that the letter was written in the cause of "unity and *koinonia*. Our aim is fraternal for we believe that within our family of faith, heart should speak to heart and speak the truth in love."

The letter was signed by six primates: David Gitari of Kenya, Emmanuel Kolini of Rwanda, Ghais Malik of Jerusalem and the Middle East, Donald Mtetemela of Tanzania, Maurice Sinclair of the Southern Cone of America, and Moses Tay of South East Asia. They were joined by Colin Bazley, former Presiding Bishop of the Southern Cone, and Archbishop Harry Goodhew of Sydney.

Fourteen bishops of the American Anglican Council, meeting in Florida February 24-26, said that the AACOM petitions "signal some troubling realities. They reveal—and may understate—the post-Lambeth condition" of the Episcopal Church. In fact, the actions "may well represent the leading edge of an impending realignment in the Anglican Communion." Their statement, issued a week before the church's bishops met for retreat in Texas, called on Griswold "to promote the kind of community that resists the use of force, the one against the other."

In a statement they released March 2, the AAC bishops said that they were "unanimous in our embrace of the reports and resolutions of the 1998 Lambeth Conference. We believe Lambeth's teaching is authoritative for Anglican Christians and the clear starting point for a new era of mission in the twenty-first century."

According to Doug LeBlanc's coverage for *Anglican Voice*, Chuck Murphy of First Promise told the bishops of what he perceived as "a tear" in the fabric of Anglicanism, predicting that a realignment would unfold slowly over the next decade.

Anticipating that possibility, at a meeting the first week of February in Atlanta, First Promise nominated the Rev. John Rodgers, former dean of Trinity Episcopal School for Ministry in Pennsylvania, as a potential bishop for a new province. Rodgers, who serves as general secretary of AACOM, said that he still held out hope that the church would repent, making such a radical action unnecessary. But he did admit that it "would require a major miracle, similar to the parting of the Red Sea."

Conservatives have raised the possibility of a diocese or province of traditionalist Episcopalians before but Archbishop of Canterbury George Carey has sent clear signals that he would not recognize such a jurisdiction. "Are they aware they would not ever be recognized by the Archbishop of Canterbury?" Bishop Mark Dyer of Virginia Seminary asked a Washington reporter. "There isn't the slightest chance. Whatever differences the Archbishop has with some practices in the Episcopal Church, he would never recognize this group."

In a parallel development, traditionalists in the Church of England began to lay plans for a major rally of priests and bishops still opposed to women in the priesthood. Provoked by a fear that the church is moving toward the consecration of women to the episcopate, the October "sacred synod" would be followed by a meeting of Forward in Faith, the umbrella group for traditionalists, who would discuss plans for a breakaway "free province" within the church. "We have enough parishes to create a province that would be bigger than Scotland or Wales," said the Rev. Geoffrey Kirk, secretary of Forward in Faith. "The bishops are more frightened of us than we are of them."

Christina Rees, a member of the new Archbishops' Council for the Church of England and a strong proponent for women bishops, told the *Daily Telegraph* that women priests "are accepted almost everywhere, and it is no longer an issue."

The Church of England's General Synod is expected to debate the issue of women in the episcopate at its July and November 1999 meetings. The church's most senior female priest, Archdeacon Judith Rose of Tonbridge, has prepared a resolution asking the House of Bishops to consider the theological implications of the consecration of women.

Meanwhile, the leadership of the American church remained resolute in its position that Lambeth was the beginning, not the end, of the conversation on sexuality. On March 10, Griswold, joined by nine bishops who serve as his Council of Advice, responded to the primates' letter. The letter of response began, "The bonds of communion which we enjoy with other provinces are precious to us, and the mutual sharing of the gifts between us is both a privilege and a blessing."

The letter emphasized the "divergent opinions on the question of homosexuality" in many provinces of the Anglican Communion. It quoted from the four understandings that emerged from the Lambeth Conference report on human sexuality, ranging from those who believe homosexual orientation is "a disorder" that might be changed to "those who believe that the church should accept and support or bless monogamous covenant relationships between homosexual people and that they may be ordained."

Griswold said the Episcopal Church is in a process of discernment, "testing the spirits," and he quoted from a letter of Archbishop Carey to another primate. In that letter Carey pointed out that the issue was discussed at Lambeth for "the very first time" and the resolution stating that homosexual activity is contrary to Scripture "indicates where bishops stand now on the issue; it does not indicate that we shall ever rest there."

Carey said in the letter that the debate at Lambeth "showed me more powerfully than I had ever seen before that argument and controversy solves nothing." He called for a new kind of conversation, "one that begins with respect for the integrity of another and a willingness to study the scriptures together, to reflect on our experience—including the experience of homosexuals—and to share in a process" of moral discourse.

Griswold and his nine advisors ended their letter by inviting the primates "to visit those parts of our church which cause you concern so that you may inquire and learn directly what has animated certain responses" to the Lambeth resolutions. "Such visits will afford you the opportunity not only to query some of our bishops and representatives of their dioceses but also to listen to the experience of homosexual persons, which is mandated by the Lambeth resolution on human sexuality."

The other bishops who signed the letter were: J. Clark Grew II of Ohio; Robert H. Johnson of Western North Carolina; James Krotz of Nebraska; Julio Holuguin of the Dominican Republic; Jack McKelvey of Newark; Robert D. Rowley, Jr., of Northwestern Pennsylvania; Richard Shimpfky of El Camino Real; William Smalley of Kansas; and Douglas Theuner of New Hampshire.

HOUSEHOLD OF FAITH FOR THE FUTURE?

"The future of the Anglican Communion, as is customary with futures, remains unreadable," said a September editorial in *Foundations*, the magazine of the Episcopal Synod of America. "What bears watching in the short run, anyway for Americans, is the attitude of the U.S. bishops. These returned, angry, disgruntled and defiant, to their dioceses. Backlash could be coming, for whatever good it does."

As many had predicted, it did not take long for the fallout from Lambeth to ripple through the Episcopal Church, pointing to a new confrontation at the General Convention in 2000.

At its November convention in Boston, for example, the Diocese of Massachusetts overwhelmingly passed a six-part resolution that affirmed that "God calls some homosexual people to live together in committed relationships and the church can and does appropriately bless such unions, and that God calls some homosexual people in such relationships to ordained ministry and that the church can and does appropriately ordain them."

While upholding traditional marriage and the commitment to listen to the experience of homosexuals in the church, key elements of the Lambeth resolution, the Massachusetts resolution states "regret that the Lambeth resolution seems to rely on Scripture alone," asking for "further study of Scripture in light of the tradition of the church and in light of our God-given reason on the issues of sexual expression, Christian marriage, the meaning of ordination and specifically on the issue of homosexuality."

At the same time, the diocesan resolution pledged the diocese "to a greater level of awareness of the cultural and spiritual contexts of our fellow Anglicans throughout the world, and a greater level of response where there is identified need. We ask for the same level of awareness and response to our own context by others in the Communion."

Florida Bishop Stephen Jecko warned Shaw in an October 21 letter that "the resolutions you propose in Massachusetts will trigger an international response in the Anglican Communion that could tear us apart—not to mention the further strife that will be set loose in ECUSA."

The Diocese of Dallas also addressed the Lambeth resolutions, voting that it would "be guided by the moral authority of the 1998 Lambeth Conference." In another resolution, the diocesan convention also noted that Lambeth had voted that "there should be no compulsion on any bishop in matters concerning ordination or licensing" of women. The diocese called on the General Convention to "remove all provisions of the canons of the Episcopal Church as are inconsistent" with that Lambeth resolution.

So the interpretations of Lambeth at the local level will depend a great deal on whose ox is being gored. In some areas of the Communion, the implications of Lambeth will be discussed earnestly, but in other areas those implications may sink out of sight rather quickly.

A difficult job: Bishop Duncan Buchanan of Johannesburg, South Africa, chaired the volatile Lambeth sub-section on human sexuality. (Photo: Episcopal News Service)

While sexuality remains the hot-button issue, especially in the Episcopal Church, Lambeth exposed even deeper strains on the unity of the Anglican Communion. Carey raised the issue at the beginning of the conference, when he said that unity suggests a "voluntary curtailment of freedom." For Carey, "the greatest heresy" would be to allow issues to divide the church. The Archbishop knows as well as anyone how crucial a time this is for the Anglican Communion, leading him at one point to ask, "In what way can we realistically claim to be a Communion?"

At the 1988 Lambeth Conference, Archbishop of Canterbury Robert Runcie expressed his deep fear that instead of unity the Anglican Communion was headed for "gradual fragmentation." And in his closing sermon at that conference, Edmond Browning asked if Anglicans were ready to embrace diversity and become "not a museum of the past but the household of faith for the future."

How large is the Anglican tent anyway? Who decides where the boundaries are drawn, determining who is inside and who is outside of the fellowship? How broad and deep are the divisions, the fissures that were so apparent in Canterbury? Is it even possible to talk about a new relationship that leaves room for churches in widely divergent cultures, facing very different challenges, to respond in a way that makes sense to them—and yet support each other? If not, doesn't the Lambeth Conference, and the other signs of unity which hold Anglicans together, become a sign of disunity? Is the ultimate choice between diversity based on common respect or disunity?

In an address to the November meeting of the Church of England's General Synod, Bishop Josiah Idowu-Fearon of Nigeria said that he "came away from Lambeth more convinced of the need to keep to biblical principles than when I went in." He emerged with "a resolve to work harder in my part of our Communion to see that we continue to keep both the Western and developing minds together so as to checkmate each other." Yet he welcomed the call for a way "we might set limits on Anglican diversity in submission to the sovereign authority of Holy Scripture and in loyalty to our Anglican traditions and formularies." He concluded, "We are hoping and believing that under the guidance of the Holy Spirit, there will eventually emerge within this Communion an enhanced and centralized body that will speak for and to the entire Communion to offer guidance on doctrinal, moral, and pastoral matters."

Idowu-Fearon was speaking for many bishops at Lambeth who want a different kind of Anglican Communion, one that would require a different definition of authority, with more authority invested in the Primates' Meeting and the office of the Archbishop of Canterbury. But what kind of Communion, what kind of *koinonia*, is based on the implied stalemate?

In an address to the same General Synod, Bishop Graham James of St. Germans said, "The office and ministry of the Archbishop of Canterbury is visibly the greatest single means of holding our Communion together." Yet he expressed the frustration of many bishops when he asked, "If Lambeth has no binding authority, why do we have resolutions debated under rules which were bewildering to most bishops there...And where lies the authority of that much-publicized resolution on human sexuality? Whom does it bind?"

J. Robert Wright of New York's General Theological Seminary, wrote on the authority of Lambeth in *Anglican and Episcopal History*. He said the reports of Lambeth in 1968 and 1978 made it clear that "even the resolutions have no legislative authority unless or until they are accepted by individual synods of the member churches....The intention of the warnings, as well as the distinctions between resolutions and reports, is not the positive one of helping to clarify the provincial process whereby the Lambeth resolutions can be synodically received, but rather the negative one of showing how thoroughly non-authoritative the conference, even in its resolutions, really is." Is that changing as the result of Lambeth '98?

The Rev. John Peterson, secretary general of the Anglican Communion Office, said in his column in *Anglican World*, that the conference "was not about resolutions and pronouncements. It is about encounter—learning and being one with those who exist in states of struggle and pressure." Something powerful did happen in those Bible study groups, across cultural and theological divides. Perhaps the seeds were sown for new bonds of affection that could influence the next Lambeth Conference.

Maybe Bishop Richard Grein of New York was close to the mark when he told his diocese that he thought that this Lambeth "was a transitional conference." Or was he being optimistic when he added, "I believe history will remember this conference for the way it strengthened the bonds of our life together as a Communion of churches"?

Even though it was seldom invoked during the conference, the Virginia Report's probing theological examination of unity and diversity, what it means to be a Communion, may provide the fodder for the future. How does the Anglican Communion hold in tension the independence of the provinces and the commitment to seek God's will—together? Lambeth 1998 did indeed "test the truth of our unity," as Bishop Mark Dyer suggested, raising the possibility of holding together the Communion "in the creative tension of provincial autonomy and interdependence."

But then there is the plaintive question of Bishop Duncan Buchanan of Johannesburg, who asked when the sub-section on sexuality was about to dissolve in disagreement, "Is anybody listening?"

APPENDIX

The following is an annotated list of the resolutions passed at the Lambeth Conference by sections. Resolutions mentioned in the text of the book are included in their entirety. The complete text of resolutions is available on line at the Anglican Communion Website: http://www.anglicancommunion.org/acns/

SECTION I RESOLUTIONS

Resolution I.1
Affirmation and Adoption of the United Nations Universal Declaration of Human Rights

Resolution I.2
Religious Freedom and Tolerance

Resolution I.3
Justice for Women and Children

Resolution I.4
A Faithful Response to Aggression and War
This Conference:

(a) abhors the evil of war;

(b) repudiates and condemns the use of violence for settling religious, economic, cultural or political disputes;

(c) encourages the use of peacekeeping forces to prevent or forestall the escalation of conflicts, and to assist in their resolution;

(d) repudiates and condemns the use of terrorism;

(e) decries the production and proliferation of arms;

(f) commits its members to prayer, mediation, and any active, non-violent means we can employ to end current conflicts and wars and to prevent others; and

(g) urges the nations represented by our Churches and all those on whom we have any influence whatsoever to join us in this endeavour.

Resolution I.5
Uprooted and Displaced Persons

Resolution I.6
The Plight of the People of Northern and Western Uganda

This Conference, acknowledging the appalling suffering of the people of Northern and Western Uganda as a result of continued civil war waged by rebels, known as LRA and ADF (Lord's Resistance Army and Allied Democratic Forces), backed by forces from outside Uganda:

(a) urges the government of Uganda to continue to engage in a process which will lead to reconciliation, peace and justice. The process must include the Governments of Sudan and the Democratic Republic of Congo, representatives of the Rebels, representatives of main Religious bodies and Opinion Leaders of the areas affected; and

(b) calls upon the Anglican Consultative Council and appeals to the United Nations organisations to assist in bringing about a quick settlement of this armed conflict.

Resolution I.7
The Plight of the People of the Sudan, Rwanda and Burundi

This Conference, expressing its horror at the human disaster in the Sudan and
Rwanda, urges that:

(a) the Episcopal Church of the Sudan be encouraged to establish a dynamic network of reciprocal communications with government bodies, sympathetic Muslims, and non-governmental organisations, including the All Africa Conference of Churches, the Anglican Consultative Council, the Primates of the Anglican Communion, the Anglican Observer at the UN, and specialised organs of the UN and the UN Security Council;

(b) the member Churches of the Anglican Communion find ways to help provide technology, equipment, vehicles and administrative support in order to make publicity about and response to the urgent situation in the Sudan, Rwanda and Burundi possible;

(c) the member Churches of the Anglican Communion contribute as generously as possible of expertise, labour, money, and material goods to aid in necessary rebuilding of these nations on all levels; and

(d) help be sought from existing organisations whose mission is the facilitation of peace processes, to aid in the implementation of this resolution.

Resolution I.8
Creation

Resolution I.9
Ecology

This Conference:

(a) calls upon all ecumenical partners and other faith communities, governments and transnational companies:

(i) to work for sustainable society in a sustainable world;

(ii) to recognise the dignity and rights of all people and the sanctity of all life, especially the rights of future generations;

(iii) to ensure the responsible use and re-cycling of natural resources;

(iv) to bring about economic reforms which will establish a just and fair trading system both for people and for the environment.

(b) calls upon the United Nations to incorporate the right of future generations to a sustainable future in the Universal Declaration of Human Rights.

(c) asks the Joint Standing Committee of the ACC and the Primates to consider the appointment of a co-ordinator of an international ecological network within the Anglican Communion, who would:

(i) work in co-operation with other ecumenical and interfaith agencies;

(ii) be funded through and responsible to the Anglican Consultative Council;

(iii) support those engaged in grass-roots environmental initiatives;

(iv) gather and disseminate data and information on environmental issues so that the Church can play an informed role in lobbying for ecological justice in both the public and private sectors; and

(v) contribute to the development of environmental educational programmes for use in the training of Christian leaders.

Resolution I.10

Human Sexuality

This Conference:

(a) commends to the Church the subsection report on human sexuality;

(b) in view of the teaching of Scripture, upholds faithfulness in marriage between a man and a woman in lifelong union, and believes that abstinence is right for those who are not called to marriage;

(c) recognises that there are among us persons who experience themselves as having a homosexual orientation. Many of these are members of the Church and are seeking the pastoral care, moral direction of the Church, and God's transforming power for the living of their lives and the ordering of relationships. We commit ourselves to listen to the experience of homosexual persons and we wish to assure them that they are loved by God and that all baptised, believing and faithful persons, regardless of sexual orientation, are full members of the Body of Christ;

(d) while rejecting homosexual practice as incompatible with Scripture, calls on all our people to minister pastorally and sensitively to all irrespective of sexual orientation and to condemn irrational fear of homosexuals, violence within marriage and any trivialisation and commercialisation of sex;

(e) cannot advise the legitimising or blessing of same sex unions nor ordaining those involved in same gender unions;

(f) requests the Primates and the ACC to establish a means of monitoring the work done on the subject of human sexuality in the Communion and to share statements and resources among us;

(g) notes the significance of the Kuala Lumpur Statement on Human Sexuality and the concerns expressed in resolutions IV.26, V.1, V.10, V.23 and V.35 on the authority of Scripture in matters of marriage and sexuality and asks the Primates and the ACC to include them in their monitoring process.

Resolution I.11
Nuclear Weapons

This Conference resolves to call upon our respective governments and through our governments, the United Nations and other instruments:
(a) to urge all nations to agree by treaty to stop the production, testing, stock-piling and usage of nuclear weapons; and

(b) to press for an international mandate for all member states to prohibit nuclear warfare.

Resolution I.12
Calling for a Commission on Technology and Ethics

This Conference:
(a) calls for consideration to be given to the establishment of a commission through the Anglican Consultative Council to track technological developments, to reflect on them theologically and ethically, and to inform bishops and other church leaders as to what is taking place; and

(b) recommends that such a commission does its work and informs the church of it, as far as possible, through e-mail and Internet conferencing.

Resolution I.13
Landmines

This Conference - attended both by bishops from nations suffering acutely from the presence of landmines in their own countries (Mrs. Winifred Ochola, wife of the Bishop of Kitgum in Uganda was killed by a landmine), and by bishops from countries that have profited from the manufacture of landmines:

(a) calls upon all signatory Governments to ratify the Ottawa Convention (without exceptions) at the earliest possible date;

(b) calls upon all non-signatory Governments to sign and ratify the Ottawa Convention at the earliest possible date;

(c) calls upon all Governments to provide extra funding for mine clearance programmes, and to encourage the development of appropriate technology for mine clearance initiatives; and;

(d) calls upon international organisations, all Governments, community level and local Government initiatives, NGOs, Churches and other people of good will, to engage in educational work on this issue, provide practical assistance to alleviate the consequences of the massive level of previous landmine deployment, and engage in practical schemes to reintegrate landmine survivors and their families into their communities.

Resolution I.14
Euthanasia

In the light of current debate and proposals for the legalisation of euthanasia in several countries, this Conference:

(a) affirms that life is God-given and has intrinsic sanctity, significance and worth;

(b) defines euthanasia as the act by which one person intentionally causes or assists in causing the death of another who is terminally or seriously ill in order to end the other's pain and suffering;

(c) resolves that euthanasia, as precisely defined, is neither compatible with the Christian faith nor should be permitted in civil legislation;

(d) distinguishes between euthanasia and withholding, withdrawing, declining or terminating excessive medical treatment and intervention, all of which may be consonant with Christian faith in enabling a person to die with dignity. When a person is in a permanent vegetative state, to sustain him or her with artificial nutrition and hydration may be seen as constituting medical intervention; and

(e) commends the Section Report on euthanasia as a suitable introduction for study of such matters in all Provinces of the Communion.

Resolution I.15
International Debt and Economic Justice

Recognising the importance and urgency of issues of international debt and economic justice, this Conference adopts the following statement:

(a) We see the issues of international debt and economic justice in the light of our belief in creation: God has created a world in which we are bound together in a common humanity in which each person has equal dignity and value. God has generously given to the nations immense resources which are to be held in trust and used for the wellbeing of all and also offered us in Christ Jesus liberation from all that which destroys healthy human life – a pattern of giving which God desires all to follow. The healthy pattern for relationships is of mutual giving and receiving of God's gifts. Borrowing has its place only in as much as it releases growth for human well being. When we ignore this pattern, money becomes a force that destroys human community and God's creation. The vast expansion in the power and quantity of money in recent decades, the huge increase in borrowing among rich and poor alike, the damaging material and spiritual consequences to many, bear testimony to this destructive force.

(b) Mindful of the work done by the political leaders, finance ministers, church leaders and people of creditor nations, we welcome the framework provided by the historic Heavily Indebted Poor Country Initiative (HIPC) of 1996. We particularly welcome the approach of bringing all creditors together to agree upon debt relief, and the emphasis on debtor participation. We welcome unilateral initiatives taken by governments to write off loans owed to Overseas Development Departments; and initiatives by governments and international financial institutions to strengthen the capacity of debtor nations to manage debt portfolios, and to co-operate together. We welcome the commitment by leaders of the eight most powerful economies (the G8) in Birmingham May 1998; to consider withholding future taxpayer-subsidised loans intended for arms sales and other unproductive purposes.

(c) While recognising these achievements, we wish to assert that these measures do not as yet provide sufficient release for the hundreds of millions of people whose governments are diverting scarce resources away from health, education, sanitation and clean water.

(d) We have heard and understood the point of view that poverty reduction is more important than debt cancellation. Nevertheless we conclude that substantial debt relief, including cancellation of unpayable debts of the poorest nations under an independent, fair and transparent process, is a necessary, while not sufficient precondition for freeing these nations, and their people, from the hopeless downward spiral of poverty. Because indebted nations lose their autonomy to international creditors, debt cancellation is also a necessary step if these governments are to be given the dignity, autonomy and independence essential to the growth and development of democracy. We believe it vital that all of God's people should participate, on the basis of equal dignity, in the fruits of our interdependent world.

(e) The need for debt relief for the poorest nations is urgent. Children are dying, and societies are unraveling under the burden of debt. We call for negotiations to be speeded up so that the poorest nations may benefit from such cancellation by the birth of the new millennium. The imagination of many, rich and poor alike, has already been gripped by the stark simplicity of this call. This response can be harnessed for the cause of development.

(f) We call on the political, corporate and church leaders and people of creditor nations:

• to accept equal dignity for debtor nations in negotiations over loan agreements and debt relief;

• to ensure that the legislatures of lending nations are given the power to scrutinise taxpayer-subsidised loans; and to devise methods of regular legislative scrutiny that hold to account government-financed creditors, including the multilateral financial institutions, for lending decisions;

• to introduce into the design of international financial systems mechanisms that will impose discipline on lenders, introduce accountability for bad lending, and challenge corruption effectively, thus preventing future recurrence of debt crises;

• to introduce measures that will enable debtor nations to trade fairly with creditor nations. Fair trade will allow debtor nations to develop their domestic economies. This in turn will allow them to pay those debts which remain and to take their rightful place in the community of nations;

• to ensure that each of the OECD (Organisation for Economic Co-operation and Development) nations honour their commitment to set aside 0.7% of their GNP for international development.

(g) We call on political leaders, finance ministers, corporate executives traditional rulers, religious leaders and the people of debtor nation:

• to accept independent, fair and transparent procedures for agreeing debt relief;

• to adopt much greater transparency and accountability in the process of accepting and agreeing new loans, particularly as the burden of repayment of these loans will fall largely on the poorest; ensuring proper scrutiny by legislative bodies of each loan contract signed by government ministers;

• to adopt measures for disciplining elected and paid government officials who corruptly divert public funds and also to provide for sanctions against private sector persons and bodies who act corruptly;

• to adopt measures for ensuring that additional resources generated from debt relief are allocated to projects that genuinely benefit the poorest sections of society.

(h) We call on political leaders and finance ministers in both creditor and debtor nations to develop, in a spirit of partnership, a new, independent, open and transparent forum for the negotiation and agreement of debt relief for highly indebted nations. In particular, we call on them to co-operate with the United Nations in the establishment of a Mediation Council whose purpose would be:

· to respond to appeals from debtor nations unable to service their debts, except at great human cost;

· to identify those debts that are odious, and therefore not to be considered as debts.

· to assess, independently and fairly, the assets and liabilities of indebted nations;

· to determine that debt repayments are set at levels which prioritise basic human development needs over the demands of creditors;

· to hold to account those in authority in borrowing countries for the way in which loans have been spent;

· to hold to account those in authority in lending nations for the nature of their lending decisions;

· to demand repayment of public funds corruptly diverted to private accounts;

· to consult widely over local development needs and the country's capacity to pay; and

· to ensure, through public monitoring and evaluation, that any additional resources made available from debt relief are allocated to projects that genuinely benefit the poor.

(i) We, commit ourselves to supporting the objectives outlined above, in the countries in which we live, whether they are debtor nations or creditor nations. We will seek also to highlight the moral and theological implications. Mindful of the wisdom held within other faith traditions we shall work with them, as we are able, to examine the issues of credit and debit and the nature of the economy.

(j) Furthermore we call upon members of the Communion to co-operate with other people of faith in programmes of education and advocacy within our dioceses, so that we may help to raise public awareness of these vital economic issues that impact so deeply on the daily lives of the poor.

(k) Finally, we call on all Primates to challenge their dioceses to fund international development programmes, recognised by provinces, at a level of at least 0.7% of annual total diocesan income.

SECTION II RESOLUTIONS

Resolution II.1
The Theological Foundations of Mission

Resolution II.2
Mission and The Structures of the Anglican Communion

This Conference:

(a) acknowledges gratefully the contribution of many individuals and agencies in serving, stimulating and assessing the work of the Decade of Evangelism, particularly the Church of Nigeria for its gift to the whole church through its role in initially resourcing the involvement of the ACC in this work by seconding Canon Dr Cyril Okorocha, the continuing contribution of MISSIO whose report we received, and whose work we wish to see continued, and the Anglican Communion Global Conference on Dynamic Evangelism beyond 2000 at Kanuga in 1995;

(b) believes that the instruments of unity (the Archbishop of Canterbury; the Lambeth Conference; the ACC and the Primates' Meeting) need to work much more closely together and to review their mutual accountability (e.g. the ACC and the Primates' Meetings should consider communicating the results of their deliberations to all Bishops in the Communion);

(c) considers that regional networks and relationships should be reinforced and encouraged and their work be fully publicised;

(d) requests that the Joint Standing Committee of the Primates' Meeting and the ACC consider, as a matter of urgency, how the budget and staffing of the Communion's official networks might come to reflect the priorities of mission and evangelism;

(e) similarly requests that the MISSIO be instructed to study further the most efficient and effective ways for the Communion to extend mission and evangelism (e.g. through a mission and evangelism secretary);

(f) suggests that the Lambeth Conference be recognised as a significant consultative body which gives a sense of unity and direction to the whole Communion, which should receive and review reports of significant activities carried out as part of the work of the Communion.

Resolution II.3
Companion Dioceses

Resolution II.4
Christianity in Islamic Societies

This Conference;

(a) mindful of the great changes that have taken place in many nations with a substantial or majority Islamic population, and recognising the historic contributions of Islamic culture to ideals of justice and religious freedom;

(b) views with concern the tendency in some such nations to seek to enforce a legal code which encourages discrimination against, or harassment of, non-Muslim communities;

(c) resolves:

(i.) respectfully to request the governments of nations where such discriminations and harassment are common occurrences to affirm their commitment to religious liberty; and

(ii.) to pledge ourselves to support the civil and religious liberties of Muslims in situations where they are in a minority, and to combat prejudice and ignorance about Islam among Christians and others.

Resolution II.5

Iran—This resolution was not moved in view of a similar resolution from the South Asia/Middle East Region

Resolution II.6

Future Priorities in Mission

As it moves towards the third millennium of Christian Witness, this conference;

(a) gives thanks to God for all the experience so far of the Decade of Evangelism, noting the Testimonies and challenges from many churches across the Communion;

(b) repents of our failures in mission and evangelism;

(c) expresses its determination that the impetus should not be lost. The primary task of every bishop, diocese and congregation in the Anglican Communion is to share in and show the love of God in Jesus Christ – by worship, by the proclamation to everyone of the gospel of salvation through Christ, through the announcing of good news to the poor and the continuing effort to witness to God's Kingdom and God's justice in act and word and to do so in partnership with Christians of all traditions;

(d) urges that priority should be given at every level in our Communion to reaching out to those who have never heard, or never responded to the gospel of Christ, and to reawakening those whose love has grown cold;

(e) commits ourselves to call our people to be a transforming church by practising Jubilee, and by sharing financial resources between different regions of our Communion, not only for responding to crises or disasters, but to enable local initiatives in outreach, service and evangelism;

(f) commits ourselves in the light of what is said in this Report to work to transform the dioceses we serve into communities that share fully at every level in the mission of God.

Resolution II.7
Urbanisation

Resolution II.8
Young People

This Conference;

(a) recognises and celebrates the dynamic work of God among young people, and their infinite value in the human family. They are for us in the church, as they were for Jesus, signs of the Kingdom of God among us. Their presence and ministry in the church is essential for the whole family of God to be complete. As adults, we confess with deep humility and sorrow that the adult world has created children of war, children abused by neglect and sexual exploitation, and children who are victims of aggressive advertising. In joyful obedience to God we reaffirm our apostolic commitment to all young people everywhere;

(b) recognises the faithful and creative work by many Church members in ministry with children both within and beyond the church's borders;

(c) resolves, for the health and welfare of the whole Church;

(i.) that the bishops of the Anglican Communion will commit themselves, and will give leadership in their diocese, to ensure that the church is a safe, healthy, and spiritually enriching community for children and young people;

(ii.) that the bishops will give more attention to the furtherance of ministry to children as a recognition of their importance to God and as a foundation for all future ministry;

(iii.) that the bishops will commit themselves to give significant time over the next twelve months to meet with young people in their dioceses, listening to them, praying with them searching the Scriptures and breaking bread together with them, and providing ways for them to be trained in leadership skills and to exercise that leadership in the life and mission of the church;

(iv.) that such meetings should open out into attempts to meet and hear young people who have not yet been touched by the Gospel;

(v.) that teams of adults and young people in as many congregations as possible be trained for holistic ministry to young people outside the church, so as to speak of God's love in Christ in ways that can be heard, and that Christian young people be equipped, in the power of the Holy Spirit, for service in Church and Community;

(vi.) that young people should be helped to find or maintain their spiritual home in the Anglican Church by giving particular attention to matters of liturgy including the use of music and silence; and

(vii.) That urgent consideration be given to how best international Anglican networks of young people may be strengthened and serviced by the structures of the Communion.

SECTION III RESOLUTIONS
Resolution III.1
The Bible

This Conference, recognising the need in our Communion for fuller agreement on how to interpret and apply the message of the Bible in a world of rapid change and widespread cultural interaction, (a) reaffirms the primary authority of the Scriptures, according to their testimony and supported by our own historic formularies;

(b) urges that the Biblical text should be handled respectfully, coherently, and consistently, building upon our best traditions and scholarship believing that the Scriptural revelation must continue to illuminate, challenge and transform cultures, structures, and ways of thinking, especially those that predominate today;

(c) invites our provinces, as we open ourselves afresh to a vision of a Church full of the Word and full of the Spirit, to promote at every level biblical study programmes, which can inform and nourish the life of dioceses, congregations, seminaries, communities, and members of all ages.

Resolution III.2
The unity of the Anglican Communion

This Conference, committed to maintaining the overall unity of the Anglican Communion, including the unity of each diocese under the jurisdiction of the diocesan bishop,

(a) believes such unity is essential to the overall effectiveness of the Church's mission to bring the Gospel of Christ to all people;

(b) for the purpose of maintaining this unity, calls upon the provinces of the Communion to uphold the principle of 'Open Reception' as it relates to the ordination of women to the priesthood as indicated by the Eames Commission; noting that "reception is a long and spiritual process." (Grindrod Report);

(c) in particular calls upon the provinces of the Communion to affirm that those who dissent from, as well as those who assent to, the ordination of women to the priesthood and episcopate are both loyal Anglicans;

(d) therefore calls upon the Provinces of the Communion to make such provision, including appropriate episcopal ministry, as will enable them to live in the highest degree of Communion possible, recognising that there is and should be no compulsion on any bishop in matters concerning ordination or licensing;

(e) also affirms that "although some of the means by which communion is expressed may be strained or broken, there is a need for courtesy, tolerance, mutual respect, and prayer for one another, and we confirm that our desire to know or be with one another, remains binding on us as Christians". (Eames, p.119).

Resolution III.3
Subsidiarity

This Conference affirms the principle of "subsidiarity," articulated in Chapter 4, The Virginia Report, which provides that "a central authority should have a subsidiary function, performing only those tasks which cannot be performed at a more immediate or local level", provided that these tasks can be adequately performed at such levels.

Resolution III.4
Eames Commission

Noting that Resolution 1 of the 1988 Lambeth Conference (The ordination or consecration of women to the episcopate) recommended that the Archbishop of Canterbury, in consultation with the Primates appoint a commission

(a) to provide for an examination of the relationships between the provinces of the Anglican Communion and ensure that the process of reception includes continuing consultation with other Churches as well;

(b) to monitor and enumerate the process of consultation within the Communion and to offer further pastoral guidelines; and noting that the Archbishop of Canterbury and the Primates having now received the completed work of the commission chaired by the Most Revd Robin Eames: this Conference

(a) accepts and endorses the report and thanks the members of the Commission;

(b) recognises the ongoing, open process of reception within the Communion;

(c) recommends the guidelines to every Province; and

(d) urges continuing monitoring within the Communion with regular reporting to the Primates' Meeting.

Resolution III.5

The Authority of Holy Scriptures

This Conference

(a) affirms that our creator God, transcendent as well as immanent, communicates with us authoritatively through the Holy Scriptures of the Old and New Testaments; and

(b) in agreement with the Lambeth Quadrilateral, and in solidarity with the Lambeth Conference of 1888, affirms that these Holy Scriptures contain 'all things necessary to salvation' and are for us the 'rule and ultimate standard' of faith and practice.

Resolution III.6

Instruments of the Anglican Communion

This Conference, noting the need to strengthen mutual accountability and interdependence among the Provinces of the Anglican Communion,

(a) reaffirms Resolution 18.2(a) of Lambeth 1988 which "urges that encouragement be given to a developing collegial role for the Primates' Meeting under the presidency of the Archbishop of Canterbury, so that the Primates' Meeting is able to exercise an enhanced responsibility in offering guidance on doctrinal, moral and pastoral matters";

(b) asks that the Primates' Meeting, under the presidency of the Archbishop of Canterbury, include among its responsibilities positive encouragement to mission, intervention in cases of exceptional emergency which are incapable of internal resolution within provinces, and giving of guidelines on the limits of Anglican diversity in submission to the sovereign authority of Holy Scripture and in loyalty to our Anglican tradition and formularies;

(c) recommends that these responsibilities should be exercised in sensitive consultation with the relevant provinces and with the Anglican Consultative Council (ACC) or in cases of emergency the Executive of the ACC and that, while not interfering with the juridical authority of the provinces, the exercise of these responsibilities by the Primates' Meeting should carry moral authority calling for ready acceptance throughout the Communion, and to this end it is further recommended that the Primates should meet more frequently than the ACC;

(d) believing that there should be a clearer integration of the roles of the Anglican Consultative Council and the Primates' Meeting, recommends that the bishops representing each province in the Anglican Consultative Council should be the primates of the provinces and that(i) equal representation in the ACC from each province, one presbyter or deacon and one lay person from each province should join the primates in the triennial ACC gathering;(ii) an executive committee of the ACC should be reflective of this broad membership, and; (iii) there should be a change in the name of the Anglican Consultative Council to the Anglican Communion Council, reflecting the evolving needs and structures to which the foregoing changes speak;

(e) reaffirms the role of the Archbishop of Canterbury as a personal sign of our unity and communion, and the role of the decennial Lambeth Conference and of extraordinary Anglican Congresses as called, together with inter-provincial gatherings and cross-provincial diocesan partnerships, as collegial and communal signs of the unity of our Communion.

Resolution III.7

The Lambeth Conference

Noting that -

(a) the members of the Anglican Consultative Council (ACC) were invited to Lambeth Conference 1988 and Lambeth Conference 1998;

(b) some assistant bishops were invited in 1978 and 1988 and that in 1998 all assistants were invited; and

(c) that in ten years' times numbers and costs will inevitably be much greater; this Conference requests that those planning for the next Conference actively consider

(a) the optimal size for the Conference;

(b) possible alternative locations; and

(c) optional Conference designs.

Resolution III.8

The Virginia Report

This Conference

(a) welcomes the 1997 Report of the Inter Anglican Theological and Doctrinal Commission (The Virginia Report) as a helpful statement of the characteristics of our Communion;

(b) recognises that the report, the fruit if ten years of careful work accomplished since the 12th Lambeth Conference, identifies and explores important questions about unity, interdependence and mutual accountability in the Anglican Communion;

(c) commends its discussion of our Trinitarian faith as the basis of our koinonia and interdependence, while recommending the need for further work to be done with respect to the report's discussion of reason in relation to the primacy of Holy Scripture;

(d) affirms that the Churches of our Anglican Communion are joined in the communion of God through Our Lord Jesus Christ by the gracious power of the Holy Spirit, celebrating the fact that our communion together is maintained in the life and truth of Christ by the gift to us of the Holy Scriptures, the Apostles and Nicene Creeds, the sacraments of Baptism and Eucharist, and the historic episcopate, and commending the fundamental importance of these to the consideration of our partners in ecumenical dialogue;

(e) values the instruments of Anglican unity as they are described in the Virginia Report, the Archbishop of Canterbury, the Lambeth Conference, the Anglican Consultative Council, and the meeting of Primates;

(f) values and discerns the Church to be held in koinonia by our liturgical tradition and common patterns of worship, by prayer and the communion of the saints, the witness of the heroes and heroines of our history, the sharing of the stories of our faith, and by our interdependence through exchanges of friendship between our dioceses and by service to others in the name of Christ;

(g) calls upon member Churches and the ACC in the next decade to facilitate the sharing of resources of theological education and training in ministry and to promote exchanges amongst the theological colleges and seminaries of our Communion so as to minister to a deepening unity of heart and mind;

(h) requests the Primates to initiate and monitor a decade of study in each province on the report, and in particular on "whether effective communion, at all levels, does not require appropriate instruments, with due safeguards, not only for legislation, but also for oversight" (para. 5.20) as well as on the issue of a universal ministry in the service if Christian unity (cf. Agros Report, para. 162, and the Encyclical Letter of Pope John Paul II, Ut unum sint 96);

(i) requests that this study should include consideration of the ecumenical implications involved and that the Primates should make specific recommendations for the development of instruments of communion not later than the 14th Lambeth Conference.

Resolution III.9
Inter-regional groupings

This Conference requests that at a forthcoming meeting of the Anglican Consultative Council ways and means be explored for bishops to gather in inter-regional groupings at convenient intervals for communion, exchange, renewal and theological reflection whereby they might be enabled to take back home ideas for guidance distilled from the global experience of fellow bishops.

Resolution III.10
Marriage and Family Life

Resolution III.11
Religious Freedom

This Conference challenges Anglicans, as servants of Jesus Christ, our Lord and Saviour -

(a) to respect the rights and freedom of all faiths to worship and practise their ways of life;

(b) to work with all people of good will to extend these freedoms of worship, religious practice and conversion throughout the world;

(c) to stand by those who are being persecuted for their faith by our prayers, protests and practical support;

(d) to enter into dialogue with members of other faiths, to increase our mutual respect and explore the truths we hold in common and those on which we differ;

(e) to witness to our faith in the reconciling and saving activity of God in our Lord Jesus Christ working in us now through the power of the Holy Spirit; and

(f) to equip ourselves for our witness, dialogue and service by becoming better versed in the teaching and practice of our own faith, and of at least one other faith.

Resolution III.12
The Monitoring of Inter-Faith Relations

This Conference requests the Anglican Consultative Council to consider setting up a body in the Anglican Communion to monitor Christian/ Muslim and other faith relations throughout the world for the purpose of, promoting, educating, and advising on inter-faith dialogue with Muslim and other faiths and to arrange for adequate support and relief for Christians who are persecuted.

Resolution III.13
Marriage and Family Life
This Resolution was not moved, having been conflated with Resolution III.10.

Resolution III.14
Inculturation of worship

Resolution III.15
Co-ordinator for Liturgy

Resolution III.16
International Anglican Liturgical Consultations

Resolution III.17
Liturgical revision
This Resolution was not moved, having been conflated with Resolution III.15.

Resolution III.18
The Mothers' Union

Resolution III.19
Urbanisation
This resolution was not moved in view of the similar Resolution II.7.

Resolution III.20
The daily offices

Resolution III.21
Young people
This resolution was not moved in view of the similar Resolution II.8.

Resolution III.22
Discipleship

SECTION IV RESOLUTIONS

Resolution IV.1
Commitment to full, visible unity

This Conference:

(a) reaffirms the Anglican commitment to the full, visible unity of the Church as the goal of the Ecumenical Movement;

(b) encourages the further explication of the characteristics which belong to the full, visible unity of the Church (described variously as the goal, the marks, or the portrait of visible unity); and

(c) recognises that the process of moving towards full, visible unity may entail temporary anomalies, and believes that some anomalies may be bearable when there is an agreed goal of visible unity, but that there should always be an impetus towards their resolution and, thus, towards the removal of the principal anomaly of disunity.

Resolution IV.2
The Chicago-Lambeth Quadrilateral
This Conference:

(a) reaffirms the Chicago-Lambeth Quadrilateral (1888) as a basis on which Anglicans seek the full, visible unity of the Church, and also recognises it as a statement of Anglican unity and identity;

(b) acknowledges that ecumenical dialogues and experience have led to a developing understanding of each of the elements of the Quadrilateral, including the significance of apostolicity, pastoral oversight (episcope), the office of bishop and the historic episcopate; and

(c) commends continuing reflection upon the Quadrilateral's contribution to the search for the full, visible unity of the Church, and in particular the role within visible unity of a common ministry of oversight exercised in personal, collegial and communal ways at every level.

Resolution IV.3
An Inter-Anglican Standing Commission on Ecumenical Relations

Resolution IV.4
Local ecumenism

Resolution IV.5
Ecclesiology and Ethics

Resolution IV.6
Churches in Communion

This Conference:

(a) recommends that the proposed Inter-Anglican Standing Commission on Ecumenical Relations reflect upon the implications of being in communion with the See of Canterbury with particular reference to the United Churches and Churches in Communion;

(b) welcomes the fact that the International Bishops' Conference of the Union of Utrecht and the ACC have agreed to the establishment of an Anglican-Old Catholic International Co-ordinating Council;

(c) recommends that consideration be given to ways of deepening our communion with the Old Catholic Churches beyond the Bonn Agreement, including means of taking counsel and making decisions together; the anomaly of overlapping jurisdictions; the implications of wider ecumenical relationships, particularly with the Roman Catholic, Orthodox and Lutheran Churches; and the importance of work together on issues of mission and common witness;

(d) welcomes the adoption by both churches of the Concordat between the Episcopal Church in the Philippines and the Philippine Independent Church (1997), which establishes a relationship of full communion;

(e) welcomes the relationship of communion established in Northern Europe between six Lutheran churches (Estonia, Finland, Iceland, Lithuania, Norway and Sweden) and four Anglican churches (England, Ireland, Scotland and Wales) by the signing of the Porvoo Declaration in 1996, and recognises the enrichment brought through the presence of Finnish, Norwegian and Swedish bishops at this Conference as bishops in communion; and

(f) welcomes the decision by the Porvoo Church Leaders meeting in 1998 that the Lusitanian Catholic Apostolic Evangelical Church of Portugal and the Spanish Episcopal Reformed Church should be regarded as being covered by the Preamble to the Porvoo Declaration subject to their Synods' approval of the Declaration.

Resolution IV. 7

World Council of Churches

This Conference:

(a) greets the 8th Assembly of the World Council of Churches in Harare and congratulates the Council as it celebrates its Fiftieth Anniversary in 1998;

(b) expresses its gratitude to the WCC, which has enriched the Anglican Communion not least through the work of the Faith and Order Commission;

(c) commends the achievements and insights of the Ecumenical Decade of Churches in Solidarity with Women;

(d) affirms the importance of the study Towards a Common Understanding and Vision of the WCC as a first step in the renewal of the Council's life and work;

(e) recommends that the Assembly mandate the incoming Central Committee to undertake more focused work on:

(i) the vision of unity the Council should seek to nurture, building on the Canberra Statement adopted by the Seventh Assembly;

(ii) renewed structures of the Council which would most effectively promote that vision;

(iii) a radical reassessment of the basis and categories of membership in the WCC and what changes in the WCC would be required to make it possible for the Roman Catholic Church to be a full member;

(iv) the nature of the fellowship shared by members of the Council;

(f) invites the Joint Working Group between the WCC and the Roman Catholic Church to consider what changes in the WCC would be required to make it possible for the Roman Catholic Church to be a full member; and

(g) requests that the Harare Assembly makes provision for a consideration of the concerns of the Orthodox Churches, expressed at the meeting at Thessaloniki (May 1998).

Resolution IV.8
A Common Date for Easter

Resolution IV.9
The Virginia Report

This Resolution was not moved, having been conflated with Resolution III.8.

Resolution IV.10
Eames Commission

This Resolution was not moved, having been conflated with Resolution III.4.

Resolution IV.11
'Continuing' Churches

This Conference:

(a) believes that important questions are posed by the emergence of groups who call themselves 'continuing Anglican Churches' which have separated from the Anglican Communion in recent years; and

(b) asks the Archbishop of Canterbury and the Primates' Meeting to consider how best to initiate and maintain dialogue with such groups with a view to the reconciliation of all who own the Anglican tradition.

Resolution IV.12
Implications of Ecumenical Agreements

Resolution IV.13
Unity within Provinces of the Anglican Communion

This Conference:

(a) notes with gratitude the ministry of support which the Archbishop of Canterbury has been able to give in Sudan and Rwanda, and recognises that he is called upon to render assistance from time to time in a variety of situations;

(b) in view of the very grave difficulties encountered in the internal affairs of some Provinces of the Communion, invites the Archbishop of Canterbury to appoint a Commission to make recommendations to the Primates and the Anglican Consultative Council, as to the exceptional circumstances and conditions under which, and the means by which, it would be appropriate for him to exercise an extra-ordinary ministry of episcope (pastoral oversight), support and reconciliation with regard to the internal affairs of a

Province other than his own for the sake of maintaining communion within the said Province and between the said Province and the rest of the Anglican Communion.

Resolution IV.14
Assyrian Church of the East

Resolution IV.15
The Baptist Churches

Resolution IV.16
The Lutheran Churches

This Conference:

(a) welcomes the remarkable progress in Anglican-Lutheran relationships during the last decade in many parts of the world;

(b) commends for study the report of the Anglican-Lutheran International Commission, The Diaconate as Ecumenical Opportunity (1996);

(c) noting the approval by the Episcopal Church in the United States of America of the Concordat of Agreement with the Evangelical Lutheran Church in America and the narrow vote against the Concordat by the ELCA, hopes that the draft revision of the Concordat, currently being undertaken by the ELCA in consultation with representatives from ECUSA, will provide a firm basis for the two churches to move to full communion;

(d) commends the progress toward full communion between the Anglican Church of Canada and the Evangelical Lutheran Church in Canada as set forth in the Waterloo Declaration (1997) for consideration by both churches in 2001;

(e) encourages the continuation of close relations with the Lutheran Churches of Denmark and Latvia, which participated fully in the Porvoo Conversations but have not so far become signatories;

(f) welcomes the development of dialogue in Australia, and of dialogue and collaboration in the search for justice and human rights and the joint pastoral care of scattered Christian communities in Africa;

(g) affirms the growing fellowship between churches of the Anglican and Lutheran Communions in other regions of the world, and encourages further steps toward agreement in faith, eucharistic sharing and common mission on the way to the goal of full, visible unity;

(h) rejoices not only in the Porvoo Common Statement between the Anglican Churches of Britain and Ireland and the Lutheran Churches of the Nordic and Baltic region, but also in the Meissen Common Statement with the Evangelical Church in Germany, which includes Lutheran,

Reformed and United Churches, and looks forward to the proposed agreement between the Anglican churches of Britain and Ireland and the French Lutheran and Reformed churches; and

(i) recommends consultation with the Lutheran World Federation about the continuation of the work of the Anglican-Lutheran International Commission.

Resolution IV.17
The Methodist Churches

Resolution IV.18
The Moravian Church

Resolution IV.19
The Oriental Orthodox Churches

Resolution IV.20
The Orthodox Churches

Resolution IV.21
Pentecostal Churches

Resolution IV.22
The Reformed Churches

Resolution IV.23
The Roman Catholic Church

This Conference:

(a) continues to be grateful for the achievements of the Anglican Roman Catholic International Commission and, recognising that there are a number of outstanding issues which still need to be addressed, strongly encourages its continuation;

(b) welcomes the proposal for a high-level consultation to review Anglican-Roman Catholic relationships in the light of the agreements reached and the 'real though imperfect communion' already existing between the churches of the Anglican Communion and the Roman Catholic Church. The Conference requests that the consultation should include different local situations, including the movement of clergy from one Church to another; the experience of Christian solidarity under persecution [e.g., in the Sudan]; discussions of the implications of having agreed statements on Eucharistic Doctrine and Ministry and Ordination, and the status of Apostolicae curae in the new context brought about by the work of ARCIC;

(c) recognises the special status of those Agreements which have been affirmed by the Lambeth Conference 1988 as 'consonant in substance with the faith of Anglicans' (Eucharistic Doctrine, Ministry and Ordination, and their Elucidations) and urges the provinces to receive them into their life;

(d) encourages the referral of Salvation and the Church (1987), Church as Communion (1991), Life in Christ (1994), and the anticipated completion of ARCIC's work on authority in the Church to the provinces for study and response back to the proposed Inter-Anglican Standing Commission on Ecumenical Relations and (through the Primates' Meeting and the Anglican Consultative Council) to the next Lambeth Conference; and

(e) welcomes warmly the invitation of Pope John Paul II in his Encyclical Letter Ut unum sint (1995) to consider the ministry of unity of the Bishop of Rome in the service of the unity of the Universal Church, strongly encourages the provinces to respond and asks the proposed Inter-Anglican Standing Commission on Ecumenical Relations to collate the provincial responses.

Resolution IV.24
WCC Faith and Order Commission

Resolution IV.25
New Churches and Independent Church Groups

This Conference:

(a) encourages the development of relationships between members of Anglican Churches and members of New Churches and Independent Christian Groups bilaterally, multilaterally, locally and informally, where this is appropriate and possible; and

(b) asks the Primates to investigate ways and means of monitoring the development of New Churches and Independent Christian Groups, studying their characteristics, and offering advice to provinces and dioceses about initiating and developing relationships with them.

Resolution IV.26
Kuala Lumpur Statement

This Resolution was not voted upon, as the Conference agreed to move to next business.